BUSINESS POLICY AND STRATEGIC MANAGEMENT

BUSINESS POLICY AND STRATEGIC MANAGEMENT

Dr. Anil Tandon

ANMOL PUBLICATIONS PVT. LTD.
NEW DELHI-110 002 (INDIA)

ANMOL PUBLICATIONS PVT. LTD.

Regd. Office: 4360/4, Ansari Road, Daryaganj,
New Delhi-110002 (India)
Tel.: 23278000, 23261597, 23286875, 23255577
Fax: 91-11-23280289
Email: anmolpub@gmail.com
Visit us at: www.anmolpublications.com

Branch Office: No. 1015, Ist Main Road, BSK IIIrd Stage
IIIrd Phase, IIIrd Block, Bangalore-560 085 (India)
Tel.: 080-41723429 • Fax: 080-26723604
Email: anmolpublicationsbangalore@gmail.com

Business Policy and Strategic Management

First Edition, 2010

ISBN 978-81-261-4506-5

PRINTED IN INDIA

Printed at Mehra Offset Press, Delhi.

Contents

Contents

Preface

The book presents the Fundamentals of Strategic Management in comprehensive manner and relates its concepts and techniques to the Indian context. The ideas are basically inspired from the writings of several luminaries in the field. The book exhibits a balanced combination of theory and application. This book is designed to support and enhance both learning and teaching. An important aspect of the style adopted for this book is the use of exhibits, presenting a vast gamut of information regarding special theoretical matter.

The knowledge of business policy and techniques of strategic management is the need of the hour to prospective business managers. The present competitive environment has brought several drastic changes in policy making and strategic management. Hence, there is necessity of theoretical understanding about the business policy as well as strategic management. Most of the organizations have started adopting strategic management system. This book focuses on conceptual approach to the subject as well as some select case studies, which make a foundation to the knowledge of strategic management.

Author

Chapter 1

Introduction

BACKGROUND

This chapter introduces strategic management and provides an overview of the rest of the book. Following a review of the history of strategic management as it has evolved into the form presented here, the research that has tested the advantages to organizations of strategic management is outlined.

That an organization's mission statement is a manifestation of the culture intended for it by top-level management or owners is discussed next.

Mission, or purpose, is an explanation of why the organization exits and of the guiding philosophies to be followed in the development of strategy at each major organizational level.

Then, these four levels of strategy—enterprise, corporate, business, and functional—are explained. When strategic management is practiced effectively, formulation and implementation of strategies at the appropriate levels become the management processes that establish competitive advantage and drive the company forward.

In the final two sections, the nature of strategic decisions is discussed, followed by an explanation of contingency strategies.

EVOLUTION

Accept for a moment that strategic management is a way of running an organization that recognizes the complexity of its environment and seeks to establish competitive advantage at all levels.

It is a process by which the manager can transform environmental factors, along with various internal, personal, and political considerations, into decisions that result in strategies (goals and plans of action for reaching them) to help guide the organization into the future in a dominant competitive position.

Over the past few decades, the nature of strategic management as a management technique has changed in two important ways with the changing environment.

It has increased both in its level of detail and in its importance as the complexity of the environment has increased. Between World War II and the early 1960s, *business policy*, following the so-called prestrategy paradigm, addressed the problem of coordinating the operations of the various functional departments of the firm. Policies were established by top management to integrate activities that each department was to carry out.

Thus policy served to standardize and specify behaviour within functional departments. Strategy was usually viewed as an implicit concept reserved for the topmost managers.

In the top manager's mind, this concept, environmental characteristics, certain organizational goals, and political circumstances, along with years of management experience, all came together to produce what was hoped would be the right collection of policies.

Strategy was seldom analyzed, once it was decided on by top management, and rarely changed. When operations did not meet expectations, it was policy that typically was analyzed and modified. Most firms were single-line businesses; business policy making was conducted in large part at what is known today as the business level.

The rapid rise during the 1950s and early 1960s in the number of interest groups making demands on organizations of all kinds, along with the proliferation of mergers and acquisitions, began to strain the applicability of the relatively simple business-policy approach to management.

Divisionaiized firms no longer had a single line of business. Thus a different set of policies was needed for each subsidiary and managers sought a common thread that might bind them together.

The internal complexity of firms had increased in an attempt to deal with the complexity of a pluralistic society. Davis and Blomstrom describe social pluralism as a society "in which diverse groups maintain autonomous participation and influence in the social system."

Business is merely one such influence (interest group) and competes with many other groups for time, money, interest, allegiance, or attention. Increasingly organizations that were operated without an understanding of, or respect for, the various interest-group influences have been subjected to successful attacks by these groups.

Electric utilities were forced by many interest groups to cease or radically change the nature of nuclear power plant construction projects. Through the pressure of consumer groups, automobile manufactures have been made to correct deficiencies in their products.

Industrial polluters were required by environmental groups to clean up or stop harmful discharges. Product labeling requirements were tightened, Equal Employment Opportunity assurances became stricter and product safety standards were improved. These changes, and hundreds of others, were brought about largely by the political actions of interest groups. Their activities often resulted in enactment of legislation that today regulates the conduct of business.

In response to this growth in the dimensions of firms' environments, and also to the growth in the number of Divisionalized firms, strategy increasingly became interpreted as the link between an organization and its environment. All of the "policy" problems remained, but they were compounded by a baffling set of external claims, and also by the needs imposed by multiple product lines and business-level activities.

Because of its inability to deal with these factors, the business-policy model underwent several evolutionary changes and emerged as what was later called strategic planning.

Dubbed the *initial strategy paradigm*, this view of corporate management focused heavily on the process of strategy formulation with emphasis on environmental pressures, yet it had four major shortcomings.

First, it did not clearly differentiate between corporate-level strategy (questions related to the collection of business activities a divisionalized company owned) and business level strategy (how to compete within a particular business activity).

Second, the initial strategy paradigm was unclear about the nature of relationships between strategy and the operation of the various functional areas of business.

How does the task of marketing management, for example, change with different strategic focuses and how can the functional areas be integrated into an effective whole? Such questions largely went unanswered.

Third, this paradigm was incomplete in its discussion of the role of general management. Some authors contended that strategic planning was the province of only top managers, whereas others claimed that all managers should be involved in strategic planning.

Finally, there was disagreement about whether strategy included both goals and action plans, or just action plans. The *strategic management* paradigm, although still in its infancy, is the third step in the evolution of thought about strategy, and it addresses the shortcomings of strategic planning.

As initially codified by Schendel and Hofer, strategic management is far from representing a consensus. Yet there is a perceptible movement toward consolidation around many of its principles.

In particular, there is now a widely accepted distinction between corporate-level, business-level, and functional-level strategy. A fourth strategy level, enterprise strategy, has been proposed by Ansoff, but the concept has not endured (enterprise strategy was defined as describing the interaction of a firm with its environment—it is now felt by many that this interaction is best incorporated in each of the other strategy levels and not reserved only for a separate category of strategy.)

In some ways related to Ansoff's concept of enterprise strategy, a more global strategic orientation is described by Magaziner and Reich; they call it international strategy. Here too, during the early 1990s the idea of isolating global issues and direction in a separate strategy level has given way to the practice of incorporating international competitive matters into all levels of strategic decision making.

The strategic management paradigm not only distinguishes among different levels of strategy but is sufficiently adaptable to accommodate the need for this expanded scope of strategic thinking.

Next, strategic management addresses the issue of functional integration by identifying various functional strategies. At the same time, responsibility for strategic thinking is viewed within this paradigm as the responsibility of all managers, not just top-level executives. Although there is much work to be done in learning how best to integrate functional strategy with other strategy levels, the strategic management paradigm lays the groundwork for the conduct of such research.

Finally, by separating the steps of goal formulation and strategy (action plan) formulation, this paradigm is more objective, more teachable, and less mysterious than earlier interpretations. It may help to continue the increase in popularity of strategy-focused management and thus expand the competitiveness of U.S. business in the international marketplace.

BENEFITS OF PRACTICING

One would expect that the primary benefit of practicing strategic management would be higher profitability. But the evidence of this is still inconclusive in a wide variety of applications, and there have been many attempts to resolve the issue.

We therefore shall present examples of research results on both sides of this question, along with a discussion of the problems encountered in conducting this kind of research. We are confident you will agree not only that strategic management is beneficial in many ways, but also that it is nearly indispensable for most organizations.

Researching Strategic Management's Effectiveness

The weight of numbers tends to favour the studies that have supported the positive effects of strategic management. Only a few have not supported it.

In 1957 the Stanford Research Institute analyzed some 400 firms and concluded that those that plan outperform those that do not in terms of sales and profit growth. One of the most convincing studies was undertaken by Thune and House in 1970. They identified two groups, formal planners and informal planners, among eighteen matched pairs of companies in six industries.

The two groups were then compared by sales, return on stockholders' equity and total capital, earnings per share and stock prices. One result that is important for our purposes is that the formal planners were significantly better performers on the three profit-related ratios that were the informal planners.

Another test of the formal planners compared their performance before planning with their performance after planning was begun. After-planning performance was superior to preplanning performance. Also in 1970, Eastlack and McDonald showed correlation between planning and performance.

In a replication of the Thune and House study by Herold in 1972, the previous findings were upheld—formal planners continued to outperform informal planners.

Another often-cited study, by Rue and Fulmer in, also lends support to the planning-performance relationship, at least for producers of durable goods. However, for businesses in service and nondurable product industries, planners were not significantly better performers than nonplanners. In 1974 Wood and LaForge found that banks that planned formally performed better than those that did not. More support was offered by Karger and Amalik in 1975, when they showed the same results for the machinery, chemicals, drugs, and electronics industries. However, drug and electronic firms in their sample did not show as strong a relationship between planning and performance as did the other two types.

Later studies in this area have tended not to support the findings of the earlier work. In research conducted by Kallman and Shapiero and Kudla, and Leontiades and Tezel during 1980, no positive relationship was seen between planning and performance.

The only study since the mid-1970s we found which showed a positive relationship was one by Burt in Australia. He showed that the higher the quality of the planning programme, the better was performance.

Research Problems

The major problem encountered when trying to test the effectiveness of strategic management is research methodology. Although many studies have shown that companies that plan perform better than those that do not, the simultaneous presence of planning and good performance does not prove that one causes the other.

It is especially difficult to demonstrate the effectiveness of strategic management when one considers the many variables that would have to be controlled for to focus on the effects of planning. Among these are the type of industry, the size of the firm and the industry, management experience and personality, cultural factors, and various accounting conventions such as inventory valuation methods used and income tax expectations.

If its results are to be conclusive, a study of the effectiveness of strategic management would have to involve firms matched according to many factors such as these.

Another problem with this line of research is ascertaining what is meant by strategic management in individual firms. Much of the work already done has used the presence of "formal planning" as the independent variable to test for variations in measures of performance, the dependent variable.

Mangers often maintain they are performing formal planning when in fact they are not. Indeed, one of our recent executives in residence claimed to do formal planning. When questioned further about his methods, he admitted that he plans while driving his car.

The fact that planning has, or has not, had an effect on a certain dependent variable chosen by the researcher does not mean that management did not perceive a positive effect on some other variable not tested by the researcher.

For example, a management group might institute strategic management as a way to decentralize management functions. That no effect was demonstrated on, say, return on assets, would not mean that the process had not been "successful" or beneficial in some other way.

Another explanation for the lack of overwhelming consistency among planning-performance studies is the contention that financially successful firms are the ones that can afford the start-up costs incurred in initiating strategic management.

Therefore, the argument goes, such studies are biased in favour of planning companies that were successful first and planners second.

STRATEGIC MANAGEMENT MODEL

We can look at strategic management as a process that generates certain outputs and requires certain informational inputs. Understanding strategic management is a matter of understanding the contents of and the relationship among these three components.

To develop that understanding in this book, we take the strategic management process as our focus and discuss each stage by explaining its management activities, its input requirements, and the nature of the results or outputs of each stage. Thus the chapters correspond to stages in the strategic management process, and each chapter discusses the various inputs and outputs of each stage.

Of course, in practice one does not necessarily follow the sequence of strategic management stages in this fashion. Managers might formulate goals and the means for achieving them (action plans) simultaneously, rather than attempt to accomplish one completely and then the other.

Or some might view organization structure as a prerequisite for strategy; that is, structure might be established before strategy rather than strategy before structure. Still others might prefer to establish the portions of a control system first, before turning attention to the details of strategy formulation.

This could be the case, for example, where strict federal reporting requirements, such as for defence contracting, necessitate structuring the organization and its strategy around particular control features.

This sequence is also similar to structures prepared by other authors. Whereas it serves to identify the milestones for students being introduced to it for the first time, it also could be used as the outline for analyzing an ongoing strategic management system or one portrayed in a case study.

The strategy formulation block contains a section representing the process of goal formulation and another section for the process of action-plan formulation. When we discuss strategy formulation, we mean the development of both goals and action plans, or, as others have said, ends *and* means. An early concern in strategic management is constructing a set of data (facts and supporting information) that defines present and expected influences on, and characteristics of, the organization.

The major categories of information sources for this process are the organization's present strategic management elements (mission and goals and action plans for each of the various levels of strategy), relevant characteristics of present and forecast environment, and pertinent features of internal operations.

Information generated by these analyses can be organized in a strategic data set according to whether it constitutes threats and weaknesses, or strengths and opportunities.

These, in turn, can be further categorized as internal or external factors that are either positive or negative in nature. Mintzberg distinguishes between goal formation and goal formulation by noting that formulation involves a conscious individual decision process. Goal formation is accomplished by implication; individuals form goals implicitly by the decisions they make.

In the first part of Chapter, we are concerned with the process of goal formulation. It results in goals for an organization's performance that apply to the corporate, business, and functional levels of its operation.

Refinement of goals requires understanding of the political processes at work in the organization as well as of the system of individual values and preferences that characterize its managers. Whatever facts and predictions make up a firm's strategic data set, they are filtered through these two influences.

The activity of deriving action-plan choices for the overall process of strategy formulation is described in the second part of Chapter. Just as political processes and personal values and preferences influence goal formulation, they also shape the ways in which strategy choices are made.

Also, relevant portions of the firm's strategic data set constitutes vital information inputs to this process.

Chapter discusses several approaches that have appeared in the literature to explain the processes by which strategies are evaluated and selected.

Both existing and new strategies have to be evaluated to:

- Determine their acceptability in the present time frame,
- Estimate how well they can be expected to meet future goals in light of the firm's pro forma data set,
- Ultimately select the particular strategy set to be implemented.

Thus either an existing or a new strategy can be rejected as a whole, retained as is, or retained with alterations. Of course, evaluation of existing strategy ideally would take place during the first stage of the strategic management process as part of the internal analysis; proposed new strategies could be evaluated only after formulation.

The formulation and content of six areas of functional strategy—marketing, finance, personnel, research and development, production, and external relations—are addressed in chapter.

Since functional strategy is formulated to put into motion strategies developed at higher levels, it logically could be called either a formulation or an implementation process. We have chosen the former for two reasons.

First, there is a necessary interplay between the formulation of functional strategy and the formulation of the other levels of strategy. Second, even for those who consider functional strategy an implementation problem, it still must be formulated before it can be used to implement business and corporate strategy.

The next stage in strategic management is to implement the entire set of strategies. This process is explained in the first part of Chapter. Strategy implementation is essentially an administrative process; the other processes of strategic management are primarily analytical in nature.

Strategy implementation involves the structural and behavioral aspects of assigning responsibility for carrying out strategic components. It results in an organization structure, complete with appropriate vertical and lateral linkages specifically related to the strategy elements selected.

The final strategic management process, control, is discussed in the second part of Chapter. In practice, strategic control might be the first concern of the manager. Certainly the issues of how to establish performance standards, how to measure results, what corrective actions to take at what time, and other control problems should be considered throughout the strategic management process and not ignored until everything else is decided.

Indeed, control issues may significantly influence the content of strategy. It is discussed last simply to be consistent with tradition. In addition to all the other strategic management process outputs, strategic control takes as an input the technology of control available to the organization. For example, the advent of sophisticated microprocessor-based decision support systems (DSS), customized to the needs of a particular set of strategies, has resulted in many new control method possibilities. The absence of this technology in a particular firm, however, may severely limit the strategic control options available to its managers.

Output of the strategic control process consists of a feedback system that can modify strategic implementation and organization operations so as to alter either strategies or performance as might be reasonably necessary.

Thus one category of input information at each stage of strategic management consists of control system output. In this way evaluation of current performance vis-a-vis the organization's current strategy is always included in the analysis of each stage.

ELEMENTS OF STRATEGIC MANAGEMENT

Mission

Mission is the description of an organization's reasons for existence, its fundamental purpose. It is the guiding principle that drives the processes of goal and action plan formulation, "a pervasive, although general, expression of the philosophical objectives of the enterprise."

Mission should focus on "long-range economic potentials, attitudes toward customers, product and service quality, employee relations, and attitudes toward owners."

It provides identity, continuity of purpose, and overall definition, and should convey the following categories of information.

- Precisely why the organization exists, its purpose, in terms of
  - Its basic product or service,
  - Its primary markets,
  - Its major production technology.
- The moral and ethical principles that will shape the philosophy and character of the organization.

- The ethical climate within the organization.

Thus mission outlines the firm's identity and provides a guide for shaping strategies at all organizational levels. The role played by mission in guiding the organization is an important one.

Specifically it:

- Serves as a basis for consolidation around the organization's purpose.
- Pro :ides impetus to and guidelines for resource allocation.
- Defines the internal atmosphere of the organization, its climate.
- Serves as a set of guidelines for the assignment of job responsibilities.
- Facilitates the design of key variables for a control system.

Deal and Kennedy claim that a strong culture is the key to long-term corporate success and that culture has five elements: business environment, values, heroes (people who personify values), rites and rituals (routines of day-to-day corporate life), and the cultural network (communication systems).

The mission statement describes primarily the second of these cultural factors, corporate values. The strong cultural companies studied by Deal and Kennedy all had "a rich and complex system of values that were shared by the employees."

The mission statement must be believable in that the company's behaviour should correspond to it over both the short and long term. In this way it can serve as the foundation for the development of respect for and pride in the firm by management, employees, owners, customers, suppliers, and others who interact with it. Broad-based acceptance of the values represented by mission can lead to three characteristics of firms that accomplish this acceptance:

- They stand for something—the way in which business is to be conducted is widely understood.
- From the topmost levels of management down through the firm's organization structure to the

lowest level of production jobs, the values are accepted by all employees.

- "Employees feel special because of a sense of identity which distinguishes the firm from other firms."

Many examples of firms that have these characteristics as a result of a finely honed sense of cooperation and value acceptance are presented by Deal and Kennedy. A few of these are listed here, along with the slogans that have come to represent their value systems.

- *Dupont*: "Better things for better living through chemistry—a belief that product innovation, arising out of chemical engineering...
- *Sears, Roebuck*: "Quality at a good price—the mass merchandiser from Middle America.
- *Dana Corporation*: "Productivity Though people—enlisting the ideas and commitment of employees at every level in support of Dana's strategy of competing largely on cost and dependability rather than product differentiation...
- *Chubb Insurance Company*: "Underwriting excellence—an overriding commitment to excellence in a critical function.
- *Price Waterhouse and Company*: "Strive for technical perfection" (in accounting).

Mission typically is not considered a part of a firm's strategy set. It reflects the essential preferences of owners and managers for what the firm will do. Strategy will accomplish the task of reducing mission to operational terms.

As such mission is somewhat a personal choice of a firm's dominant group of actors and is an *input* to the strategy formulation process.

LEVELS OF STRATEGY

There is wide diversity in the strategic management literature of labels attached to the different levels of strategy that may exist in a firm. For example, Thompson and Strickland propose four levels: corporate strategy, business strategy, functional area support strategy, and operating-level strategy.

They go on to say,"Each layer is...progressively more detailed to provide strategic guidance ot the next level of subordinate managers." Lorange defines three levels for a typical divisionalized corporation: Portfolio strategy (corporate level), business strategy (division level), and strategic programs (functional level).

He defines the focus of each as follows:

- Portfolio strategy: Developing the desired risk/return balance among the businesses of the firm.
- Business strategy: Source of competitive advantage of a particular business relative to its competition.
- Strategic programs: Bringing to bear functional managers' specialized skills on the development of programs.

He notes that smaller firms may involve only the last two of these, but in any firm there rarely would be more than three. Hofer, et al list four levels of strategy for business organizations.First, strategy at the societal level is concerned with the definition of a firm's role in society.

It would specify the nature of corporate governance, political involvement of the firm, and trade-offs sought between economic and social objectives.

The second strategy level is corporate strategy which addresses:

- The nature of the firm's business
- Management of the set of businesses necessary to achieve its goals.

Third, business strategy addresses how the firm should be positioned and managed so as to compete in a given business or industry. Finally, functional area strategy is the lowest level of corporate strategy. It is concerned with their respective functional area environments.

Newman and Logan present two levels—business strategy and functional policy—for nondiversified firms, and a total of three (with the addition of corporate strategy) for diversified firms.

Higgins identifies four levels of strategy: Societal response strategy (enterprise strategy), mission determination strategy (corporate level), primary mission strategy (business level), and mission supportive strategy (functional level). He defines their contents as follows:

- *Societal response strategy:* How the firm relates to its societal constituents.
- *Mission determination strategy:* The organization's field of endeavor.
- *Primary mission strategy:* How the organization will achieve its primary mission.
- *Mission supportive strategies:* How primary mission strategy will be supported.

Another model proposes five levels of strategy but the levels are not tied to organizational structure. Gluck, et al suggest that the levels of planning activity consist of corporate, sector, shared resource unit (SRU), natural business unit (NBU), and product market unit (PMU).

The advantages of this system are:

- It separates the strategic management process from organization structure to a large degree
- Pushes it farther down the organization than traditional systems do.

These characteristics stem from focusing planning level selection on strategic issues or problems shared by the organization's activities rather than on the organization levels of its business activities.

Corporate level planning is that which involves identifying trends and formulating strategy in global, technical, and market arenas, responsibility for which rests with corporate headquarters in most cases.

Sector level planning, where sectors represent national and technological boundaries, may involve several SBU's, product categories, or even product/service-based divisions of an organization. Shared resource unit planning calls for the development of strategies for activities of the business that are shared by SBU's or the various product-market focuses which the company might have.

Natural business units, "...are largely self-contained businesses with control over the key factors that govern their success in the marketplace—their market position and cost structure". Finally, product-market unit planning is the lowest level at which planning takes place and those activities that directly relate the company's output to its markets.

There are many other interpretations of the levels of strategy. They differ primarily in terms of the organizational levels to which they apply. Those discussed above and most of the others have a number of commonalities.

First, the uppermost levels in each scheme tend to concern the problem of fitting the organization to its environment; lower levels address the problem of integrating functional areas in ways consistent with upper-level strategy. Second, the topmost level tends to involve structuring the set of acquisitions of divisionalized firms and is usually called corporate-level strategy. Third, they contain a business or strategic business unit (SBU) level of strategy that applies almost equally to a firm comprised of only one line of business and to the individual subsidiaries of multibusiness corporations.

Finally, the various schemes include a functional level of strategy that represents the ways in which functional departments are expected to respond to business-level and, in turn, corporate-level goals and action plans.

During the mid-1980s some authors began to include the fourth level: enterprise or societal goals and action plans. Societal strategy was intended to capture the essential ways in which the firm was expected to respond to goals related to the major social issues confronting it.

Interpreted fundamentally, then, there are four primary levels of strategy: societal-level, corporate- level, business-level, and functional-level. The concerns of societal-, corporate-, and business-level strategy are clearly cross-functional. That is, they contain implications for each of a firm's functional areas (although more distantly removed in the case of societal-and corporate-level strategy), whatever they may be and regardless of the type of firm.

By contrast, functional area strategies are more operationally focused than the others. The process of determining how each functional area should be managed is a more specialized problem, defined largely by the practice and theory applicable to each functional (or operational) area.

That is, the content of marketing strategy is the subject of marketing texts and courses, finance strategy can be found in finance texts and courses, personal strategy in personal texts and courses, and so on.

Societal Strategy

Societal strategy consists of goals and action plans of which the overall purpose is to guide the ways in which management intends the organization to respond to the major social demands placed on it.

It is an explicit definition of the organization's social responsibilities: how it is expected to react to the demands of particular groups of external constituents. The recent emergence of this level deserves further explanation.

The idea of isolating social responsibility in a separate (from corporate, business, and functional) strategy level was introduced in 1979 by Ansoff and modified by Schendel and Hofer. Ansoff presented it as follows.

The original concept of product/market strategy appears as only one component of a much broader concept. We might call it *enterprise strategy,* which is needed to integrate and relate the new dimensions of the strategic problems.

The development of societal legitimacy (or enterprise) strategy is Ansoff's proposed solution to the increasing importance of... socio-political variables in the life of the firm. Included in these variables are "new consumer attitudes, new dimensions of social control and, above all, a questioning of the firm's role in society."

In other words, Ansoff suggests concentrating managers' attempts to deal with new liberal views about the social role of business, growing egalitarianism, and the proliferation of constrictive regulation, among other social demands, in a societal legitimacy strategy that specializes in matters of social responsibility. Actually Ansoff's proposal for enterprise strategy goes beyond social responsibility issues to include other substrategy areas. Schendel and Hofer limit its contents to social-legitimacy concerns because of their belief that the other strategy areas are effectively addressed within prevailing definitions of corporate-business-and functional-level strategies.

Thus they recommend, Enterprise strategy attempts to integrate the firm with its broader noncontrollable environment, not in terms of product/market matches in a narrower economic sense, but in the sense of the overall role that business, as one of society's important institutions, should play in the everyday affairs of society... More explicit attention will have to be given to (societal legitimacy strategy) in the future, just as Ansoff suggests, just as it has been necessary to separate corporate and business strategy considerations from the problems of functional area interpretation, over the past two decades.

However, some strategists may prefer not to institute this new strategy level, for reasons explained by Dill: "There has been less turbulence in the environment for companies which have spent time over the years listening to and assessing what various internal and external constituencies have to say about the powers they are and are not willing to delegate to corporations and corporate management."

Stated differently, some managers may prefer to address *all* social legitimacy issues within the rubric of existing strategy levels.

For them social responsibility concerns would be addressed within the fabric of goals and action plans at the corporate, business, and functional levels.

Our conclusion about the usefulness of enterprise strategy is that it should be employed by organizations that have particularly sensitive relationships with the environment.

Firms such as utility companies, toy manufacturers, and educational institutions, for which an especially sharply focused public scrutiny has devolved, would be well suited for development of separate social-legitimacy goals and action plans.

For others, whose society interaction is less controversial, matters of social responsibility might be handled more efficiently, and even effectively, within goals and action plans at the corporate, business, and functional levels alone.

However, the advisability of their formulation for a given firm as a distinct activity is intended to be a matter of judgment depending upon whether or not sufficiently poignant social issues either confront the firm at present, or are expected to do so in the future.

Corporate-Level Strategy

A corporation's portfolio of business units (SBUs) can vary in its desirability just as a financial manager's portfolio of investments can.

The acceptability of a particular*business portfolio* is determined by assessing whether it reflects mission and expected strengths, weaknesses, threats, and opportunities (determined through environmental, industry, and internal analyses of each business unit) as well as values and political exigencies.

Additions to and deletions from the present portfolio would then be expressed in merger and/or divestment strategy. Finally, these strategies would be implemented by the appropriate organizational units and the machinery would thus be activated to adjust the present portfolio.

The content of corporate-level strategy is a set of action plans and corresponding corporate-level goals expressed in terms of the firm's collection of subsidiaries. By comparison, business strategy focuses on expected operational results of a business unit. However, it also consists of action plans that relate to goals (at the business level).

The substance of corporate-level goals and action plans can be summarized as follows:

- *Corporate-level goals*: The desired portfolio of business units by the end of the firm's planning period.
- *Corporate-level action plans*: How to get from the present portfolio to that targeted in terms of:
  - Business unit strategies to be retained.
  - Additions of business units expressed as either growth strategy parameters (for "home grown"

units) or merger and acquisition strategy.
- Business units to be divested.

Business-Level Strategy

The content of business-level strategy is also a combination of goals and action plans. Business-level goals should be stated in such a way that for each one, the following four components are evident:

- *Identifying, characteristics* of each objective or target.
- Each target's *substantive threshold value;* that is, the hurdle value upon reaching which the target will be considered attained (often stated as a specific value of the evaluative criteria).
- *Evaluative criteria* to be monitored in order to measure the firms progress toward the target.
- *Time frame threshold value;* that is, the date by which, or the elapsed time during which, the substantive threshold value would be reached.

Business-level action specifications should be devolved so that collectively they define the following elements:

- The firm's *product market scope;* that is, the nature of the products or services provided and the markets served by the firm.
- *Input-output transformations* in which the firm is engaged; that is, the nature of the activities with which the firm adds value to its labour and material inputs and what those inputs are.
- What *synergies* are sought in the operation of the firm.

Whether a strategy is being analyzed from within or outside the firm, these characteristics should be present. The outside analyst may use them as dimensions along which a firm's strategy can be described. The inside analyst or strategist may use them as guidelines for determining the comprehensiveness of strategy.

When taken together, these elements of business-level strategy should combine uniquely to:

- Define the business of the SBU or firm,
- Describe its competitive edge.

Thus strategy aligns the strategic business unit or firm relative to its competitors, distinguishes it from them, and hopefully propels it beyond them.

Functional-Level Strategy

In contrast with the other levels of strategy, functional strategies serve as guidelines for the employees of each of the firms's subdivisions. Which ones of these segments or functional areas are included in a firm's functional strategy set is itself a matter of strategy. For example, whether to have an R&D department or not in the first place is a strategic decision.

Functional goals and action plans are developed for each of the functional parts of the firm to guide the behaviour of people in a way that would put the other strategies into motion. If part of a firm's business-level strategy were a target of a 10 per cent increase in sales to be brought about by market penetration, for example, marketing strategy might include a change in compensation policy for salespersons and a specified increase in the advertising budget.

In that way marketing strategy would provide some detail about how the marketing aspects of the market penetration action plan would be implemented. Similarly, financial strategy would consist of a set of guidelines on how the financial elements of the firm would be put into effect. Personal strategy, production strategy, research and development strategy, and appropriate other functional strategy areas would do the same.

Nature of Strategic Decisions And Strategic Thinking

Although the process of creating strategy is often discussed as if it were an unconstrained design process, keep in mind that while strategists evaluate strategy, the firm is operating.

This evaluation involves assessing the extent to which present strategy is meeting expectations. It may be the case that only a small part of, say, marketing strategy would have to be changed to correct a problem. In effect, then, such a change would constitute an acceptance of corporate- and business-level strategy, and also of the firm's functional strategy set. Marketing strategy would be all that was rejected. When a firm's performance is less than satisfactory, the reason often is a functional strategy shortcoming. One might say that a "good" business-level strategy would have been poorly implemented by part of its functional strategy set. For this simple example, a change in marketing strategy could improve performance while other levels of strategy would remain unchanged.

Alternatively, a problem with the nature of a firm's or SBU's business brought about by a major environmental opportunity or threat, a change in that level's goals set, or the development of some internal capability or weakness could necessitate a business-level strategy change.

The new strategy would probably include vestiges of the old along with some unfamiliar elements. In most cases a whole new functional strategy set would likely have to be designed and put into effect to implement the new business-level strategy.

More generally, one could conceivably change parts of a firm's functional strategy set without changing business-level strategy. However, rarely would one expect to encounter the case in which a change in business-level strategy did not trigger the necessity to alter functional-level strategy in some way, at least not in a successfully managed business.

There is a risk of incorrectly identifying the strategy level at which a problem exists. A tendency exists in business to change functional-level strategies or organizational structure in a attempt to remedy any problem.

Of course, if the problem existed within the firm's corporate-or business-level strategy, for example, changing functional-level strategy would not correct it. In fact, this move would most likely aggravate the situation. The reason for this tendency is probably that functional strategy changes are potentially less disruptive than changes in the other levels. They certainly would affect fewer people than modifications at the corporate or business levels. The results of trying to solve a business-level strategic problem with a functional-level solution is well illustrated by the "big four" U.S. automobile companies.

With overseas competitors exporting fuel-efficient automobiles to the United States, and with widely acknowledged shrinkages of fossil fuel supplies, they still stubbornly tried to retain their old business and corporate strategies, well into the 1970s, by changing market strategy only. A set of major environmental threats, particularly at the business level, was met by minor model changes and increased efforts to convince the car-buying public that big autos were what we all really wanted. During the 1970s and early 1980s, these companies finally began to respond to their business strategy problems with business strategy changes—major philosophical alterations in the nature of their businesses.

If U.S. auto firms were to rely on small cars instead of traditional American big cars as their primary sources of growth, far-reaching changes in their functional strategy sets were also necessary.

New growth rates, profit targets, market-share goals, and the like, along with related broad action plans that centered around contraction in many forms, were implemented along with new functional strategy.

They included such things as cash rebates, Chrysler's government-guaranteed loan, employee layoffs, close cooperation with UAW officials, R&D efforts focused on producing smaller, less powerful engines as a primary effort rather than as an inconvenience.

The U.S. auto firms' strategy changes were finally implemented during a period of chaos. However, by then they were all in the red, and the doomsayers were having a heyday.

South claims that the key to successful strategic decisions is the creation of competitive advantage—selection of competitive areas within which success is clearly achievable. The Japanese have taught us that there are really two very different forms of competition: Reciprocal and strategic. Reciprocal competition is the traditional form in which companies in mature industries compete with other firms having similar strategic positions while attempting to distinguish themselves on the basis of operations.

Many colleges and universities offer similar programs, with traditional facilities and are significantly different only in terms of the geographical areas within which they operate. Strategic competition, on the other hand, involves competing primarily by establishing superior strategic position.

That is, the main concern of strategists is selection of a strategically advantageous posture which affords their organization a position of strength from which to do battle. Lincoln Electric Company has successfully differentiated itself on the basis of price and quality.

Their industrial welding equipment is regarded as the top quality product of its kind and the firm has consistently passed along cost savings to customers in the form of low prices. As a result, Lincoln is very difficult to compete with because of its strong price position.

Following this set of ideas, then, strategic decisions are those which involve "clear and favorable differentiation from competitors," so that one's competitive advantage is tangible, measurable, and preservable.

Defining strategic thinking is made especially difficult by the absence of a consensus on what strategic management is. On the latter point, Gluck, et al commented, "hardly anyone yet fully understands what strategic management is, knows exactly how to do it, or can clearly define its benefits." Their explanation of strategic management is that it is an approach to management which fuses strategic planning (plan development through analysis of environment, competition, and strategy choices) and the firm's system of operational decision making. This process has five dimensions.

First, strategic management requires a widely understood strategic planning process tightly interwoven with a strategically centered organization structure. Second, it requires widely discussed, analyzed and negotiated goal choices from which are culled out the ones that are not adoptable. Third, strategic management relies on the shared ability to think strategically by managers throughout the company.

Fourth, a performance evaluation system is necessary that focuses top level evaluators' attention on critical positive and negative strategic factors. Finally, it requires a strategy supportive motivational system and value orientation among managers.

These qualities, they say, define a strategically managed organization. Four of these qualities are readily understandable. But still subject to question is what is meant by the ability to think strategically.

Strategic thinking is that which generates:

- Creative, environmentally relevant ideas
- Concepts about how to turn them into systematically managed action plans.

It has the following prerequisites:

- Input information is based on facts and logical data.
- Previously unquestioned assumptions are sought out and examined.
- A burning desire for resource conservation, and
- Indirect, spontaneous, and unexpected thought processes which are hard for competitors to predict.

These requirements of strategic thinking set it apart from other kinds of decision making. First, strategic thinking requires factual and logical input data because it is competitively dangerous to base strategy formulation on erroneous information.

The stakes are too high to "hoof it." Second, long-held assumptions should be identified and analyzed to make sure they still apply. This is especially true about goals which are in force, understandings about the environment and competitors, market acceptance and image, etc.

Third, the manager attempting to think strategically should be committed to conservation of the organization's resources rather than expecting that a good idea will precipitate a cornucopia of funds, people, and support. It is easy to be creative while assuming that most resource requirements can be taken care of.

A greater degree of creativity is required when one must conserve resources. Finally, strategic thinking must be done without setting patterns which competitors can identify and anticipate. The problems of predictable strategic thinking are analogous to the football coach sending in plays to his quarterback using hand signals that are understood by the opposing team's coaches.

EVOLUTION OF STRATEGIC MANAGEMENT

Gluck, Kaufman, and Walleck propose a model of the evolution of strategic management within organizations whose managers have a propensity to plan. The model is based on a study undertaken by McKinsey and Company. Part of the reason for including a summary of their model here is to help students recognize the strategic management stage in which a particular organization might be.

Such information may provide additional insight into the operation of the firm and help understand the degree of strategic management progress made by managers. More importantly, however, it may be useful in helping students understand strategic management as the highest level of a hierarchy of management activities.

The McKinsey analysis discovered four quite distinct phases of strategic management evolution. In Phase 1, financial planning, management focuses on the preparation of budgets with an emphasis on functional operations. Most organizations have a budgeting process, in at least rudimentary form, as a way of allocating resources among functional units, subsidiaries, or projects.

The second, forecast-based planning, follows naturally from the first as managers project budget requirements beyond the one-year cycle.

This phase represents an effort to extend managers' attention beyond the immediate future as scenarios are developed which describe their expectations about future time periods.

Budgets are often constructed for several years at a time and are rolled over annually so that the appropriateness of a budgeted amount can be reviewed several times before it is operationalized. Phase 2 planning is very "now" oriented.

Current operations and characteristics are stressed in analyses of the firm and there is little attention to or patience for considering operational options or development of strategic changes. The business portfolio of a Phase 2 firm is often viewed as the final expression of strategy rather than as an input to the strategy formulation process. Current structure and business activities may be considered fixed, not as strategic variables.

Planners are required to adopt an external orientation and tools and procedures for environmental and internal assessment.

Concern centers on understanding the organization's environment and competitive position and generating ideas about how the company might better fit its environment. Several choices, contingency plans, are often devised for how the company might fit its environment. Lower level planners and managers are often involved in the process of generating choices, an activity that soon puts top management in the position of choosing a plan in which it had little involvement in developing.

Strategic management, evolves as top management senses the need to more heavily invest in the planning process because of its lack of understanding of or involvement in the details of earlier plan development. Strategic management is the meshing of Phase 3 planning and operational management into one process.

It is analysis and conclusion that takes place year-round and ties performance evaluation and motivational programs to strategy.

Deliberateness of Strategy

Sometimes outsiders impute strategy to the behaviour of firms. Obviously, students analyzing case studies are placed in this position when they impute strategy from the data they are able to generate on the firm's operations. Similarly, journalists and the managers of competing firms may impute strategy to a firm's behaviour; and it may or may not accurately reflect the real strategy in place.

Outsiders may also imply intent to an imputed strategy. That is, they assume not only that the strategy they imputed from the firm's behaviour is the real strategy its employees are implementing, but they imply that this strategy is the one intended for the firm by its management. Seldom is this the case.

Mintzberg developed a taxonomy which is useful for discussing the realism and deliberateness of strategy. First, he distinguished between strategy that is the result of a plan, and of a pattern of behaviour.

He referred to them as "strategy as plan" and "strategy as pattern," respectively. Strategy as plan is a chosen course of action; it could be a real strategy (one intended for implementation) or a ploy (a tactical move whereby a competitor may be influenced into making a mistake). Some people think that Coca-Cola's rumored change in Coke's formula in the mid-1980s was such a ploy.

The implication is that Coca-Cola had not intended to really change the formula. Instead, it is thought, they publicized their plan to change formula, intoduced a new product with a different formula that tasted a lot like a competitor's product, and finally graciously conceded to continue producing the old formula product when the public demonstrated a preference for it over the new—"similar to a competitor's—" formula.

Incidentally, if this was in fact a ploy, it has to rank among the top marketing moves ever attempted by any business. Coca-Cola reaped an immediate increase in market share of about 15 per cent that thrust them once again into unquestioned dominance in the huge U.S. softdrink market.

Strategy as plan, when implemented, may or may not be what the firm ends up with. That is, the planned strategy could ultimately be either realized or unrealized.

If it is realized, then the entire process would be a textbook case of strategy formulation and implementation in the sense that the firm successfully implemented what was intended.

But what happens if the planned strategy is implemented and, for some reason, the strategy that is realized is not the intended one? We might say that the planned strategy was unrealized, and the realized strategy (the one that seems to describe what the company is actually doing) arises out of some consistency in the behaviour of the company.

Mintzberg and Waters call this unintended realized strategy, "strategy as pattern," or a pattern in a series of actions by the organization. Strategy as pattern is what you will end up with when you impute strategy to the behaviour of a company you are analyzing in a case study, or what journalists produce when they attribute a strategy to a company based only on its actions.

Thus, a realized strategy could be either a deliberate strategy as plan, or an "undeliberate" strategy as pattern. If the realized strategy was planned and also accurately described the firm's actions, then strategy as pattern and strategy as plan would be synonymous. However, when realized strategy is not intended strategy (that is, it was either not what was intended by management when they drafted a planned strategy, or they drafted no strategy at all), then it simply "grew" out of the activities of the company. In Mintzberg's terms, it "emerged" as a pattern of behaviour in the absence of intension, or despite unrealized intentions.

A realized strategy is what a company is actually doing. If it is the one intended by management, then it is deliberate If not, then the intended strategy wasunrealized, and the realized strategy is emergent. An emergent strategy is, by definition, not deliberate.

However, a manager may choose not to consciously formulate strategy and, instead, "go with" the emergent one. But even here, the resultant emergent strategy would not have been deliberate in the same way an intended strategy would have been.

Often it is convenient to distinguish between intended and emergent strategies. When management performs no strategic management at all, they still will have a realized strategy that is emergent.

This emergent strategy could be recognized by outsiders (and insiders for that matter) even though it may not have been intended my management.

Contingency Strategies

Managers may develop several versions of strategy, each of which is intended to fit a different environmental scenario. An environmental scenario consists of a set of environmental characteristics that describe a firm's external circumstances. By structuring external variables into sets of related variables, different scenarios result.

Thus several scenarios (usually three) can be arrayed on a probability distribution for which the horizonal axis is a measure of the extent to which they are viewed as "good" or "bad"—supportive or not supportive—to the firm.

In the scenarios that fall on the left side of the distribution are considered pessimistic (undesirable but only a small probability that they might have to be dealt with); those on the right as optimistic (desirable but probably will not materialize either); and those in the middle as most likely to occur and having some good and bad features.

Next a strategy set is established for each scenario. These could be entirely different strategies or variations of one. Evaluative criteria then are formulated for each scenario. These are variables to be monitored in order to figure out which of the scenarios is going to apply in the future.

Actually this is a matter of deciding whether the present scenario will continue to be the best description of the firm's environment or, instead, if one of the others seems to be emerging as most correct. By identifying critical values for evaluative criteria, the strategist knows beforehand under what set of conditions to switch from the present strategy set to the pessimistic or optimistic set.

Summary

This chapter serves to familiarize the reader with the underlying principles of strategic management and to outline the path through that field taken by the chapters. First, the history of strategic management as an academic discipline is reviewed to provide perspective on its current stage of development. Next, summarizes the results of some of the major studies conducted to answer the question "Does strategic management pay off?" Also discussed in this section are the primary methodological problems encountered in doing such research.

The mission statement is considered an input to the strategy formulation process, which is outlined in the next section. Strategy at four organizational levels comprise the focus of this section and the book's text. They are the enterprise, corporate, business, and functional levels.

STRATEGIC THINKING

When a roomful of executives is asked, is it fair to say that your business is getting more competitive? A resounding Yes! From each one echoes in response. This happens regardless of industry or service sector, the size of the executive's organization, whether it is domestic or global, or even whether it is from the public or private sector.

All organizations face competition—for resources, people, cash, or customers. Likewise, all organizations face uncertain environments, because both product and technology life cycles are shortening relentlessly.

Never has it been more important for businesses and their leaders to position their organizations strategically for competing successfully in the future.

This requires that managers thoroughly understand the dynamics of their industries, the trends in their external environments, and the basic economics of their firms.

They also must think creatively enough to craft strategies that make their companies unique and inspire their organizations to perform to ever increasing standards. Finally, they must balance the multiple activities of the various functions in their organizations and galvanize them toward unified action. To accomplish all these activities simultaneously requires that managers engage in *strategic thinking* and *strategic management*.

Strategic management encompasses the activities of senior-level executives in their attempts to influence the overall direction of their corporations. This textbook covers many of the approaches that help executives increase that influence by developing successful business and corporate strategies.

Strategic thinking, on the other hand, can occur at all levels of the organization—from brand managers to production supervisors, from sales executives to financial planners and analysts. Strategic thinking at these levels involves understanding the role of one's firm in the marketplace and how one's individual function contributes to that role.

Just as a guitar player or drummer needs to know the bandleader's intent with a piece of music in order to provide masterful support to the whole, every individual in a corporation can provide better customer service, better information back to the home office, and make better personnel decisions if she or he has a good understanding of both the company's strategy and some basic strategic management principles.

This textbook provides concepts and tools to aspiring managers who wish to add value to their companies by making strategically sound decisions, whatever their functions or responsibilities may be.

EVOLUTION OF STRATEGIC THINKING

Strategic thinking evolved from the different approaches that companies utilize to plan their business activities. Prior to the 1920s, few firms did any of what today might be called "long-term planning." Most businesses were run more or less entrepreneurially, and business decisions were relatively short term in focus. Manufacturing produced products, sales sold them, and accounting counted the money. Many businesses were driven by a focus on survival.

With the advent of the modern corporation, such as General Motors and DuPont in the 1920s, larger and more far-flung enterprises needed mechanisms to plan and allocate resources. Financial planning provided senior managers with a sophisticated set of tools with which to plan annual production, expenses, and capital investments.

The methods typically involved translating sales forecasts into production schedules, estimating the costs associated with the planned volume, and deriving profit forecasts. Once capital appropriations, research, development, advertising, and administrative overhead were taken into account, projecting cash flows available for dividends was a simple and straightforward matter.

This approach, however, was based on a fundamental assumption that sales projections could be made. In a stable world, this assumption held. Sales forecasters had only to extrapolate from the past.

But when times changed—the economy slowed, markets got saturated, or other events affected demand—the limitations of this method became obvious. Also, this approach tended to treat departments within the business as separate functions (sales forecast ? manufacturing costs ? financial results) and tended to have a one-year horizon.

As a consequence, changes occurring over several years, such as shifting consumer preferences or market saturation, would go unnoticed. Finally, the driver of business behaviour under financial planning systems tended to have short-term goals, which were often oriented toward meeting the budget for the year.

To deal with longer-horizon changes, forecast-based planning was developed in the 1950s and 1960s. Here, the rigor of analyses jumped dramatically, as planners began using such tools and concepts as product life cycles, discounted cash flows and net present value analyses, and statistically valid market research of consumer preferences and buying behaviour.

Because the level of sophistication and time required by these tools was significantly greater than called for previously, managers needed assistance from a new breed of technical experts—strategic planners, business school graduates, and consulting firms. Business schools grew at unprecedented rates in the 1960s and 1970s, and the consulting profession boomed as new strategic planning firms, such as the Boston Consulting Group and Bain & Company, were founded and flourished. The behaviour driver under forecast-based planning was to predict the future and to plan strategies that would adapt the firm to that future.

In other words, it was reactive. At the same time, staff planners and consultants found that many of their strategic recommendations were not getting implemented. This occurred for two reasons.

One reason was that often the analyses and recommendations were performed by people who were not responsible for executing the strategy. Without the ownership that comes with participation, many line executives either rejected plans or, at best, were lukewarm in their compliance.

The second reason was that plans that were based on analyzing consumer trends and product acceptance often failed to take *competitor* behaviour into account. The strategic management approach was developed in response to these limitations.

Strategic *management,* in contrast to strategic *planning,* is the function of line executives—the people on the firing line who deal with the real world of customers, machines, products, and people.

The philosophy is simple: the people closest to the action are in the best position to know what is going on in the business, what works, what trends are developing, and what competitors are doing. In other words, those who must execute must be involved in developing strategy.

A second part of the philosophy is also simple: it is not sufficient to look for-ward (at potential consumer demand for a new product, for example). Managers must also look to the right and to the left—at what competitors are doing. In other words, competitive analysis becomes a key feature in strategic thinking.

The dilemma, however, is twofold:

- Usually, line managers do not have the time to do strategic analyses. As you will see in the Astral

Records case, a general manager's life is cluttered with a multitude of conflicting demands on his or her time. So, managers must either take time out—such as at a planning retreat, for example—or they must learn so much about strategy and competition that they are thinking strategically on the job.

- Even if managers create the time for strategic planning, they often lack the tools. Their training may have been thorough in the *functional* areas of marketing, accounting, engineering, or human resources, but it may have been insufficient in *strategic* concepts, frameworks, and tools. As stated earlier, the purpose of this book is to provide these tools.

In a firm equipped with strategic management tools and strategic thinking managers and executives, the behaviour driver shifts from a mentality of survival, meeting the budget, or merely forecasting the future, to one of *creating* the future by shaping one's industry and markets rather than reacting to them.

A firm that is truly thinking strategically can be identified in a number of ways. First, its executives know and understand what the firm's mission and strategy are. Second, they know their core competencies and capabilities as an organization.

Third, they can identify their competitors and predict their reactions to the firm's strategic moves. Fourth, they have developed a culture that supports their strategy.

Finally, they are constantly developing new capabilities for renewing their strategies and for competing successfully in the future.

BECOMING A STRATEGIC THINKER

So, how do managers and their companies develop strategic thinking? Must they go through the stages listed above, one at a time? Fortunately, no. It is essential that managers know how to do financial planning, market research, and other fundamental business analyses. But they need not wait to master these before progressing to strategic management and thinking.

ELEMENTS OF STRATEGIC THINKING

Strategic *planning* has a fairly well-established history. The first book on strategy was written in 1965 by Igor Ansoff, an executive at Lockheed Aerospace. Titled *Corporate Strategy,* it presented an extraordinarily logical, step-by-step set of concepts and approaches to making diversification decisions.

When presented with this model as a how-to-do-strategy template, most practicing managers run for cover. The thoroughness of the model forces the analyst to think through the logic and economics of the business. But this thoroughness comes at the price of appearing overwhelming to busy line executives.

All strategic planning approaches attempt to find an optimal match between the resources and capabilities available within the firm (Strengths and Weaknesses) and the external market conditions and environmental trends (Opportunities and Threats).

This match or coalignment (often called a SWOT analysis) results in a strategy, whose efficacy translates into some level of corporate performance.

A key feature in the basic strategy model is the reciprocal influence of all of the variables. For example, in the late 1960s a major science-based consulting firm, Sigma Consultants, observed that:

- The level of expenditures on health care in the United States was accelerating, a trend likely to continue,
- The firm had several competent professionals on its staff who had carried out health care related assignments such as designing hospitals and evaluating medical group acquisitions.

By responding to the market opportunity and articulating a health care strategy or consulting practice, Sigma would define a new domain.

Having chosen the new domain, the firm would now have to respond to the dictates of the marketplace (arrow from environment to strategy) by, for example, designing products and services that were in demand or adapting to whatever governmental regulation might be relevant. To implement the new strategy, Sigma might reorganize its staff so that all professionals working on health care related assignments were grouped together.

Over time, this group might increase its proficiency by sharing experience, knowledge, and the like. The degree of success would be manifested in some level of performance (arrow from strategy to performance), and, in turn, the performance level would serve as feedback, indicating that further adaptations of strategy might be in order.

In essence, then, the model represents a system of interacting parts. But the picture painted thus far is not complete. A "perfect" strategy may be found that violates managers' predispositions. Conversely, management's values may suggest strategies that are not optimal in an economic sense. For example, President Jay Monroe of the Tensor Corporation refused to change his very "functional" high-intensity Tensor lamps when new competitors started introducing style variations.

As a result, his company lost 60 per cent of the market, which it probably could have retained had Monroe's values been more economic than aesthetic.

In our Sigma Consultants example, there was strong support for the health care venture among senior management and some of the professional staff. That is, the venture fit the values of top management. However, Sigma was originally organized on the model of a research lab, in which professionals were unimpeded by bureaucratic hierarchy and were free to choose their projects.

Assignment to projects was by invitation, and, assuming the invited person was billing sufficient time to avoid the pressure to join projects indiscriminately, he or she could turn these projects down.

The health care strategy, in contrast, suggested an organizational unit in which consultants would be expected to dedicate themselves to one major type of activity. This ran smack against the prevailing culture. The strategy was abandoned.

Although it is a very "rational" model of strategy, needs to be amplified to consider the imple-mentabilityof strategy. Management needs to include the "soft" sides of strategy, political feasibility, and organizational acceptability.

The model outlined as suggests a sequence of activities in the strategic management process. These activities constitute the fundamental components of strategic management:

- Environmental trends analysis and scenario building
- Industry and competitive analysis
- Identification of past and current strategy
- Strategy evaluation
- Identification of competitive advantages
- Strategic choice
- Cultural analysis
- Strategic change

Chapter 2

Environmental, Industry, and Internal Analyses

INTRODUCTION

A great deal must be learned about an organization so that strategy formulation decisions can be based upon appropriate information. It almost goes without saying that strategists must understand all there is to know about the internal operations of an organization before strategy can be effectively formulated and implemented.

The external influences acting on the firm also must be analyzed, documented, and understood to manage the strategy process effectively. This chapter focuses on conducting both external and internal analyses for the purpose of generating information for strategy formulation.

The chapter has two major sections—environmental analysis and internal analysis. An organization's environment consists of two parts: The industry within which it operates (for multibusiness firms, the industry is usually considered the activity in which the firm generates the majority of its revenue), and other environmental dimensions—economic, political/legal, social, and technological.

The section of this chapter devoted to internal analysis first addresses financial analysis—the process of learning about the financial performance of the firm or organization. Very often financial analysis will bring to light several financial strengths and weaknesses that are indicative of strategic or operating capabilities and problems within the various strategy levels and within functional areas. Financial analysis is typically followed by internal diagnosis of functional areas. This process identifies strengths and weaknesses within such areas as marketing, personnel, research and development, and others.

Together these four analytical activities—environmental, industry, and financial analysis and internal diagnosis of functional areas—are undertaken to generate a data set consisting of strengths, weaknesses, threats, and opportunities that comprehensively describes the internal and external characteristics of the organization.

This information is then used as input to the strategy formulation process. It is factored with data about past strategies, mission, corporate culture, managers' values, and so on to evaluate the success or failure of present strategies. As a result present strategies either can be modified, left as they are, or replaced as necessary in a particular situation.

STRUCTURE OF DATA

By its nature strategic management necessitates contextual thinking—the recognition that all organization activities, whether planned or not, occur under sets of very specific and real circumstances. These circumstances or contexts often change dramatically over time, and differ substantially from firm to firm, industry to industry, and market to market.

The withdrawal of the United States from the 1980 Olympic Games left many firms in the lurch. A small specialty T-shirt manufacturer was stuck with unsalable inventory. The NBC television network found itself out hundreds of millions of dollars in lost broadcasting and advertising revenues. Under different circumstances these ventures might have proved successful, but conditions largely outside their control changed to doom their prospects to failure.

The key to effective strategic management is to make major managerial decisions that shape actions by the firm that will correspond positively with the context within which those actions ultimately take place. The financial resources of NBC allowed it to weather the Olympic storm; for the T-shirt enterprise, the lack of adequate financial strength did not.

On the other hand, the action context is dictated to a great degree by conditions external to the firm. These conditions constitute the firm's operating "environment." To some extent the firm can shape the overall environment to its advantage.

Henry Ford's introduction of mass production of automobiles stimulated the U.S. economy in a manner that invigorated consumer markets for his products. Genentech, the recombinant DNA research firm, made biotechnical advances that had profound impacts, not just on Genentech's operating circumstances, but on the future of humankind as well. Nonetheless, few firms enjoy a scale of impact that allows major shaping of the overall climate in which they operate, particularly over the long run. Instead well-managed business enterprises adapt to environmental change so that they can take advantage of opportunities that arise and minimize the otherwise adverse impacts of environmental threats.

This involves assessment of present environmental circumstances (for reaction) and the forecasting of future conditions (for proaction).

These key positive and negative factors of both the firm's external environment and its internal operations, which represents the data set developed for strategic management. A data set has both present and future time frames as internal and external, positive and negative factors are forecast into future periods. Environmental and industry analysis involves filling the right-hand sectors of the data set with information pertinent to a particular firm.

Analysis of the internal operations of the organization results in a collection of strengths and weaknesses that would fill the left-hand cells of the data set model.

Environmental conditions affect the entire strategic management process. Management's perceptions of present and future operating environments and internal strengths and weaknesses provide inputs to goal and action plan choices. They can also affect the manner in which implementation and internal circumstances will dictate the effectiveness of strategies as they are implemented (including alterations in the environment itself).

The implementation stage of strategic management provides the real, as opposed to the expected, interface between the firm and its environment.

The effects of the environment on the organization, as well as the success of its present strategies, are ultimately reflected in its financial statements.

A large part of the task of internal diagnosis is accomplished by financial analysis. Of course, there is more to analyzing the internal operations of a business than financial analysis.

By understanding the theory and practice of management, marketing, accounting, personnel, production, and other functional aspects of organizational performance, internal strengths and weaknesses beyond those found by financial analysis can be found. But financial analysis uncovers clues to functional strengths and weaknesses.

Both environmental and industry analysis procedures consist of four interrelated processes:

- Developing an assessment taxonomy to outline major environmental dimensions.
- Defining environmental boundaries (the "relevancy envelope").
- Monitoring and forecasting change in key variables.
- Assessing potential impacts on the firm (or industry) in terms of whether they are threats or opportunities.

In the sections that follow, we discuss these processes for undertaking an environmental analysis, and then explain how they apply to the task of conducting a complementary industry analysis. Application of Porter's "Five Forces Model of Competition" is explained as one element of an industry analysis. Designing strategic group maps is presented as another.

Finally, a procedure for carrying out an internal analysis is discussed that consists of two phases. The first is financial analysis. The four processes above apply to financial analysis, but with some modifications. An assessment taxonomy and a set of environmental boundaries are well established for financial analysis and are explained in that section. Key variables are the various financial entities measured during such an analysis and assessment of their potential impacts on the firm is its purpose.

In the second phase of an internal analysis, the other functions of the firm are analyzed. The financial analysis reveals many questions about the operations of functional departments, which can be answered through analysis of those departments.

However, the four processes do not apply so neatly to the other functional areas, but they do apply generally. For each area an assessment taxonomy must first be developed, although it and the boundaries of each function will be different. Consequently we present a taxonomy and a set of key variables for each major function.

FORMAL VERSUS INFORMAL SCANNING

Sensing the pulse of environmental threats and opportunities is a natural and continuous process in business planning. In many organizations it is done on an informal basis. The construction firm executive who learns from a golfing colleague of a request for bids on a major construction project is gaining information that could affect the performance of his firm—information that would be no more valuable had it been acquired through more systematic means. Discovering changes in tax statutes by perusing the Wall Street Journal is no less important than learning about them through a well-established monitoring system within the firm's tax accounting office. Indeed, the talent for acquiring valuable information through informal means often marks the successful entrepreneur and manager.

To rely totally on informal means, however, increasingly exposes the firm to missed opportunities and unforeseen threats. A rained-out golf game or an overlooked column in the Wall Street Journal can have profound implications, even if the implications themselves go unnoticed. Therefore, a systematic approach to environmental assessment is important for the management of uncertainty and risk.

One formal approach to generating data about environmental conditions is survey research. The use of both original and contracted survey research for purposes of evaluating the present corporate environment offers a lot of promise for strategists.

For analysis of external concerns in the present, survey research is a way to accurately identify the attitudes of selected population groups toward the company. In fact, virtually any external constituency's attitudes toward the organization can be assessed through survey research methods.

ENVIRONMENTAL ANALYSIS ASSESSMENT TAXONOMY

The dimensions of environment can be generally classified by a set of key factors that describe the economic, political/legal, technological, and social surroundings.

These, in turn, can be overlaid by the various constituents of the firm, including shareholders, customers, competitors, suppliers, employees, and the general public.

To assess environmental conditions, concern is focused on opportunities and threats that exist, or may arise, through impacts on and by the firm's constituents.

Key Economic Variables

Changes in economic circumstances can be as global as the new worldwide economic order initiated by petropolitics, or as localized as a small town plagued by a plant closing. Firms that anticipate economic change and identify the constituents through which that change will be applied, can better adapt goals and action plans.

By the late-1990s, major oil producing firms has shifted their source of supply from middle-eastern countries to Venezuela because of uncertainties about the political and economic environment of the middle east. Shareholder expectations of financial return are dictated in part by alternative investments and their associated returns and risks. Interest rates, tax policies, shareholder incomes, availability of funds for margin-purchased equity investments, and expectations of future economic circumstances will shape changes in equity investor profiles and/or the financial performance expectations of the firm's owners.

In the early 1980s, high returns on money market instruments (representing corporate and government debt) led to massive shifts from equity holdings by private investors to those shorter-term debt instruments. In many cases this disturbed long-standing shareholder composites (making more room for institutional investors, for example) and pressured management to focus more closely on generating higher short-term returns.

Personal income, savings, employment, and price-level trends can have dramatic effects on the attractiveness of a firm's products or services in output markets—not only final markets, but intermediate markets as well. In efforts to reduce costs during inflationary periods, automotive manufacturers during the 1980s reduced their reliance on outside suppliers for automobile components. This, in turn, led many component manufacturers to retrench or redirect their marketing efforts elsewhere (e.g., replacement parts).

Similarly, total sectoral outputs, movements in private-sector capital replacement and expansion, government spending, and the allocation of the consumer dollar can have dramatic impacts between and within industrial sectors. Each can be set off as macroeconomic changes well outside the control of the firm, yet may be buffered by appropriate strategic action.

Twenty years of inflation, for example, increased consumer use of $50 and $100 bills in retail trade. Among other implications, this meant that many retailers had to replace cash drawers, or entire cash registers, to accommodate these denominations.

More significantly, the collapse of the Soviet Union has led to decreased government spending in the U.S. on defence items. Many thousands of prime defence contractors and their subcontractors spent the early-1990s trying to develop new strategies based on non-military products.

Economic conditions faced by competitors can play a large part in shaping a firm's strategies and policies. The movement of manufacturers out of the "snow belt" to areas of the country with lower energy costs could provide decisive competitive advantages vis-a-vis those who remain. Transportation costs, on the other hand, could reduce those savings. Competitors selling to diverse markets might realise less volatility in their capital bases and abilities to compete across economic cycles than might a firm with a narrow product/market scope.

In any case it is important to recognize that the economic conditions faced by the competition may be different in form and substance from those faced by the target firm. The capacity, reliability, and, in some case, the survivability of suppliers are largely a function of their economic climate. Both debt and equity capital markets often realise significant swings as a result of overall economic conditions. The firm accessing these markets experiences the repercussions.

Federal discount rates and changes in reserve requirements have both short-term and long-term implications in primary capital markets, and often affect the private sector borrower through secondary markets.

The available supply of goods and services can be affected by the overall economic health of suppliers, including their productivity, alternative markets, and cost structures.

To the extent that the target firm represents a major market for a supplier, that firm becomes a significant factor in the economic climate the supplier experiences.

The choice of multiple versus singular sources of supply might be dictated by assessments of suppliers' economic bases as well as by the degree of control the buying firm can maintain over them.

Though adverse economic circumstances could threaten sources of supply, They could also provide buying leverage for the firm or represent new opportunities for backward integration.

The economic climate of the firm is also manifested through employees. Wage and benefit escalations are often as much a function of the overall economic circumstances employees face as they are unilateral policy set forth by employers.

Rising consumer prices are usually translated into expectations and/or demands for increased compensation. Shifts in employment status, including societal and regional unemployment levels, can increase or decrease these pressures.

Economic conditions usually affect employees unevenly, thus requiring creative policy adaptation. Depression of housing markets in the early 1980s, for example, led a number of large employers to buy homes from transferred executives, who were unable to sell them at reasonable prices, if at all. This inadvertently put a number of these firms into the real estate "business" (albeit on a relatively small scale), tying up capital and effort.

Clearly, economic conditions have wide-reaching effects on the general public. These can be as abstract as alterations in high birth rate trends or as direct as changes in personal income.

Conversely, public expectations and behaviour substantially determine the health or inadequacy of the economy, through earning, spending, and saving patterns. In any case the general public is so intertwined in the mechanics and psychology of a firm's economic climate that movement by one can have dramatic implications for the other.

Kinder-Care Learning Centers, Inc., a chain of child-care centers, both profited by the economic (and social) trend toward working mothers and contributed to the trend by providing necessary child care at reasonable cost. The overall impact was synergistic.

Finally, in assessing the economic dimension of a firm's environment, it is important to recognize the interrelated nature of the participants.

The multiplier effect in macroeconomics has its micro counterpart. Raw data on prices, wages, savings, government spending, manufacturers' shipments, and the like are valuable in themselves, but represent only the front line of a truly comprehensive analysis.

Key Political/Legal Variables

Business firms, like people, are touched directly and indirectly by political/legal influences at all levels of government (federal, state, and local). These influences run the alphabetic gamut from antitrust to zoning.

The scale of federal intervention in business is matched only by its turbulence. The Centre for the Study of American Business concluded that federal regulation of business "cost the American economy more than $100 billion in 1980. Approximately $5 billion represented the administrative costs of the major regulatory agencies, and the balance, compliance costs." In addition to serving as regulatory bodies, governments also represent a major factor in the private sector through fiscal policy. Taxation and government spending can represent both opportunities and threats, depending upon the nature, timing, and position of the impacted enterprise. And, of course, fiscal policy can have dramatic impacts on the overall economic climate of the firm.

Shareholders are affected by governments in a variety of ways. Changes in tax structures can affect tax exposure on corporate payouts when treatments of capital recovery versus earnings distributions are considered.

To the extent that corporations themselves are shareholders, intercorporate shareholding can be constrained by antitrust laws. Security and Exchange Commission regulations can affect the "tradability" of shares as well as dictate corporate disclosures. Laws dealing with pension funds and other forms of institutional investing can exhilarate or impair changes in investor profiles.

Incorporation laws often constrain flexibility in capital restructuring. All of these impositions, in turn, create the need for corporate adaptation to shareholder expectations and requirements. Government-mandated sales prohibitions (e.g., on certain firearms) can limit markets. Similarly, export restrictions (national and interstate) can impose market constraints.

Conversely, public policies targeting industries for rejuvenation or expansion can open up a host of market opportunities (such as trade-adjustment programs in energy and steel). Social legislation (e.g., environmental protection, health, consumer protection) can create markets for new classes of products and services as well as limit those where noncompliance exists.

Politics and law are influenced by, and have an impact on, competitors. Antitrust can sustain or impair industry structures and thereby affect the nature of present and future competition. Import restrictions can limit foreign competition. Patent laws provide competitive protection for patent holders.

Governments themselves can be suppliers (e.g., mineral rights). And, of course, the viability of suppliers as a whole can be affected by all forms of political/legal influences. During mid-1993, hospital administrators in the state of Maine estimated that they were experiencing about a 20 per cent vacancy rate in their facilities.

Retrenchment became necessary to survival for a large number of facilities. The Maine legislature then passed a law freeing their state's hospitals from antitrust provisions that prohibited asset-sharing among institutions.

This minor legal change alone may save countless millions of dollars in Maine's health care industry by eliminating unnecessary duplication of equipment purchases and operations.

Cooperation among hospitals is no longer an antitrust violation. Similarly, state legislatures adopting mandatory automobile insurance laws have had dramatic affects on their states' insurance industries.

Protection of employees is clearly a major matter in any firm. Wage laws, labour statutes, equal employment opportunity, occupational safety and health, employee privacy, and pension fund controls all represent areas of strategy concern. Further, the public sector competes with the private sector for employees. Through support of education and training programs, the public sector also represents a source of labour.

Finally, the political/legal climate is both a function and a determinant of public sentiments. Federal regulatory reform (including deregulation) is a prime example. Public expectations of business behaviour can cause, and be caused by, shifts in partisan politics, which in turn can affect the overall socioeconomic climate in which private sector enterprises operate.

Expansionary and technologically aggressive moods on the part of the general public have their counterparts in business and industry, though they need not always be similarly timed (Wall Street, the public, and Washington are occasionally out of phase in this regard).

Assessing and forecasting the political/legal environment require creativity and a sensitivity to industry-specific matters. Unlike the economic environment, the political/legal environment requires a largely "soft" calculus where numerical relationships and extrapolations are often unavailable or inappropriate.

Key Technological Variables

Electronics, bioengineering, chemicals, energy, medicine, and space are but a few of the fields in which major technological change have opened new areas to private enterprise. In some cases entire industries have emerged seemingly overnight (such as genetic engineering), bringing with them new opportunities, and new threats, in the marketplace.

In other cases technological changes within industries have brought new forms of product competition (e.g., micro technologies in electronics) that require an openness to new applications. In still others technological process changes (as in the use of robots in automobile manufacturing) have led to different competitive advantages in production costs and product quality.

In all instances the firm subject to technological obsolescence or intent on maintaining some form of technological leadership must stay abreast of technological innovation, and to the extent possible, forecast future technological change and its potential for acceptance. That Timex vastly underestimated market acceptance of the digital watch early in its life cycle is but one of many instances of technological displacement having adverse effects on those caught unaware.

Technological change has had implications for shareholders, primarily through communications and information processing. High-speed, computer-based market reports are reaching increasingly larger proportions of stock market participants. On-line office and in-the-home displays mean quicker reaction time in market "plays," and the proliferation of FAX machines and worldwide e-mail systems make round-the-clock real-time communications commonplace.

New products and processes resulting from technological innovation can result in redefinition of customer bases or customer demands. The design of new, relatively lightweight diesel engines opened up a host of opportunities in the passenger-car industry.

Computer-aided design and computer-aided manufacturing (CAD/CAM) have led to the expectation of shorter lead times and much closer tolerances in many industrial and consumer products industries (e.g., aerospace and automobiles).

The home information revolution not only may expand markets for consumer product retailers, but may well lead to better informed, more discerning retail customers.

So too the nature of competition can be redefined as technological advances unfold. In the oil-well wire-line (or "logging") industry, new techniques allow in-the-well sensing of critical geophysical characteristics (temperatures, pressures, etc.) while drilling gear is in place.

Older technologies require expensive and time-consuming removal of the gear before these measurements can be made. Thus those firms with access to the new technology have a marked, competitive advantage. Price is no longer a significant factor when the competition for business is between those with and those without the technology.

In acquiring the advantages of new technology, a firm might rely heavily on its suppliers. Manufacturers may turn to equipment suppliers for the latest in robotics, or food processors to pharmaceutical or chemical firms for the latest in preservatives. In each case technological advantage is passed through the production chain, with competitive differentials possible at each stage.

Sources of supply can also be redefined with technological innovation. Fibre optics, for example, may well displace metal wire as a primary medium in telecommunications. Telecommunications firms thus would turn to the glass industry instead of the wire industry for this critical material.

Employees continually experience the impact of technology by virtue of changes in requisite skills and job assignments. Automation has led to the conversion of hand labour to higher skills needed in machine design, operation, and maintenance. Even work routines are affected. As telecommunicating attracts ever-greater interest, more and more types of work may be accomplished more effectively and efficiently away from the traditional workplace (at home or at local offices). Finally, technological change looms large in the overall picture of public experiences and expectations. Dissatisfaction with technological lags in the steel industry led to government investigations. Fear about runaway advances in bioengineering have resulted in self-imposed restraint among firms involved.

Expectations of technological solutions to serious socioeconomic problems (e.g., energy) may have implications for public policy and for strategic adaptations within affected industries. And of course everyday life is changed permanently by technology.

The spread of Automatic Teller Machines in banking has dramatically changed our banking habits. Not many people under-thirty remember the pre-ATM days when consumers had difficulty accessing their cash on weekends because the banks were closed. The time we save preparing food by microwave oven we now lose by watching video-taped movies at home!

Few firms are left untouched by technological change, although some may be more severely or rapidly affected than others. To the extent that technological innovation is a key factor of success in a given industry, it must be monitored and forecast aggressively. In all cases at least a general sensitivity to the technological environment is a primary component of successful strategic planning.

Key Social Variables

The overall social climate in which business operates has broad systemic implications for U.S. firms rooted in the free enterprise system. Under the doctrine of "enlightened self-interest," business enterprise exists to satisfy the needs and wants of society, which can sustain or impair the enterprise's existence through public pressure.

On a more micro level, it is clear that public wants and needs can significantly determine the effectiveness of a given firm's strategy. The marketing concept is designed to deal with one facet of the business-society relationship on a firm-by-firm and product-by-product basis.

As with the other dimensions of a firm's environment, social conditions can pose both opportunities and threats. Computer crime, for example, has become a major concern in industry, and is expensive to control. At the same time, a new field within the computer industry has emerged to provide computer crime control services and systems. Thus one profits from the social circumstances from which the others suffer economically.

Since present and future shareholders are drawn from segments of the general public, demographic shifts hold the potential for redefining shareholder profiles. To the extent that age or marital status distribution may be related to preferences for income-yielding as opposed to capital-appreciation equity investments, overall growth strategies and dividend payout policies may be affected. Increased education and greater awareness of stock and debt investments provide the potential for expanding capital markets. Clearly pension programs are affected by age distributions of the participants, which in turn affect the availability of debt and equity funds.

Institutional investors have also placed immediate demands (albeit with limited success in some instances) on individual firm's operating strategy. A number of religious groups, in their capacity as institutional investors, took issue with the involvement by U.S. firms in the Union of South Africa. As shareholders the groups called for complete withdrawal from that country or the reformation of personnel strategy in branches there so that they would not conform to the host government's apartheid mandates.

Demographic research within marketing circles is precisely designed to assess population characteristics as they relate to market potential and threats. An aging population, for example, represents a distinct opportunity for a firm selling geriatric products.

Increases in the number of "live alones," and therefore households, represent many opportunities for firms selling household products. Similarly, data on consumer buying habits might allow a firm to reposition its marketing channels or alter its advertising mix.

Changing consumer awareness and concomitant market responses might call for changes in product quality or positioning. Consumer perceptions of the quality of Japanese-made products, for example, have changed so dramatically over the past fifteen years as to give the Japanese an a priori differential competitive advantage, as opposed to an earlier disadvantage, in this regard. Perceived quality differentials have reversed in many industries so that domestic manufacturers must now compete on the basis of price.

Special trends and fads also have marked implications for product/market choices. Increased interest in personal health has led to major market opportunities in products and services from health foods to jogging clothes to in-the-home medical equipment. Athletic clubs became a booming new industry in some parts of the U.S. Greater concern over crime has allowed industrial security firms to expand to consumer markets with home security devices. And certainly success in the apparel industry is closely linked to fads and styles in the marketplace.

Competitors may be positively or negatively affected by social change, depending upon how they have adapted to it. Regional shifts in population have given some firms in the housing industry a distinct locational advantage (e.g., those in the sun belt), which also is true for firms that rely on population increases for market expansion. United States firms hold a distinct advantage over overseas competitors among buyers whose nationalistic spirit inspires a preference for U.S.-made products.

Suppliers face similar social constraints and promises. The existence of cooperatives, particularly in agriculture, reflects a collectivist approach toward the marketplace, the binds of which the buying firm may have to tolerate.

Aside from strictly labour pool concerns, modern enterprise must also consider the changing needs of employees in developing effective strategies.

Flexible hours, the four-day work week, job sharing, the cafeteria approach to employee benefits, and other personnel strategy matters are largely responses to changing employee requirements.

Increased demands for leisure time, individual privacy, freedom from harassment, equal opportunity, personal safety, and job protection all represent fundamental social expectations that have become manifest in the management of the workplace.

Finally, the general aura of social change, including shifts in basic ideologies, can have profound implications for the propriety of strategic choice. Social consciences can bring with them challenges that call the most successful business enterprises to task. Dow Chemical's napalm production during the Vietnam era resulted in unwanted visibility that led to a deemphasis of the Dow name on its consumer products.

Concern over the ability of both the public and private sectors to control nuclear power safely has set the entire industry back on its heels. In both cases the strategic implications have been real and monumental.

Identifying Environmental Boundaries

Defining environmental boundaries involves the choice of criteria or constraints that will bound the breadth, depth, and forecasting horizon of the analysis. Breadth refers to the topical coverage of the scan.

A narrow assessment for a metal products firm might entail heavy concentration on domestic raw material sources, whereas a broader assessment for an international conglomerate could involve identification of geopolitical instabilities worldwide. In an extreme case, the breadth could be largely unbounded—an open-ended search for commercial opportunities, for example.

The depth of environmental assessment determines the degree of detail in the data sought and analyzed. Assessing Mideast geopolitics could be undertaken rather generally by identifying competing power bases and gaining a general understanding of regional political history.

On the other hand, such an assessment may be most useful for a textile machinery firm only when brought to the level of examining specific trade restrictions on soft-goods production equipment.

The appropriate breadth, depth, and forecasting horizon of an environmental scan is dictated n large part by a firm's present overall strategy. Geographic boundaries for a multinational firm would normally transcend those of a regional retail chain, particularly if the latter intends to remain a regional business.

A firm whose strategy is built around high technology would likely be much more concerned with the details of "cutting edge" technologies than would a wholesaler of durable goods. A firm with substantial fixed commitments with long payback periods will normally have a longer assessment horizon than will a low fixed asset firm.

Environmental boundaries can be at least generally established by examining the firm's strategic postures regarding:

- Geographic diversity
- Product/market scope
- Sources of supply
- Sources of capital
- Technology/innovation
- Regulatory vulnerability
- Return horizon on fixed commitments
- Overall flexibility

The depth and breadth of environmental scanning also are constrained by available resources. Larger firms can often make substantial resource commitments within planning units to conduct formalized scans on a continual basis. Smaller enterprises, however, rarely can make such commitments and must rely on intermittent or more closely focused analyses.

FORECASTING

Implicit in all of our discussions thus far is the need to translate environmental observations into forecasts of the environment within which future goal and action plan formulation and implementation will take place.

This is not to suggest that business planning calls for determination of the future. That is largely impossible. Instead we attempt to forecast or predict environmental conditions (in the context of opportunities and threats) for the purpose of establishing a strategic data set. This data (often called "planning premises") becomes the basis for goal and action plan selection decisions.

In many cases the environmental forecaster needs to make multiple forecasts so that contingency goals and action plans can be developed. For example, a single-point forecast of interest rates one year hence may be a dangerous premise upon which to base an expansion strategy. Instead well-reasoned multiple forecasts of interest rates can lead to contingency expansion strategies, one of which could be implemented as certain economic conditions unfold.

Forecasts can be made in the context of reasonable ranges. Here the analyst is less concerned with anticipation of precisely what the future will bring than with the likely future nature of environmental conditions.

This is especially useful when the forecasting horizon is more distant. For example, one might predict a decrease in federal defence spending in the range of 5-10 per cent per year over the next five years or continued Japanese investment in U.S. industry, but at a level not to exceed that of, say, 1989. The general direction of change is addressed within the confines of anticipated limits.

Forecasting Techniques

Though a multitude of forecasting techniques might be catalogued, only a few have received recognition in strategic management circles. These techniques can often be used in conjunction with each other to identify opportunities and threats.

Trend extrapolation is probably the most widely used. Most simply put, this involves picking a tracking factor or environmental variable, noting its trend (statistically or otherwise), and extending that trend into the future. Lead and lag correlates often are used in the process.

Linear and nonlinear statistical models and techniques can be used when hard numerical data exist. This normally involves line fitting to historical data, and extending the line into future periods. Most spreadsheet programs and some operating systems have easy-to-use trend line extrapolation routines built into them.

Of course, more sophisticated packages like SPSS (Statistical Package for the Social Sciences) and SAS (Statistical Analysis Software), installed on most computer mainframe systems and also available in microcomputer versions, allow detailed trend line analyses.

As with other forecasting techniques, the validity and reliability of trend extrapolation must be carefully evaluated in each application. Parameters must be appropriately selected, and intrinsic or environmental constraints identified.

If this is not done, incorrect forecasts can result - extrapolating the growth of a young blade of grass could easily yield a tree.

Forecasting by analogy is another widely used technique, although it is not a formal forecasting method. It involves identification of precursor or concurrent events and simple recognition of the relationship. For example, one might have been able to forecast a decline in public interest in the Space Shuttle programme after the first launch since there was a similar decline reaction to Columbus' unspectacular second voyage to the New World. In this case the forecaster is really examining a series of analogous (though not identical) events.

Because forecasting by analogy is used where historical data are inadequate for the more formal trend extrapolation, its validity and reliability are open to challenge.

Delphi represents yet another forecasting procedure. Developed by the Rand Corporation, it basically involves the use of expert opinion through anonymous, iterative, controlled feedback among a group of participants (the expert panel). Normally the panel is polled by questionnaires in a search for opinions on reasonably well-defined issues. Each member responds with a forecast and reasons for it. These responses are then statistically compiled and fed back anonymously to all members of the panel.

This routine continues through subsequent iterations as the information is reprocessed by the experts and new forecasts are generated. Ideally the composite results will move toward a consensus. Though this technique is employed fairly widely in public and private sector planning, it would be of limited use to the student case analyst.

Simulations and econometric models are designed as numerical interpretations of real-world systems (e.g., national economies, ecologies, production systems). They involve the estimation of theoretical and empirically based relationships, which, when taken together, interact quantitatively to produce forecast outcomes. Computers are normally used to make the calculations.

A particular advantage of these techniques is the ability to perform sensitivity analyses. Here the analyst changes assumptions or estimations within the model to generate varying outcomes.

For example, in a dynamic population forecasting model, one might wish to assess the impact of changes in personal income on population mobility.

By varying the income variables in the model, the analyst examines this impact on whatever mobility variables the model contains, thus assessing their sensitivity to income changes. In doing so the analyst is able to evaluate the model itself, as well as gain some understanding of contingency outcomes.

Cross-impact analysis is a forecasting technique designed to assess the interactions among future environmental conditions. The analyst begins by assuming that a set of future environmental circumstances will come true (e.g., four new industry entrants, each holding a 5 per cent market share within six years).

Through the use of matrix analysis, the analyst then attempts to assess the impact of these circumstances on the possibility and timing of others (such as price competition). If nothing else, the analyst is able to expose forecasting inconsistencies and to clarify underlying assumptions in the forecasts themselves.

Finally, scanning and monitoring are forecasting methods insofar as they involve future thinking. The scan is the equivalent of a 360-degree radar sweep, but monitoring is the choice for specific environmental variables or factors that are tracked over time.

The latter merely helps refine and make the gathering and processing of environmental information more efficient. For example, an environmental scan may identify a somewhat subtle shift in the packaging industry toward paper containers for liquid consumer products.

A firm interested in this matter might then choose to monitor industry shipments in that product category closely, and ultimately generate a forecast of future volume. The forecast could involve any of the other techniques. An Important Caveat. Forecasting is not crystal ball gazing. It is conjecture! The analyst must be prepared to revise forecasts as necessary so that appropriate strategy adjustments can be considered.

A forecast that is right in its substance but wrong in its timing can destroy attempts to attain goals. Firms that anticipated, indeed relied on, a second postwar baby boom are still waiting. Understanding the present and anticipating the future are key ingredients of strategic management.

INDUSTRY ANALYSIS

Industry analysis complements analyses of the other dimensions of a firm's environment. It focuses on the industries in which the firm competes.

The breadth and depth of industry analysis and the boundaries for information gathering are defined by these industries.

Thus industry analysis involves the same processes as those identified earlier for environmental analysis, except that it logically must be preceded by identification of the appropriate industries for analysis along with descriptions of the various characteristics of those industries.

Industry analysis is relevant in any of these situations:

- The firm's strategy defines the business in terms of specific industries.
- The firm is facing new forms of extra-industry competition.
- The firm is contemplating entry into a new industry.

An industry perspective is also useful for the student case analyst in that it provides the basis for gaining familiarity with the products, competition, resource requirements, and constraints peculiar to a line of business.

The industry perspective must be used cautiously since an individual firm or business unit can hardly be considered completely protected from direct extra-industry influences.

For example, relaxation in occupational safety and health standards for an industry may come at the same time that an individual firm is singled out for stricter compliance enforcement. The analyst, therefore, is cautioned to assess direct environmental influences as well as the portion of the environment that affects overall industry conditions.

Michael E. Porter developed an assessment model for analyzing industry structure that focuses on the forces imposed on the process of competing by five influences: The intensity of rivalry among competitors, the threat of new entrants, the threat of substitute products, the bargaining power of suppliers, and the bargaining power of buyers or customers. This "Five Forces Model of Competition" is presented in this section.

Some environmental influences affect a firm through the industries in which it competes. These influences, the nature of their present and future effects on the appropriate industries, and characteristics of the relationships between the firm's relevant industries and the firm itself are the subjects of industry analysis. Multiple product/service firms, particularly those that are diversified, will often hold "membership" in more than one industry. This will obviously require multiple analyses and creative cross-cutting of industries in the compilation and analysis of data.

Defining an Industry

In general an industry is nothing more than a cluster of economic units (firms or business units within firms) that are grouped together for analytical or cooperative purposes. Trade associations are the purest manifestation of the latter purpose. Trade associations themselves define criteria for membership and establish networks for information sharing and cooperation.

Thus the American Boat Builders and Repairers Association defines its own industry scope and becomes a private sector information depository (among other functions) within the confines of that scope.

A more universal taxonomy for analytical purposes is that provided by the U.S. Government's Standard Industrial Classification (SIC) scheme. It is designed to furnish a common framework for gathering, tabulating, analyzing, and cross-referencing data in a uniform fashion. The SIC clusters "establishments" (as opposed to legal entities or firms) together on the basis of the primary type of activity in which they are engaged (normally defined by product or service category). These clusters are named and coded to provide the needed uniformity and comparability. The more digits in the code, the more narrowly defined is the cluster.

The coding scheme results in a nesting arrangement of "divisions," "major groups," "groups," and "industries". Industries are assigned a four-digit code. Additional digits are used for subdivisions within industries.

The SIC is useful in a number of respects. First, it provides rather detailed descriptions of the many industries it includes. Perusal of these descriptions can offer the analyst interesting insights into product/market opportunities. Second, the assignment of establishments to specific industries and groups is internally consistent.

This allows comparable data referencing from a variety of public and private sector sources wherever the SIC has been used. Finally, the nesting feature of the SIC places somewhat narrowly defined industries in broader contexts (clusters with fewer digits). This can aid the strategist in overcoming myopic perceptions of a business and can serve as one basis for identifying forms of strategic growth (e.g., concentric versus conglomerate diversification).

As a practical matter, the definition of an industry is left to the analyst and need not be confined to institutional classifications.

Geographic boundaries, customers, suppliers, technologies, or other peculiar dimensions of a business may better serve the purposes of clustering enterprises for competitive analysis. Indeed the creative strategist in search of new product/market opportunities and threats will define and redefine industries at will.

Levels of Analysis

Industry analysis focuses interest on two primary levels:

- The structure and performance of the industry as a whole.

- The strategies and performance of individual competitors.

On the first level, aggregate data are often available from public and private sources that can be used to assess industry trends.

Although U.S. Industry Outlook has not been published since 1994, it has been replaced by several sources of similar information.

Other information of relevance at this level for the industry might be as follows:

- The industry includes about seventy-five companies operating 200 establishments.
- Industry sales are heavily concentrated among four large producers.
- Plastic containers represent a threat to industry volume.
- Use of paper containers in microwave ovens represents significant opportunities.
- Real growth has been limited; rising volume of shipments has resulted largely from price increases.
- Exports are increasing.

These and other data can be used to assess common threats and opportunities across the industry. They may be internally imposed by the industry itself (e.g., sluggishness in adopting new technologies) or may be due to other environmental circumstances (e.g., general economic conditions).

At the second level of analysis, the actions of individual competitors are of interest so that the analyst can identify:

- Competitive differentials
- Key success factors. In essence a search is made to uncover basic prerequisites for success in the industry (e.g., access to well-established distribution channels) and to examine the competitive weaponry wielded by the industry's players (e.g., product modifications).

Here the focus is on the manner in which industry members position themselves vis-a-vis one another in the broader context of overall industry change.

An Industry Study Guide

As with the more broadly based environmental analysis, the output of the industry study should be in the form of prognoses.

That is, assessment of industry conditions should be forward looking, representing opportunities and threats to which the firm might adapt its goals and action plans. This can be expedited in part by focusing on changes in industry structures and practices.

Finally, the analyst is cautioned that there are no single "cookbook" sources of data for a truly comprehensive industry analysis. Gathering and analyzing industry data is a long and arduous process that requires creativity and patience.

Porter's Five Forces Model of Competition

The nature of competition in an industry in large part determines the content of strategy, especially business-level strategy.

Based as it is on the fundamental economics of the industry, the very profit potential of an industry is determined by competitive interactions.

Where these interactions are intense, profits tend to be whittled away by the activities of competing. Where they are mild and competitors appear docile, profit potential tends to be high. Yet a full understanding of the elements of competition within an industry is easy to overlook and often difficult to comprehend.

Porter has identified five basic forces that collectively describe the state of competition in an industry:

- The intensity of rivalry among competitors
- The threat of new entrants to the market
- The amount of bargaining power possessed by the firm's/industry's suppliers
- The amount of bargaining power possessed by the firm's/industry's customers
- The extent that substitute products present a threat to a firm's/industry's products

These forces assist in identifying the presence or absence of potential high returns. The weaker are Porter's five forces, the greater is the opportunity for firms in an industry to experience superior profitability.

More generally, understanding how these forces affect competition within an industry allows the strategist to identify the most advantageous strategic position.

The actors within an industry on whom these forces exert pressure are, respectively, the industry's competing firms themselves, potential new entrants to the industry's markets, suppliers (vendors), customers, and makers of substitute products.

Obviously, the starting point for conducting an analysis of the five forces of competition is to identify all the competitors, potential new entrants, major suppliers, the demographics of customers, and makers of and nature of substitute products.

Competitors would not only have to be identified, but various distinguishing data about the industry would also have to be specified.

For each competitor this data would include market share, product line differences/similarities, market segments served, price/quality relationships represented by products, growth/decline trends, financial strength differences, and any other information that will help describe the industry.

Arranging the five forces and the major actors within an industry produces the "five forces model" as follows:

Porter's Model

Using Porter's model to analyse an industry for a particular firm, involves estimating the strength of each force, identifying its underlying source, and then formulating a strategy that will create an advantage for the firm.

An advantage could be established by defining a position from which to defend itself against strong forces somewhere in the model, drafting an offensive posture to take advantage of weak forces in the industry, or designing a way to favorably alter the forces. The key task of the analyst is to understand the underlying causes of each of the competitive forces at work. With this knowledge, a company's strengths or weaknesses can be clarified, and the most fertile areas for drafting competitive thrusts can be defined. Also, knowing the magnitude of competitive forces allows the strategist to identify the most important trends that are emerging as opportunities and threats.

Next, we'll identify typical characteristics of each competitive force, and the kinds of factors that can create strength for the five sets of competitors.

Intensity of Rivalry among Competitors

Some industries appear "sleepy" because of a low level of rivalry among competitors. An example might be industrial fasteners, the manufacturers of nuts and bolts and other devices used to connect the components of products.

A large number of quite small manufacturers accept low levels of profitability as a cost of staying in business. Competition is low key with little effort and expense devoted to differentiating brands or single products.

Such firms often produce a catalog and send representatives to trade shows to demonstrate products, or use sales forces or independent sales representatives for selling. They usually compete on the basis of price, delivery times, or the convenience of either large or small lot sizes.

There are virtually no screw machine companies advertising on television! On the other hand, some industries are characterized by a high level of competitive activity. For example, the brewing industry has many competitors who battle fiercely with each other over market share.

There is little natural differentiability in beer, so brewing firms develop complex promotional and advertising programs to try to gain the upper hand in consumer awareness.

We have seen ads, appeals, posters, jingles, demonstrations, sales, and many other types of promotional and advertising programme by beer brewers and distributors to differentiate their product on the basis of taste, brewing process, alcohol content, social acceptance, ingredients, price, "naturalness," similarity to foreign beer brands, dissimilarity to foreign beer brands, strength of flavour, weakness of flavour, and so on.

Lately, small retail location-based breweries have been popping up all over the country who make their own beer.

For breweries of a given revenue size, capital investment is large so exit barriers are high. There are few alternative uses of a defunct brewery. So participants fight it out intensely for a share of the huge beer market.

Generally, the factors that tend to precipitate intense rivalry in an industry are the following:

- Relative equilibrium in size and power among a large number of competitors
- Slow or stagnant growth of industry demand such that expansion of one competitor would come at the expense of others
- Undifferentiated products and low switching costs
- High fixed costs or product perishability
- Even small capacity additions generate large volume increases which raise pressure to cut prices
- High exit barriers causing firms to bear low or negative returns on investment
- Wide spectrum of strategies and types of firms which generates confusion and frequent "collisions" in the market. The opposite case might be an oligolopy like the automobile industry where most actions are reactions to another competitor and rivalry is somewhat orderly, albeit intense.

Buyers

For an industry, buyers can usually be broken into three categories: Consumer, industrial, and commercial customers. Consumers, or purchasers of the firm's service or product for their own use, are further divided into "bundles" of demographics which collectively identify all the various market segments that are present.

Firestone, for example, sells tires directly to the people who will be driving on them through its own retail outlets.

The various products that make up its line cater to the needs of different sets of demographic descriptions of people.

Industrial buyers are companies that purchase the firm's product or service to be used as a component in its product. Continuing with the Firestone example, automobile manufacturers who put Firestone tires on new cars, would be one group of its set of industrial buyers. By contrast, commercial buyers would be other companies that sell Firestone's products to consumers. An example would be any of the large discount store chains that handle Firestone tires, like Wal-Mart, K-Mart, Sears, etc.

Buyers, whether consumer, industrial, or commercial, can enjoy positions of strength over the firm from which they purchase products by superior bargaining power.

ZFor example, a large retailer ("commercial buyer" to its supplier) with a loyal customer base and high volume of sales of the product in question, may be able to virtually dictate price, shipping arrangements, order quantity, quality level, and other factors to its vendors.

Similarly, an automobile manufacturer could have a powerful bargaining position over a tire maker or the entire tire industry if a large volume of tires was sought for installation on a popular auto line.

Of course, the wise tire maker would prevent itself from becoming too dependent on one buyer by strenuously developing similar relationships with other companies. Toyota uses "multiple sourcing"—buying from several producers of the same components—to prevent dependency on too few suppliers.

Thus it has a strong bargaining position on matters of price, quality, delivery times, etc., as its suppliers compete with one another to gain favour with its buyers.

An industry's buyers tend to be powerful relative to the firms they are buying from when the conditions listed below apply (keep in mind that these factors apply as well to a group of consumers and to industrial and commercial buyers):

- Buyers are concentrated as in cooperatives, or they account for a large volume of purchases.

- Products are undifferentiated or standardized.
- The seller's component represents a large portion of the total cost of the buyer's finished product. When the seller's product has a small cost share, buyers tend to be less price sensitive.
- Buyers are earning low profits and are thus more price sensitive than if they were highly profitable.
- The sellers' product is not critical in one way or another to the buyer. If it's critical to the quality, price, appeal, etc., of an industrial buyer group's finished product, for example, then the sellers will have power over the buyers.
- There is a threat that buyers can integrate backward to make the suppliers' product.

An industry's commercial buyers (retailers) have, in some cases, an additional source of bargaining power over their manufacturing vendors. They can influence customers' purchase decisions.

This capability allows retailers to gain price, delivery time, order quantity, and other concessions from their suppliers that other classes of buyers might not receive.

Suppliers

Providers of goods and services to an industry have power over their customers through their ability to set price and control quality, delivery time, and order quantity.

If these customers cannot successfully play off one supplier against another to protect themselves, then the industry's profits can be drained off by suppliers.

- The power of suppliers is high in the following situations:
- There are few suppliers who are more concentrated than their customers
- Suppliers' product is differentiated
- Customers' switching costs are high
- There is little pressure on suppliers to protect themselves from substitutes or replacements for their product

- When suppliers have the capability to integrate forward. A supplier of engines to a manufacturer of lawnmowers would have a strong bargaining position if the mower company realized the engine supplier's ability to make the whole lawnmower.
- The industry is not one of the major customers of the supplier. Important customers would be protected from aggressive moves by the supplier because of their mutual interests; unimportant customers would not enjoy this position.

An interesting example of the power of suppliers is the unusual relationship between the growers of seed shrimp and the growers of mature shrimp in the shrimp mariculture industry in the country of Ecuador.

The preferred seed stock (baby shrimp placed in growth ponds to grow to a marketable size) are wild post- larval shrimp (called "PLs") netted in the country's estuarine areas by fishermen. These PL shrimp are much hardier than their hatchery-grown substitutes—as many as 80 per cent of the hatchery-grown PLs die before reaching maturity compared with a mortality rate of about 20 per cent for the wild ones.

The problem is that the supply of wild PLs fluctuates dramatically from year-to-year with climatic conditions. In some years there are not enough wild PLs to stock all the growth farms. In other years there is an oversupply of wild PLs. During the years of wild PL undersupply, the price of hatchery-grown PLs skyrockets and the PL hatchery operators thrive. Indeed, they have the power during these years to control the profitability of the much larger (in terms of revenue) mature shrimp mariculture industry.

But during the wild PL oversupply years, they may receive no revenue at all. For Ecuadorian shrimp hatchery operators, periods of extremely high bargaining power and virtually no bargaining power may be separated by only a few months.

Substitute Products

The shrimp industry example above also demonstrates

the plight of an industry facing a substitute for its product. Although it is an extreme case, seed shrimp hatchery operators really only have an industry at all during the years when their product's substitute, wild seed shrimp, are in short supply. Hatchery operators are spending heavily on research to increase the survival rate of their product.

If they are successful in this endeavor, then they may be able to displace the wild seed shrimp industry altogether.

During years when there are not quite enough wild seed shrimp to go around, shrimp growers use some hatchery grown seed stock. Their availability limits the price that the wild PL fishermen can charge for their product. This price ceiling is typical of all industries facing substitutes.

Manufacturers of products and suppliers of services must constantly scan their environments for the potential emergence of substitutes.

The most dangerous substitutes are those that show potential for improving price-performance trade-offs and those made by firms or industries earning high profits. In these cases, strategies must be formulated to protect against displacement by the substitute product/service.

Potential Entrants

New entrants to an industry pose several threats to existing competitors. New competitors can reduce the market share of all participants by dividing the "pie" into more pieces. They also may bring new technology or greater resources not available to present competitors and achieve a high market share position quickly to the detriment of all existing participants.

Corporate parent firms that diversify into an industry by acquisition are especially dangerous to existing competitors both because of their "deep pockets" and potential management expertise.

A restaurant in the tourism-driven town of Newport, Rhode Island, rapidly gained market share from other restaurants in town when it was acquired by a large international corporation.

The parent made capital available to the restaurant and after a major facilities overhaul, hiring of professional management, and implementation of other profit oriented moves, the restaurant quickly became the "industry leader" in Newport.

Although corporate ownership does not guarantee success of a restaurant, this example points out the threat to current participants presented by corporate diversification into their industry.

The threat of new entrants to an industry is high when barriers to entry are low. Low entry barriers would apply in the following situations:

- *Low economies of scale*: That small independent pizza parlors exists side-by-side with the units of national chains of pizza stores indicates that there are few economies of scale in his industry. Thus, one finds and would expect frequent appearance of new pizza places in just about every town and neighborhood.
- Undifferentiated products in an industry leads to new entrants. Most Americans can't tell a good shrimp from a bad one. As a result, Ecuador's dominant market position in the lucrative U.S. shrimp market is under attack by shrimp growers from all over the world.
- Low capital requirements for start-up in an industry leads to new entrants. An extreme example is the house painting business where capital costs are minimal. Every community sees the appearance of a large number of new house painters every year.
- Low switching costs leads to new entrants because customers sense little incentive to stay with current suppliers. Homeowners frequently change rubbish pickup companies because there is little incentive to stay with current provider. Compare this situation with the costs of changing from an oil heating system to gas, or visa versa.
- Easy access to distribution channels
- Low familiarization costs—where "learning the

ropes" in the industry is easy or inexpensive for new entrants.

- Conducting an industry analysis following Porter's model involves collecting data and developing explanations for the ways in which industry competition is affected by the five forces.

Strategic Group Mapping

The firms that make up an industry are not all alike. They have different products, market shares, life cycle stage, profitability, and so on. Indeed, each one has a different strategy, at least in its details.

But there are always some similarities. There may be several who are striving to be market leaders. Some may be pursuing low profit margin-high volume pricing. Others may have succeeded in lowering per unit costs, or creating a high-value-for-price image in the market. They may consist of several groups that represent different extents of geographical coverage or breadth of product line.

Depending on what similarities exist, industry participants can be organized by them into a set of strategic groups. For mapping strategic groups, the best bases for organizing participants are key dimensions of competition. By arraying competitors according to two key competitive factors on a two-dimensional chart (where each axis represents one of the factors), their relative positions on those factors can be analyzed.

Then conclusions about market openings and closed segments can be drawn so that the analyst can plan offensive or defensive moves. The following strategic group map of product price versus geographical coverage shows room for potential growth in the high price-wide coverage part of the market:

STRATEGIC GROUP MAP FOR HYPOTHETICAL INDUSTRY

In this simplified strategic group map, none of the competitors (Firms A-J) offers a high-priced version of the industry product for wide geographical distribution. Therefore, a competitor might formulate a strategy to enter this segment much like Toyota and Nissan did with the Lexus and Infiniti car models.

The factors used to identify the axes could be any strategic variables that are measurable and important dimensions of competition within the industry. Probably the most often used axis titles are price and perceived quality.

For purposes of preparing this map, 100 college students were asked their opinions of relative quality of the set of restaurants within their geographical area. As such, relative vertical position is a result of respondents' perceptions, not of an absolute measure. One might conclude from the map that the "holes" in the market are for high quality, moderately wide menu restaurants (top centre) and wide menu choices of low price/low quality items, possibly cafeteria style places (bottom right).

INTERNAL DIAGNOSIS BY FINANCIAL ANALYSIS

Financial statements can reveal much about a firm's operating strengths and weaknesses. They also serve as a basis for predicting future financial developments. To the extent that the performance of all parts of an organization is ultimately reflected in the magnitude of entries in a firm's financial statements, financial analysis can structure or bound the question of how well a strategy is working.

Comprehensive financial analysis consists of four elements: ratio analysis of the firm's historical financial performance, interpretation of cash flow position, analysis of retained earnings position, and predictions of future financial statements.

All findings of the financial analysis should be reduced to strengths and weaknesses of the firm and located accordingly in the data set for the present time frame. Then expected changes in each item can be forecast.

Financial Ratio Analysis

Financial ratio analysis (FRA) is a process whereby the

analyst or manager determines the degree of financial health represented by the firm's financial statements. Toward that goal there are a number of ways in which FRA can be useful.

First, it can aid in interpreting and evaluating income statements and balance sheets by reducing the amount of data contained in them to a workable amount. After computing several key ratios whose numerators and denominators are made up of selected items from the statements, a comprehensive analysis of the firm's financial position can be conducted by evaluating the resulting ratios.

Second, FRA can make financial data more meaningful. Any ratio strikes a relationship between the numbers in its numerator and denominator. By selecting sets of numbers that are logically related, only a few ratios may be necessary to comprehensively analyse a set of financial statements.

Third, ratios help to determine relative magnitudes of financial quantities. For example, the magnitude of a firm's debt has little meaning unless it is compared with the owner's investment in the business. Thus the debt/equity ratio strikes a relationship between these quantities such that their relative magnitudes can be established.

Because of these advantages, FRA can help managers or external analysts make effective decisions about the firm's credit worthiness, potential earnings, and financial strengths and weaknesses. It involves simply selecting the financial entities to be compared from either the income statement or the balance sheet, dividing one by the other, and comparing the product with a base. This comparative base could be a history of ratios for the firm (trend analysis), average ratio values from past periods computed from financial statements of other firms in the same industry (industry average comparison), or a combination of the two.

To use the first of these approaches, a ratio's historical values are computed to determine whether its trend is increasing, decreasing, or constant. The second approach requires availability of industry average financial ratios that were computed in the same way as those of the firm under analysis.

There are several published sources of data for such comparisons. The major ones are Dun and Bradstreet's Key Business Ratios, The Troy Almanac, and Robert Morris Associates' Annual Statement Studies. Trade associations also publish financial data computed on their member organizations. This data is very useful but unfortunately ordinarily available only to members.

Financial Dimensions

The financial structure of a business has several dimensions. Each financial dimension may be measured by several ratios, but the financial dimensions themselves normally are not directly measurable.

To analyse a firm's financial structure comprehensively, then, one must select a set of ratios made up of subsets, each of which represents a dimension. In this section financial dimensions are explained first. Then the ratios that collectively measure each dimension are discussed. The method of computation for each one is presented, followed by its interpretation.

Liquidity: The liquidity of a firm is its ability to pay current liabilities as they come due (current liabilities are debts due within one year).

The only funds available for payment of short-term debt are either cash or other current assets readily convertible to cash. Consequently liquidity is measured by ratios that strike a relationship between current liabilities and selected current assets.

$$\text{Current ratio} = \frac{\text{Current assets}}{\text{Current Liabilities}}$$

Current assets are those normally expected to flow into cash in the course of a merchandising cycle. Ordinarily they include cash, notes and accounts receivable (due within the next twelve months), inventory, and marketable securities (at current realizable values).

Current liabilities are short-term obligations for the payment of cash due on demand or within a year. Ordinarily they include short-term notes and accounts payable for merchandise, current portion of long-term debt, taxes due, and other accruals.

Interpretation: This ratio is a rough indication of a firm's ability to service its current obligations. Generally the higher the current ratio, the greater is the "cushion" between current obligations and a firm's ability to pay them. The stronger ratio reflects a numerical superiority of current assets over current liabilities. However, the composition and quality of current assets are a critical factor in the analysis of an individual firm's liquidity.

Current assets - inventories
Quick ratio = Current liabilities

Interpretation: Also known as the "acid test" ratio, this is a refinement of the current ratio and is a more conservative measure of liquidity. The ratio expresses the degree to which a company's current liabilities are covered by the most liquid current assets. Generally any value of less than one to one implies a reciprocal "dependency" on inventory to liquidate short-term debt.

Coverage: Coverage refers to a firm's ability to service debt that involves interest or premium payments. Ratios that measure coverage consist of one component to estimate flow of funds into the firm and another for periodic payments on debt.

Earnings before interest and taxes
EBIT to interest = Annual interest expense

Interpretation: This ratio is a measure of a firm's ability to meet interest payments. A high ratio may indicate that a borrower would have little difficulty in meeting the interest obligations of a loan. This ratio also serves as an indicator of a firm's capacity to take on additional debt.

Net Profit Plus Depreciation,

Cash flow to current = depletion, and amortization expenses maturities of long-term debt Current portion of long-term debt.

Interpretation: This ratio expresses the coverage of current maturities by cash flow from operations. Since cash flow is the primary source of debt retirement, this ratio measures the ability of a firm to service debt repayment and is an indicator of additional debt capacity.

Although it is misleading to think that all cash flow is available for debt service, the ratio is a valid measure of the ability to service long-term debt.

Profitability: This familiar dimension of a company's financial structure concerns management's ability to control expenses and to earn a return on committed funds. Ratios that measure profitability usually consist of a profit element and one that represents the amount of funds invested in whatever aspect of the firm is of interest to the analyst.

Net profit can be calculated either before or after taxes. Robert Morris Associates and the following explanation use net profit before taxes.

The analyst should ensure that the ratio elements used to compute the profitability ratios (and others as well) are the same as those used to compute the industry average against which the ratio's value will be compared. Also note that the following two ratios are converted to and reported as percentages.

Net profit before taxes (per cent)
Return (before taxes) Tangible Net worth

Interpretation: This ratio expresses the rate of return on tangible capital employed (called net worth or capital or owners' equity less intangibles).

While it can serve as an indicator of management performance, the analyst is cautioned to use it in conjunction with other ratios. A high return, normally associated with effective management, could indicate an undercapitalized firm. A low return, usually an indicator of inefficient management performance, could reflect a highly capitalized, conservatively operated business.

Net profit before taxes (per cent)
Return (before taxes) = Total assets
on total assets

Interpretation: This ratio expresses the return on total assets and measures the effectiveness of management in employing the resources available to it.

If a specific ratio varies considerably from the ranges found in published sources, the analyst will need to examine the makeup of the assets and take a closer look at the earnings figure. A heavily depreciated plant and a large amount of intangible assets or unusual income or expense items will cause distortions of this ratio.

Leverage: The extent to which the firm relies on debt as opposed to owner's capital (net worth) is its leverage position. A highly leveraged firm is one with a high proportion of debt relative to owner's investment.

$$\text{Debt to worth} = \frac{\text{Total liabilities}}{\text{Tangible net worth}}$$

Interpretation: This ratio expresses the relationship between capital contributed creditors and that contributed by owners. It expresses the degree of protection provided by the owners for the creditors.

A lower ratio generally indicates greater long-term financial safety. A firm with a low debt/worth ratio usually has greater flexibility to borrow in the future.

A more highly leveraged company has more limited debt capacity. Generally the order or preference given to this ratio is arranged on a continuum such that a low negative ratio is characterized as a weak debt/worth position and a high positive ratio value is perceived as a strong debt/worth position.

$$\text{Fixed assets to worth} = \frac{\text{Net fixed assets}}{\text{Tangible net worth}}$$

Interpretation: This ratio measures the extent to which owner's equity (net worth) has been invested in plant and equipment (fixed assets).

A lower ratio indicates a proportionately smaller investment in fixed assets in relation to net worth, and a better "cushion" for creditors in case of liquidation.

Similarly, a higher ratio would indicate the opposite situation. The presence of substantial leased fixed assets (not shown on the balance sheet) may lower this ratio deceptively. The order of preference normally given this ratio is the same as debt/worth.

Activity: Activity ratios, also called "efficiency" or "turnover" ratios, measure how effectively a firm's assets are managed. Examining the relationship between a measure of sales and an asset account is their purpose.

$$\text{Inventory turnover} = \frac{\text{Cost of sales}}{\text{Inventory}}$$

Interpretation: This ratio measures the number of times inventory is turned over during the year. High inventory turnover can indicate better liquidity or superior marketing. Conversely it can indicate a shortage of needed inventory for sales.

Low inventory turnover can indicate poor liquidity, possible overstocking, obsolescence, or, in contrast to these negative interpretations, a planned inventory buildup in preparation for future material shortages.

A problem with this ratio is that it compares one day's inventory (at the end of the accounting period) with cost of goods sold and does not take seasonal fluctuations into account.

One way to resolve this problem when sufficient data are available is to calculate cost of sales and average inventory by month to develop turnover ratios for each month. Further, it may prove extremely useful to break up cost of sales and inventory by different classes of products.

$$\text{Day's inventory} = \frac{365}{\text{Inventory turnover ratio}}$$

Interpretation: Division of the inventory turnover ratio into 365 days yields the average length of time units are in inventory.

$$\text{Receivables turnover} = \frac{\text{Net sales}}{\text{Accounts and notes receivable (trade)}}$$

Interpretation: This ratio measures the number of times accounts and notes receivable (trade) turn over during the year. The higher the turnover of receivables, the shorter is the time between sales and cash collection.

For example, a company with net sales (total sales less returns and/or allowances) of $720,000 and receivables of $120,000 would have a sales/receivable ratio of 6.0, which means receivables turn over six times a year.

If a company's receivables appear to be turning over more slowly than the rest of the industry, further research is needed and the quality of the receivables should be examined closely.

A problem with this ratio is that it compares one day's receivables, shown at statement date, with total annual net sales and does not take seasonal fluctuations into consideration.

An additional problem in interpretation may arise when there is a large proportion of cash sales to total sales. The latter problem may be resolved by including only those sales made on credit in the numerator.

This would tend to give a closer approximation of true receivables turnover. Note, however, that the turnover averages hereafter reported include all net sales in their calculations, regardless of cash or credit terms.

As with inventory turnover, it may prove useful to make these calculations by month so that seasonal fluctuations can be accounted for.

Average collection period = 365

or "day's receivables" Receivables turnover ratio

Interpretation: This figure expresses the average time in days that receivables are outstanding. Generally the greater the number of days outstanding, the greater is the probability of delinquencies in accounts receivable.

A comparison of a company's daily receivables may indicate the extent of a company's control over credit and collections. The terms offered by a company to its customers, however, may differ from terms within the industry, and should be taken into consideration.

In the example above, 365 – 6 = 6; that is, the average receivable is collected in sixty-one days. Again the distinction between cash sales and credit sales may prove useful in calculating this ratio.

Net sales

Sales to working capital = Net working capital where net working capital equals current assets less current liabilities.

Interpretation: Working capital is a measure of the margin of protection for current creditors. It reflects the ability to finance current operations. Relating the level of sales arising from operations to underlying working capital measures how efficiently working capital is employed.

A low ratio may indicate an inefficient use of working capital, whereas a very high ratio often signifies overtrading, a vulnerable position for creditors. Generally the order of preference given to this ratio (from strongest to weakest) is as follows: low positive, high positive, high negative, low negative.

Sales to net = Net sales

fixed assets Net fixed assets (net of accumulated depreciation)

Interpretation: This ratio is a measure of the productive use of a firm's fixed assets. Largely depreciated fixed assets of a labour-intensive operation may cause a distortion of this ratio.

Net sales

Sales to total assets = Total assets

Interpretation: This ratio is a general measure of a firm's ability to generate sales in relation to total assets. It should be used only to compare firms within specific industry groups and in conjunction with other operating ratios to determine the effective employment of assets.

STATEMENTS, REVENUE AND EXPENSE

The 100 per cent statements and revenue and expense distributions contained in Robert Morris Associates' Annual Statement Studies (RMA) present a series of accounts as percentages of a respective total. Total Assets, Total Liabilities and Net Worth, Net Sales, Total Revenues, and Total Expenses are used as bases. Component accounts are presented as percentages of each of these totals.

These "spreads" of major accounts can be used to determine the comparability of the magnitude of the same accounts in a specific firm. They are useful for spotlighting excessively large or small account totals in income statements, balance sheets, and cost accounting records. Unusual totals may indicate areas deserving close management attention.

Reading RMA Tables

Industry average data in most of the available sources, but in RMA specifically, are computed by first calculating the respective ratio for each firm in the appropriate SIC category. These ratios are then ordered from "strongest" to "weakest" (on the basis of criteria used by RMA and general banking guidelines).

The ratio that represents the midpoint in this list is the median. Note that this figure is not the typical average or "mean," but is the figure that falls halfway between the strongest and weakest in the data set. Simple interpolation is carried out when no ratio in the ordered list exactly represents the midpoint.

Similarly the figure that falls halfway between the median and the strongest ratio is the upper quartile; the figure halfway between the median and the weakest ratio is the lower quartile.

In the RMA data tables, the figures in each ratio cell are ordered as follows:

- Strongest
- 25% down the list (Upper quartile)
- 50% down the list (Median)
- 75% down the list (Lower quartile)
- Weakest

Note that the highest ratio numerical value is not always the strongest, nor is the lowest always the weakest. For example, for the debt-to-equity ratio, the higher the value goes, the weaker is the firm's financial position.

While interpreting the ratio values, keep in mind the description of each ratio presented. Remember that ratios often must be evaluated in conjunction with one another if proper conclusions are to be drawn.

Evaluating Ratios

Often the analyst can find no comparative ratios for the

SIC Code being evaluated. In these cases, there are three other evaluation techniques that may be helpful.

They are:

- Create your own comparative data,
- Trend analysis,
- Internal analysis.

Create Your Own Data. To create one's own comparative data, other firms like the one analyzed must be found. Then averages are computed of the ratios of the other firms which are most relevant to the nature of the analysis. These averages are then used for evaluation of the ratios computed on the firm in question.

Obtaining the financial information on a sufficient number of other firms to do such an analysis used to require hours of digging through hard-copy financial reports on those firms.

Today, with the availability of on-line Internet and library-based data services and such resources as Bloomberg terminals, constructing a set of industry average financial data is quite easy.

Customized data sets may even be more applicable to the firm being analyzed because the analyst can select members of the comparative base data set.

These displays for the Current and Times Interest Earned Ratios and the calculations that produced them are from an assignment completed March 7, 1994 by Steven O'Loughlin and Robert Landsfield, for the Strategic Management course in the MBA Programme, University of Rhode Island College of Business Administration. In all, eleven ratios were computed for 1990, 91, and 92 on the eight firms above for an analysis of the financial condition of Imasco, Ltd.

Holding companies normally show up in the industry average data sources under the SIC Code of their largest source of revenue.

For example, Textron would be considered an aerospace firm although they have many other subsidiaries that have nothing to do with aerospace. For the above analysis of Imasco, no suitable industry average source could be found so eleven ratios were computed on the firms listed. Then Imasco's ratios were compared to them.

This approach is obviously a lot of work, but it may be the only alternative for analyses where no suitable comparative data is already prepared, or where the analyst feels available data sets are inappropriate for one reason or another.

Trend Analysis. In the absence of comparative financial information, the analyst could also construct trend lines of the ratios of the firm being analyzed. This may only tell whether ratios are increasing or decreasing, but that is useful information even if there is nothing else. In the case of a firm with a 1.5 current ratio, for example, knowing whether this value is on an increasing or decreasing trend tells a lot about the financial health of the firm. Most analysts would have a positive reaction to this value on an increasing trend line, and a negative one on a decreasing line.

Internal Analysis. This approach calls for playing one ratio value off against others, so to speak, to see if there is balance among the financial dimensions represented by ratios. For example, suppose the firm had a current ratio of less than one (indicating that current liabilities amounted to more than current assets.) Suppose further that the quick ratio was similarly low.

One would then hope that such a firm did not carry large amounts of debt because of its weak liquidity. So next the analyst might compute the debt-to-equity and debt-to-total assets ratios to see if they were relatively high or low.

One would have to know beforehand that a value of 2.0 for the debt-to-equity ratio is generally considered to be the upper limit. If this ratio had a value of, say, 2.4, then one might conclude that the company had a heavy debt load given that it was rather illiquid.

Then, the analyst would likely look at a few profitability ratios hoping to see high values in order to support the high debt and weak liquidity. Discovering low profitability would likely precipitate a very negative evaluation given the high leverage and weak liquidity.

The internal analysis would continue in this fashion until potential weaknesses and strengths had been identified. Then additional information about the firm would be sought to either confirm or deny the financial evaluation.

Funds Flow Statements

The funds flow statement presents summaries of transactions of the firm that showed up as changes in balance sheet items from one accounting period (usually one year) to the next.

Funds flow statements, in one of several forms, became required parts of firms' financial statements by mandate of the Accounting Principles Board's Opinion. The reason for this requirement is that neither the balance sheet nor the income statement presents the nature of transactions undertaken by the firm (they show the net effects of transactions).

Funds flow statements may appear in financial reports under one of several possible names the most common of which are "sources and uses of funds statement," "statement of changes in financial position, and "cash flow statement." We will refer to them collectively as funds flow statements.

Two basic viewpoints can be used to construct a funds flow statement: changes in working capital and changes in cash. Working Capital Viewpoint. When working capital changes are the basis for the funds flow statement, changes affecting exclusively short-term assets and liabilities are not presented.

The reason is that a transaction involving two or more short-term accounts would have no effect on working capital and would not be included. Consequently a funds flow statement on the working capital basis explains how working capital was affected by noncurrent changes in sources and applications of working capital as follows:

Sources of working capital:

- Working capital from operations (net income plus noncash expenses)
- Sale of stock

- Sale of bonds (borrowing money)
- Sale of long-term assets

Uses of working capital:

- Purchase of long-term assets
- Repayment of long-term debt
- Dividend payments

Cash Flow Viewpoint. A funds flow statement prepared from the cash flow viewpoint explains all the working capital changes that the working capital statement contains plus changes in short-term accounts other than cash.

Thus, in an overall sense, it analyzes changes in the cash account between one period's balance sheet and another period's balance sheet. Examples of sources and uses of cash according to the cash flow viewpoint follow:

Sources of cash:

- Decreases in assets (other than cash)
- Increases in liabilities
- Increases in equity

Uses of cash:

- Increases in assets (other than cash)
- Decreases in liabilities
- Decreases in equity

To reiterate, changes in long-term accounts will appear the same on statements presented on the cash basis and on working capital basis. Transactions involving only short-term accounts will not appear on a working-capital-based statement, but will appear on a cash-based statement.

For example, collection of a receivable decreases accounts receivable and increases cash (and this is a source of cash) but does not change working capital.

The primary question that can be answered by cash flow analysis, even when cash is not the basis for funds flow statements, is "How much cash is generated by the profit earned by the firm's operation?" Strategy changes can have profound effects on cash balances.

Thus a pro forma funds flow statement (or "cash budget," as it is called) should be prepared to show how the strategist plans to acquire and employ funds (cash or working capital).

Sometimes the firm's expected profits (as would appear on a pro forma income statement) can be favorable while expected cash flows swing negative. This often happens in smaller firms, for example, when receivables collections are expected to be very slow and payables payments very fast.

Retained Earnings

The statement of retained earnings simply shows adjustments in retained earnings for the year. It includes the retained earnings at the beginning of the year, the addition or subtraction caused by net income, the deduction of dividends (if any were paid), and the year-end balance of retained earnings.

This statement is important because it highlights the distribution of net income between dividends and reinvestment. The difference between annual dividends and annual net income is the amount invested in operations.

The retained earnings year-end balance is the accumulation to date of the annual portions of net income that have been reinvested in the firm. Incidentally, past periods' retained earnings typically are not held in cash, but are invested in other assets.

PREDICTING FINANCIAL PERFORMANCE

The financial impact on the firm of a strategic change is presented in pro forma (predicted) financial statements. These statements include a cash budget, an income statement, and a balance sheet prepared over the appropriate planning periods.

Typically the income statement and balance sheet are projected first to show expected sales and expenses (income statement), the level of assets necessary to generate those sales (left side of the projected balance sheet), and the way in which assets will be financed (the right side of the projected balance sheet). Then a funds flow statement is prepared to give more detail on cash or working capital transactions expected to be necessary for operations to proceed as planned (although one approach calls for constructing the cash budget first).

There are four approaches to projecting financial statements: The per cent-of-sales method, the statistical-relationship method, the budgets-and-ratios method, and the breakeven sales method.

All require a sales forecast as a foundation for predicting other components. Many techniques are available for predicting sales, of which the details are inappropriate for this book. The most popular of these for the external analyst are probably the percentage-change, regression, and trend-line-extrapolation methods. For an analyst forecasting sales from inside a firm, the most popular techniques are probably the sales-force-composite, survey-of-executive-opinion, and regression approaches. We will assume that the analyst already has a sales forecast.

Percentage-of-Sales Projections

Of the methods available for constructing pro forma statements, the most popular for purposes of strategic analysis is the percentage-of-sales method.

It is discussed in more detail here than the other techniques.Detailed explanation of these is beyond the scope of this book.

Thus what follows is an outline of the appropriate financial estimation procedures. Readers are referred to the references for more detailed development of techniques.

The percentage-of-sales approach involves the following steps:

- Isolate accounts that can reasonably be expected to vary directly with sales.
- Compute each of these accounts as a percentage of historical sales for several accounting periods.
- Take a simple, moving, or weighted average of each account's percentages to reduce them to one figure per account.
- Multiply each account's average percentage of sales figure by forecasted sales for each of the appropriate periods.
- Arrange results in statement form and reconcile totals.

- On the income statement, cost of goods sold, total operating expenses, and income taxes will vary with sales with relatively high consistency.

Balance sheet items that normally vary with sales are the following:

- Assets
- Cash
- Receivables
- Inventory
- Equipment
- Liabilities
- Accounts payable
- Accruals
- Plant

Retained earnings will vary with sales as long as the firm continues to generate a profit, but it will be affected by dividend policy. By contrast, common stock, preferred stock, and the various forms of long-term debt will not necessarily increase with sales, and predicting them is less straightforward, as explained next.

An expected dollar increase in total sales has to be financed by some combination of accounts payable and accruals, long-term debt, sale of stock, and retained earnings. Of these four accounts payable and accruals (current liabilities) tend to follow sales most closely.

Thus we simply assume that the total per cent of accrued liabilities and payables to sales (B/TS × 100)—current liabilities that vary directly with sales expressed as a percentage of total sales, will be equal to the portion of total assets that they will be used to finance in the short term.

The per cent of total assets to sales (A/TS × 100) less the per cent of payables plus accruals (B/TS × 100) equals the percentage of total assets that will have to be financed with either long-term internal (retained earnings) or external (selling stock or borrowing) sources, or both.

To estimate the retained earnings portion of total asset investment, multiply the expected percentage of after-tax earnings (m—net after-tax profit margin on sales) by expected sales (TSa—total expected annual sales) to get the dollar net income figure that is predicted.

Then determine the forecast retained earnings retention ratio (d—percentage of annual retained earnings not paid out in dividends) and multiply it by expected net income. This results in the estimate for future dollar retained earnings, and also for future dividend payments.

This process may be expressed in the following simple formula:

External funds needs (EFN) =[A/TS(δTS)-B/TS(δTS)]-dm(TSa) in which,

- A/TS = net total assets that vary directly with sales expressed as a percentage of sales
- δTS = change in total sales expected (in dollars)
- B/TS = liabilities that vary directly with sales expressed as a percentage of total sales
- d = percentage of retained earnings not paid out in dividends
- m = after-tax profit expressed as a percentage of sales

  TSa = total sales predicted for the year

A positive value of EFN is the dollar amount of net total assets that must be financed by borrowing or by issuing new stock. When it is close to zero, the projected sales increase can be financed without external funds. When the value of EFN is negative, its magnitude is actually excess funds (retained earnings) for which plans should be made to pay dividends, repay debt, or otherwise invest.

An example may clarify this approach to estimating external funds needs. Assume that a change in marketing strategy for Jones Company is expected to generate a 20 per cent increase in sales from $5 million to $6 million, or $1 million.

Further, suppose that on last year's balance sheet, Jones Company's total assets amounted to 69 per cent of sales and all of its current liabilities were 15 per cent of sales. Also, its income statement for last year reported after-tax earnings of 4 per cent of sales ($200,000), 50 per cent of which was paid out in dividends.

Assuming no other financial structure changes, what amount of additional external funding would be needed to accommodate the $1 million projected sales revenue increase? To derive an estimate following the percentage of sales procedure, the following variable values apply:

A/TS	=	.69
^TS	=	$1,000,000
B/TS	=	.15
d	=	.5
m	=	.04
TSa	=	$6,000,000.

For Jones Company, then,

External Funds Needed (EFN)	=.69($1,000,000)-
	=.15($1,000,000)
	=.5(.04)($6,000,000)
	=.54($1,000,000)-
	=.02($6,000,000)
	= $540,000-$120,000
	= $420,000

In other words, to bring about a $1 million increase in sales, Jones would have to acquire $420,000 in external financing to maintain its prior internal debt relationships.

Weston and Brigham also present a modification of the EFN computation that permits the analyst to consider the effects of an increased rate of inflation on the percentage of an increase in sales that would have to be financed externally:

Percentage of external funds (PEFN) = I – ^{m}(1 + g)d

In which"

d and m are the same as in the previous example

I = (A/TS – B/TS)

g = Firm's expected growth rate—inflation rate plus or minus the firm's relative growth rate

As the growth rate rises, the percentage of financing supplied by external sources increases in this formula. Thus, in high inflation times, the role of the cost of external financing becomes more critical in the evaluation of strategic actions requiring asset investment.

To illustrate suppose that Smith Company was growing with the rate of inflation, about 6 per cent. This would mean that it would experience little real growth.

Assume the following values apply:

g =.06
I =.5
m =.05
d =.6.
Percentage of External Funds Needed =.50-.05/.06
(1+.06)(.6)
=.5 –.53 = – 3%.

Thus the percentage of the expected increase in sales that would have to be financed externally is negative three per cent. This means that the company would not only not have to acquire additional funds, but would have excess funds in the amount of three per cent of the expected sales increase, that it could distribute as dividends or invest in one way or another.

This value would rise considerably should Smith Company decide to attempt sales growth of ten per cent. The value for growth would increase by ten per cent to 16, assuming the rate of inflation remained at .06. Completing the computation reveals that 28 per cent of the firm's sales growth would be financed with external funds.

Then, were the rate of inflation to rise by 4 per cent, the percentage of external financing to sales growth would rise to 32 per cent. During inflationary times, it is more difficult to finance growth simply because more funds have to be raised to account for the influence of inflation. The PEFN computation makes it relatively easy to estimate the effect of inflation on the financing requirements that so often accompany strategy changes.

With pro forma income statement and balance sheet constructed, the analyst can then develop a pro forma funds flow statement. This is a matter of isolating the changes between the last historical statements and the pro forma statements according to the following categories:

- *Sources of funds*: Either increases in liability and capital accounts or decreases in asset accounts (excluding cash).
- *Uses of funds*: Either decreases in liability and capital accounts or increases in assets (excluding cash).

Statistical Relationship Methods

Many techniques are available for making financial forecasts on the basis of statistical relationships among variables. Normally the analyst proceeds by first making a sales forecast and then striking a relationship, account by account, between each statement item and forecasted sales with a regression line. Simple linear, nonlinear, or multiple regression can be used, depending on the user's needs and statistical sophistication.

Budgets and Ratios Methods

One technique applies to strategic management systems with comprehensive budget programs. Essentially it involves breaking out budget categories by financial statement account and then adding (subtracting) budget quantities to (from) statement quantities.

Two other variations are appropriate to strategic planning. One calls for constructing a cash budget first, and then factoring cash budget quantities into a pro forma income statement and balance sheet.

The other relies on past ratios. With a sales forecast and a set of historical ratios, the balance sheet and income statement can be constructed. Ratios with sales in either the numerator or denominator can be converted into dollar values by appropriate mathematical manipulations. For example, accounts receivable for the pro forma balance sheet is obtained by multiplying the receivables-to-sales ratio by expected sales.

Breakeven Pro Formas

Although not actually a way of predicting financial structure in the sense of forecasting what is expected to occur, breakeven pro formas can be useful for strategic analysis. According to this approach, the analyst first determines the level of sales that would be necessary for the firm to break even, that is, to generate a precisely zero profit. Then, by using accounts as percentages of sales, statistical relationships, or ratios, the pro forma statements are developed around the breakeven sales level.

This approach is especially useful for showing what the critical financial condition would be for a firm with declining sales or deteriorating financial health were it to hit breakeven point. The analyst may even compute the rate of decrease of sales and determine how much time is available for a turnaround when sales are declining.

A rough estimate is obtained by basing the breakeven computation on income statement data. This estimation procedure simply involves dividing the firm's gross margin percentage into total dollar operating expenses (which roughly approximate fixed costs).

To illustrate, for Ajax Company, gross margin is 20 per cent on sales of $100 million with total operating expenses of $15 million. Applying the following relationship,

Estimated Breakeven Sales (BE) = Total Operating Expenses/ Gross Margin Per cent.

Approximate breakeven sales is as follows:

Estimated BE = $15,000,000/.2 = $75,000,000.

Suppose Ajax Company's sales were declining at about $10,000,000 each year. About how many years, assuming the trend continues, do Ajax Company's managers have to affect a turnaround before profits start to swing negative? The difference between present sales and estimated breakeven sales is $25,000,000 ($100,000,000 - $75,000,000). With a sales decline of $10,000,000 per year, the company has roughly two and one-half years ($25,000,000/$10,000,000) within which to turn the trend around before reported income becomes negative.

In this case, a turnaround recommendation which would not be expected to begin to take affect for, say, five years, might not be welcomed if the company had insufficient resources to last that long.

Rough as it is, this estimate gives the analyst an idea of the time frame within which he/she can work. This procedure is also useful for new ventures. In this case the important decision is whether it is reasonable to expect that the approximate breakeven sales level can be reached and exceeded within a certain time period.

The detailed techniques of breakeven analysis are presented in most accounting and finance textbooks as well as in other functional textbooks. We do not discuss it here but advise students to employ this tool where possible.

DIAGNOSIS: AND OTHER FUNCTIONAL AREAS

Most strategic operating characteristics are manifested either directly or indirectly as symptoms in a firm's financial statements. These symptoms must be "dug out" of the statements and then interpreted in operational terms for strategic analysis to begin.

Through the interpretation of operational causes of financial symptoms, the strategist can identify many of the firm's strengths and weaknesses.

But, as Berg has noted, "There is a temptation to spend too much time on the analysis of financial performance and position... and not enough time on the more difficult analysis of the underlying factors... " These underlying factors are usually the strengths and weaknesses uncovered during analysis of other functional areas. In other words financial analysis can reveal symptoms of problems or evidence of strengths in the other functional areas. (It can also indicate that certain environmental factors are affecting performance).

Therefore, financial analysis can be viewed as a way to uncover questions about performance, to which the answers are likely to be found by analysis of other functional areas. For example, if financial analysis showed relatively high gross profits for a firm experiencing declining sales, the analyst would probably turn to either its marketing function (to determine if prices charged by the firm were too high) or its production systems (to see if raw materials inventory costs were leading to excessive cost of goods sold).

Similarly, where gross margin is about average but net (operating) margin is low, the analyst would likely find some operating expense accounts that were unusually large. These excessive accounts should then be traced back to the functional areas generating them to find evidence of inefficiencies.

In the sections that follow, we first explain the processes of internal analysis generally. Then an approach to the analysis of each of the major functional areas and present strategy is described.

Our decision to present internal analysis after financial analysis is not intended to imply that financial analysis should necessarily preclude functional area analysis. Indeed, we agree wholeheartedly with Professor Berg that real insight into the operating strengths and problems of organizations will come only after analysis of the operating characteristics of functional areas.

Process of Internal Analysis

There are two fundamental ways to conduct an internal analysis: vertical and horizontal. For the vertical approach, strengths and weaknesses are identified at each organizational level. The horizontal analysis corresponds to the functional areas of the SBUs. Strengths and weaknesses are identified for each function. We prefer the horizontal approach because it seems to be more universally applicable. Analysis can be focused on functional departments, or whatever basis of departmentalization has been used in a particular organization.

The major dimensions of each area are outlined and discussed in the subsections that follow. They are intended as beginning points for analysts to formulate their own evaluation systems for each case study or organization analyzed.

Stevenson found that managers seem to use three types of criteria in identifying strengths and weaknesses: historical, competitive, and normative. Analyzing functional areas by historical criteria means comparing present values with their historical counterparts and identifying strengths and weaknesses on the basis of those comparisons.

Competitive comparisons involve assessing similarities and dissimilarities with successful competitors and finding strengths and weaknesses accordingly. Similarly normative comparisons are those where present characteristics are compared with ideal values as perceived by the analyst or an expert opinion.

In practice the process of identifying strengths and weaknesses can be one of the most educational experiences top managers can have. Especially enlightening are the enumeration and discussion of weaknesses. Since responsibility for the performance of SBUs and functional departments often rests with single managers, identification of weaknesses at these levels can be painful and embarrassing for those people.

These discussions must be handled carefully to prevent alienation and to bring about constructive solutions to whatever problems are revealed. However, the analyst must make sure that all weaknesses are identified, even though some feelings may be hurt.

The process of internal analysis involves the following steps:

- Perform a complete financial analysis.
- Comprehensively identify the major functional areas that make up SBU operations.
- Enumerate the critical operational factors of each functional area.
- Identify both qualitative and quantitative variables to describe performance of the SBU on each operational factor.
- Conduct research to assign either qualitative or quantitative values to the variables.
- Organize findings by function according to whether they represent strengths or weaknesses.

Identification of Major Functional Areas

Whatever organization is analyzed, the analyst should select a comprehensive set of categories that define the firm's operations. These categories, or functional areas, can vary from one organization to another, and depend upon whether the analyst is conducting a vertical or a horizontal analysis. We have selected for discussion of horizontal analysis the common functional areas of marketing, personnel, production, and R&D, along with organization structure, present and past strategies, and external relations (in addition to finance, which was discussed earlier).

Although most organizations will have these functions in operation, the analyst should not restrict the internal analysis to them. The particular set of functions for which data are gathered should be tailored to the firm in question. The key characteristic of the set of functions selected must be comprehensiveness. Analysts should make sure that all pertinent functions are covered.

Operational Factors of Each Functional Area

After identifying the appropriate functional areas to study in the internal analysis, the next step is to decide what aspects of each one to analyse. By the time most students take a course in strategic management, they have completed courses in each functional area and topics related to them. Those courses and the texts used in them are the best sources of evaluative criteria for the functions of organizations.

Marketing. Consistent with marketing convention, this function is analyzed by examining the operating characteristics of the organizations' products/services, price, promotion, distribution, and new product development systems.

Interest is focused on all aspects of each of these systems that have not already been identified as part of the financial analysis.

Examples of checkpoints for each factor are as follows:

- Products/services
  - Market share
  - Penetration
  - Quality level
  - Market size
  - Market expansion rate
- Price
  - Relative position (leader or follower)
  - Image
  - Relationships to gross profit margin
- Promotion

- Effectiveness
- Appropriateness of emphases
- Budget as per cent of sales
- Is return measurable, acceptable?

• Distribution
- Delivery record
- Are other methods more appropriate?
- Unfilled orders
- Costs

• New product development
- New product introduction rate
- Sources of ideas effective?
- Extent of market feedback
- Success rate

The problem is not to identify simply what the organization's marketing department is doing, but instead what it is doing particularly well or poorly.

Personnel and Union Relations. The overall purpose of the personnel function is to manage the relationship between employees and the organization.

Therefore, internal analysis of the personnel function is an assessment of the strengths and weaknesses of that relationship. This function can be analyzed by examining the following factors and questions or others tailored to the organization:

• Job analysis factors
- Are necessary skills present?
- Are all necessary jobs present?
- Are selection and placement systems effective?
- Recruiting capability
- Training effectiveness

• Job evaluation factors
- Pay scales appropriate?
- Image of pay scale within labour market
- Do pay differentials reflect job content differences?
- Adequacy of benefits

• Turnover/absenteeism

- Turnover rate
- Absenteeism rate
- Attitude of employees, managers
- Seasonality a factor?
- Performance evaluation
  - Reliability
  - Validity
- Union-management relations
  - Unions representing employees
  - Bargaining positions
  - Quality of relations
  - Negotiation schedule

Production: The production or manufacturing area's strengths and weaknesses relate to the organization's ability to produce its products/services at the desired quality level on time at the planned-for-costs.

Examples of evaluative factors for production are the following:

- Facilities and equipment
  - Capacity level
  - Per-unit costs of manufacturing
  - Obsolescence; today, future
  - Level of technology applied
  - Process optimality
  - Replacement, maintenance
- Quality level
  - Defective units
  - Inspection costs
  - Remanufacturing costs
  - Competitive position
  - Consistency
- Inventory
  - Level, turnover
  - Costs and trends
  - Is inventory rationally maintained?
- Procurement
  - Sources

  - Quality of inputs
  - Constant lead times
- Planning, scheduling
  - Formal system
  - Is demand smoothed?
  - Excessive overtime charges?
  - Productivity

For most service organizations, the process of providing the service can be roughly equated to the production of a product. Costs of providing the service, as well as quality of the service delivered, can be the focus of analysis.

Wheelwright suggests evaluating production strategy by analyzing its consistency and emphasis. First, the analyst should evaluate the consistency of production strategy with business strategy, other functional strategies, and with the overall business environment.

The categories within production strategy itself should exhibit a high level of consistency as well. Then, the extent to which production strategy is focused on factors of success should be evaluated.

This involves making sure that priorities among production activities are appropriate to business strategy, that business level opportunities have been addressed, and that production strategy is communicated, understood, and integrated with other functional strategy managers.

Research and Development. Research and development (R&D) provides technical analysis and support to other departments, and designs products or processes to meet market needs and thereby generate a profit.

Operation of R&D must strike a balance between practicality and creativity in order to contribute successfully to profit goals.

Overemphasis on practical matters can impair future profitability because few innovations will be generated.

Overemphasis on creativity could result in generation of few marketable product ideas while researchers explore the frontiers of their scientific disciplines.

The correct balance between creativity and practicality for a particular firm is a strategic issue that cannot be decided absolutely. That is, this balance is a function of the extent to which the organization requires either innovation or market emphasis, and that issue is a function of business-level goals and action plans.

Conducting an internal analysis of the R&D function involves identifying strengths and weaknesses in R&D activities such as the following:

- Demand for R&D
  - Is demand for R&D services stable?
  - Is R&D funding stable?
  - Is R&D funding vulnerable to profit variations?
- Facilities and equipment
  - Are facilities and equipment state-of-the-art?
  - Is obsolete equipment expendable?
  - Is space a problem?
- Market and production inputs
  - Does market information get fed into the R&D process?
  - Does production information influence the R&D process?
  - Are marketing and production influences balanced?
- Planning and scheduling
  - Are jobs planned and scheduled?
  - Are costs effectively monitored?
  - Are human resource needs planned?
- Is the level of uncertainty associated with the type of R&D activity in which the organization is involved appropriate for the intended level of risk?

Organization: Organization structure must support strategies and facilitate their successful implementation. To do so, structure must prevent a certain set of problems from materializing.

These problems are the characteristics that are searched for to determine the appropriateness of a change in structure.

Changing structure is risky: Therefore, it should not be

tampered with unless there is either a problem present that must be corrected or one that can reasonably be expected to develop if a change is not made.

In either case, though, organization structure should be changed only because of specific problems. That is, there is no absolutely best structure, but only the structure that minimizes organization-related problems.

Some of the criteria that can be used to analyse organization structure are as follows:

- Does structure make sense?
  - Is it confusing?
  - Are there too many levels?
  - Are there horizontal communication channels?
  - Does it expedite communication?
  - Are the forms of organization used appropriate?
- Accountability and control
  - Does structure fix responsibility?
  - Are there single functions assigned to more than one person?
  - Are there too many committees?

Present Strategies

Whether present strategies are stated explicitly or must be inferred from behaviour of the organization, the goals and action plans currently applicable must be identified and analyzed.

The idea is to determine which strategies are working (that is, which action plans are being implemented in such a way that their associated goals are being met) and which ones are not.

Information about the relative success of current strategy can then be fed into the process of formulating and implementing new strategies.

In this way problems associated with existing strategies can be corrected by formulating modifications or replacements for them and effective strategies can be improved upon, retained as is, or extended so that strategic success is facilitated.

The following steps can be followed to evaluate current strategy at any of the four levels of strategy:

- Select strategy levels for analysis.
- Identify present goals and action plans at each level.
- Determine extent to which short- and long-term goals have or have not been met.
- Determine which action plans have and have not been effective.

Of course, a strategy successfully carried out constitutes a positive attribute of the firm, and one unsuccessfully implemented is a problem to be dealt with.

For an internal analysis, however, the point is to identify strategies that are particularly effective - they become strengths.

Examples include McDonald's consistency, Coca-Cola's distribution strategy, Miller Lite's marketing strategy, and Nissan's production strategy. Weaknesses are strategies that have been especially unsuccessful in their operation.

SUMMARY

This chapter discusses the processes of environmental and internal organizational analysis. Although each of these analyses consist of identifying the strengths, weaknesses, threats, or opportunities confronting the organization in the past, present, and future, the context of each is different.

Environmental analysis involves identifying the major present and future threats and opportunities to or from the organization's principal constituents (shareholders, customers, competitors, suppliers, employees, and general public) along the dimensions of the organization's economic, political/legal, technological, and social environments.

Then the same process is applied to the industry in which the firm operates. Internal analysis consists of conducting a financial analysis followed by a study of the performance characteristics of the organization's other functional areas to identify the strengths and weaknesses of its operations.

Recognizing that a firm should make a strategic change, structuring the essential goal and action-plan sets, and implementing them are risky endeavors without first analyzing the probable impact on the firm's financial condition.

It was widely understood that Chrysler had to start producing more smaller automobiles to survive. Yet the financial requirements of this new direction were especially difficult to meet and had to be planned meticulously.

Chapter 3

Strategy Formulation: Goals and Action Plans

INTRODUCTION

This chapter explains the content of goals and the processes of goal formulation. In the second, various action plan (strategic posture) choices are enumerated. This ordering of these two topics was chosen for pedagogical convenience.

It implies that managers select goals, and then array the collection of possible action plans to reach them—and in practice some strategists may indeed follow this sequence. Others, however, may reverse the order, identifying a set of possible action plans first and then setting goals. Still others may switch back and forth between goals and action plans in an incremental process, refining each one more and more as they proceed. Any one of these sequences is possible in a particular case.

First, goals are distinguished from action plans. Then the role of goals in mission statements is discussed and the content of goals for each of the four levels of strategy explained.

Next the process of goal formulation is presented. This process is a matter of factoring present goals and action plans with data set information to arrive at new goals. Various goal formulation theories are explained next, followed by discussions of how managers' power relationships and value systems can influence the process and content of the goals that are identified as possibilities.

The second section of the chapter presents a collection of possible action plan choices, divided into offensive and defensive strategic postures.

The content of merger strategy, described as one of several possible action plans available to the strategist for reaching corporate-level goals.

The addresses the process and content of global strategy. Formulation of global strategy requires the continuation of strategic management processes on a wider scale.

CLARIFICATION OF TERMS

Various authors have used the terms goal, target, and objective differently as elements of the strategic management process.

One set of differences concerns their definitions: Are they interchangeable terms or do they have distinct meanings? The second concerns their role vis-a-vis strategy: Are they part of strategy (that is, proper elements of strategy statements) or is strategy formulation a separate process that occurs after the process of goal and objective formulation?

On the first issue we have taken the position that goal and objective are interchangeable terms, but we prefer the term goal only because it seems to be most popular.

Consequently, the following distinctions apply:

- A goal is an expected result. Synonyms for goal include the words aim, end, and objective.
- A qualitative goal is an aspiration toward which effort is directed; a goal to be reached for but not necessarily grasped, rather than a quantitative level of a certain variable. Thus, a firm might aspire to be a good corporate citizen.
- A quantitative goal is one intended to be reached, a quantified expected result.

  There are two types:

  - A hurdle goal value is a certain level of a quantitative goal that is to be exceeded (synonyms include instrumental and interim goal);

– A final or overall quantitative goal is a value that should be achieved.

A final goal could be established without hurdle values or it could be the value achieved after all appropriate hurdles have been reached. Achieving a ten per cent increase in total revenue within three years would be a final goal. Hurdle goals would be the targeted revenue increase intended at the end of Years 1 and 2.

Thus the process of goal formulation involves the task of setting qualitative aspirations and establishing both hurdle and final values, all three of which are different types of goals. Examples of the kinds of goals are presented.

Resolution of the second area of disagreement (whether goals, actually are part of strategy or should stand alone in the process of strategic management) depends on what you believe should be the content of a firm's strategy. Two views are prevalent among business policy authors.

According to one view, strategy consists of both goals and action plans. Thus the statement "We intend to increase sales by 10 per cent within one year by concentrating on market development" would be deemed a strategy (or at least part of one) by adherents to this view. Strategy formulation would have consisted of establishing the quantitative goal of a 10 per cent sales increase in one year as well as the selection of the action plan of market development as the means for achieving it.

Arguing against separating goals from the activities designed to achieve them, Andrews states:

The interdependence of purposes... and action is crucial to the particularity of an individual strategy... It is theunity, coherence, and internal consistency of a company's strategic decisions that position the company in its environment and give the firm its identity, its power to mobilize its strengths, and its likelihood of success in the marketplace.

Goals	Qualitative	Final Values
Objectives		
Aimes	Quantitative	Hurdle (Interim) Values

Examples of Types of Strategic Goals and Their Definitions:

Goal Type	Definition	Examples
Qualitative	An aspiration	"Good corporate citizenship" "Ethical practices" "Improved quality of life" "Heightened awareness"
Quantitative	Numerical aim	"6 (Final Goal) per cent increase in sales "Raise ROI by per cent"
Hurdle goal	Minimum to be reached w/in a timeframe	"Increase sales by per cent per year for three

In other words advocates of this approach argue that when goals and their related action plans are arrived at by simultaneously contemplating means and ends (identified as "incrementalism" by Christensen et al.), then a stronger degree of interrelationship between the two elements will result. And this result will tend to produce a "better" strategy.

Andrews says further, "Breaking up the system of corporate goals and the character-determining major (actions) for attainment leads to narrow and mechanical conceptions of strategic management and endless logic-chopping."

According to the other view, goal setting and the formulation of means for achieving goals are distinct activities that call for the stabilization of goals followed by selection of the proper strategic alternatives.

The ultimate separation of goals and strategy results in applying the word strategy only to statements about the means for achieving goals. A set of goals would be established first and then discussions about strategy would focus on deciding the best ways to achieve them.

However, this view can result in semantic confusion. If the word strategy applies to means, then what word will be used to refer to goals plus the means for achieving them? Unfortunately for the linguist, in practice goals plus means are often also called strategy.

For example, when describing the strategy of Mesa Petroleum, Business Week includes Chairman T. Boone Pickens's goal ("to enlarge Mesa's holdings so that its reserves always outpace depletions") as well as this statement: "His strategy... remains the same:

He wants to form a partnership strong enough to buy a big company, sell off large chunks of the target to pay off acquisition debt, and then spin off oil and gas properties in the form of a royalty trust to his shareholders." Similarly, for Intermedics, Inc.,

Business Week identifies its "strategy" as consisting of both the strategy of diversification and the goal of 30 to 40 per cent annual growth over the next five years. Thus the word strategy has been applied both to means and ends, and to the means alone.

In this book strategy formulation is a process involving the formulation of goals and also action plans. The latter are treated as separate strategic management steps. Consequently we have taken a position that is somewhere between the two views but includes elements of both.

Strategy herein refers to the combination of goals and the means for achieving them. But the means for achieving goals are called action plans when discussed independently of their related goals.

The overall process of formulating both, and we believe they are complementary entities and activities, is called strategy formulation.

The strategy includes both goals and action plans, A manager might work on goal formulation problems, on action plan formulation, or simultaneously on both. A firm could change strategy by altering a goal while retaining an action plan, retaining a goal and altering an action plan, or altering both. The activity of formulating strategy requires that both goals and action plans are dealt with.

Making this distinction ultimately leads to breaking somewhat with convention in some sections of the book. Most notably we use "action plan" where others might have used "strategy." However, we do not use the two terms interchangeably as becomes necessary when the means for reaching goals are called strategy.

We chose this structure for several reasons. First, as Schendel and Hofer point out, it is more convenient to order goals and action plans sequentially during the process of describing them, even though "in practice, they are interactive, recycle and repeat themselves and do not move forward in sequence... neatly." In other words this structure is pedagogically convenient, allowing for discussion of goal and action plan setting separately.

Second, distinguishing between goals and action plans as elements of strategy avoids applying the word strategy to two different concepts. This helps reduce confusion about what strategy is.

Finally, this usage preserves the meaning of the word strategy as the means and ends of an organization's present and future activities. The preponderance of both popular and academic usages of the term implies the content of both an ends component and a means component.

When all of a firm's goals and associated action plans for a single level (typically, corporate, business, or functional) are grouped together, they constitute a set of goals and an accompanying set of action plans that together are called that level's strategy

Notice that some elements of the generalized goal have more than one action plan (e.g., quantitative goals), others have individual action plans , and still others share one action plan.

As an example of one goal reachable by more than one action plan, John Nevin, president of Firestone, set a quantitative goal for the company in late 1979 of a 9 per cent return on equity. It was to be accomplished by:

- Divestiture of subsidiaries with less than 12 per cent return on assets in the short term
- Diversification into healthier, unrelated businesses.

More common is the case in which several goals are expected to be reached by the implementation of one action plan. For example, the James River Corporation of Virginia accomplished several goals (raised its profits—presumably by a targeted amount —doubled sales,

Single Level's Strategy integrated backward, gained certain assets, and entered the consumer-oriented specialty paper products business), all by acquisition of American Can Company's Dixie Northern papermaking division.

In this book the terms master strategy, overall strategy, and strategy set are used interchangeably to identify the particular collection of strategies that characterizes the firm's major thrusts. Indeed, some people seem to apply the word strategy very loosely to just about any reference to business direction that may be at hand.

To avoid uesing the same word (strategy) for different concepts (individual action plans and overall strategy), we employ the following terms:

- *Goal set*: A collection of quantitative and qualitative goals for a particular organizational level.
- *Action plan*: A description of the means by which activity is expected to be directed toward striving for specified goals.
- *Strategy*: A set of goals and their action plans for a particular strategy level.

Organizational goals manifested as either qualitative or quantitative values would be tied to action plans that identify the appropriate ways to work toward them. A single-line business would thus have a set of goals and related action plans that together define how it should compete within its business segment.

This set of goals and action plans would be called its business-level strategy. It could also have strategies, still made up of goals and action plans, for other strategy levels. That point is covered in the next section.

"Policy" and "tactic" are other terms that have been defined in many different ways. We use policy to refer to standing directions, instructions that vary little with changes in strategy.

Thus organizations can have vacation policy, a policy on absenteeism, affirmative action policy, and so on. Policy tends to have fewer competitive implications than strategy when used in this way.

However, in many curricula the strategic management course is called business policy. A tactic is a short-term action taken by management to adjust to internal or external perturbations. They are formulated and implemented within a strategic effort, usually with the intention of keeping the organization on its strategic track.

HIERARCHY OF GOALS

The number of levels of goals appropriate for an organization is a function of its number of organizational levels. Large multi-product firms are typically configured with major goal sets established for their mission and societal, corporate, business, and functional levels. Single-business firms typically would not require corporate-level goals but would have a mission along with business- and functional-level goal sets.

Of course, variations from the simplified structure may be necessary in a particular firm. For example, a large diversified corporation may have several unrelated divisions, each of which is composed of a number of single-line businesses.

It therefore would be necessary to have a set of corporate-level goals for each division. Each corporate-level goal collection would then have a set of business-level goals for each business unit within it, and a related set of functional goals associated with each business unit's functional departments.

Further, an organization with a tall structure could have several sub-functional levels of goals below the so-called functional goals.

Mission

Mission should address the basic purpose of the firm, the reasons for which it exists. Statements of mission can be made up of goals and descriptions of the means for achieving them. However, mission-related goals are often qualitative as opposed to quantitative. Some owner groups prefer to state broad goals as the organization's purpose and defer to management to set strategy as the way to achieve them.

In some organizations questions about purpose are left solely to owners, whether widely dispersed stockholders acting through a board of directors, the small group of owners of a closely held corporation, or the sole owner of a small business.

In these cases managers are informed of the owners' expectations and these goals serve as overriding constraints or guidelines on the activities and operations of managers.

In other firms managers may participate in the process of deciding on purpose, along with owners or their representatives. Managers may even be called upon to submit basic purpose choices to owners for affirmation or veto.

The importance of a generally understood and accepted notion of purpose cannot be overstressed. The sole owner of a $30 million-a-year industrial supply firm decided, upon reaching fifty years of age, that he no longer saw the purpose of his company as primarily a generator of cash flow for him and his family.

Instead he decided its purpose was to generate wealth ultimately through acquisition by a larger company. The change in purpose from a short-term cash generator to a well-groomed acquisition target necessitated a set of dramatic alterations in the way business was conducted on a day-to-day basis by key managers.

Things that had been previously assigned low priority--market development, product development, asset reinvestment, development of career commitments by employees and managers, and so on--suddenly became essential goals, the achievement of which, over time, would serve the new mission.

Although many managers tend to develop qualitative mission statements, they can be expressed as a set of quantitative goals stated in financial terms.

As such they specify the major financial outcomes expected by owners and managers from operation of the organization. Examples include market share, market growth, cash flow, stock performance, and dividend payout.

Societal Goals

Societal goals (also called enterprise goals), in organizations that employ societal strategy, would occupy the topmost levels of an organization's hierarchy of goals.

In those that do not develop a separate societal strategy, these goals would be woven into corporate-, business-, and functional-level strategies.

Societal goals mainly address expectations about the firm's societal legitimacy. Sometimes included in statements called creeds or guiding philosophies, societal goals identify the major ways in which the organization will operate so as to stay within the legal, ethical, and cultural constraints placed on it by society. Although they guide the behaviour of people at all levels of the organization, they have particular relevance for the decisions of key managers related to balancing the claims on the firm of society's interest groups and institutions, owners, and managers.

Legitimacy goals should address the overall role of the firm in the daily functioning of society. They should include goals that pertain to the major social issues and legislation of the day. Some examples are pollution standards, the firm's antidiscrimination position, safety in working conditions, and sexual harassment.

Corporate Level Goals

Corporate-level goals consist of quantitative and qualitative outcomes that encompass management's expectations about the optimal combination and types of businesses that make up the company. They direct the integration of the particular collection of businesses that makes up the overall organization and they serve as behaviour specifications for staff members at the corporate level.

Business-Level Goals

The final goal of sales growth of 5 per cent in one year

could be achievable partly by acquisition or divestiture moves, but primarily through the contributions of sales increases by present SBUs. Therefore, in this case an average cross-SBU sales increase of 5 per cent could satisfy the corporate-level target and one would expect each business-level strategy to contain a sales growth element that defines that SBUs "contribution," so to speak, to the corporate level sales growth goal.

Business-level goals integrate the activities of the SBU's functional departments and guide the behaviour of business unit managers. In other words, business strategy defines the role of each functional area relative to each other and to resource requirements and availability. One might say that business-level strategy balances the roles of organizational functions within each business unit in terms of their contributions toward reaching higher level goals.

Functional-Level Goals

At this level goals are set for each of the functional departments into which each SBU is organized. The point of functional-level goals is to define several aims for each department in such a way that their achievement would result in achievement of business-level goals.

Thus to reach a business-level target of 5 per cent sales growth, it might be necessary for the personnel department to recruit and screen twenty-five production workers and three more clerical people; for marketing to raise advertising costs by a certain amount, increase the number of sales representatives by a specified number within a certain region, and hire one more inside salesperson; and so on. These functional requirements become, either directly or indirectly, goals of the respective functional departments to be achieved within appropriate time frames.

GOAL FORMULATION]

Four sets of factors affect the nature of an organization's collection of goals:

- The present goals (and action plans);

- The set of strengths, weaknesses, threats, and opportunities that result from environmental and internal analysis;
- The set of political influences within which individuals compete over goal preferences;
- The personal values of the organization's key managers that shape their preferences.

In this section we discuss the role of present goals, the firm's data set, various explanations of how goals are formulated, a prominent theory about the influence of power on goal selection, and the structure of value systems as goal determinants.

Present Goals and Action Plans

The degree of success experienced by an organization in reaching past or present goals and in implementing related action plans provides insight into the need for new or modified goals. Failure to meet the goal of retired Chairman Willard Rockwell, Jr., to build a $1 billion Rockwell International consumer products division led company managers, under the leadership of new chairman and CEO Robert Anderson, to adopt a new goal: $1 billion in foreign sales. This change seems to have been precipitated by the widespread realization that the previous consumer products goal was not likely to be achieved.

Direction for goal formulation at any organizational level also exists in the strategy of the next highest organizational level. These higher levels' goals have the effect of partially defining the context within which goals are to be set at lower levels. For example, when corporate goals are stated in terms of long-term profitability and sales growth, then business-level goals should be consistent with them.

Of course, more information would be required about the other factors that affect goal formulation, but at least corporate goals serve significantly to define the goal choices available for the business level. Similarly, business-level goals can structure the formulation of goals at the functional level and thereby define the context of functional-level goals. Think for a moment of the difficulties that might be encountered by a functional department manager, say, the marketing director, in trying to manage the department without any idea of what business-level goals were important to top management.

The Data Set

The contents of an organization's environmental and internal data set provide major clues for goal formulation. As explained, threats and opportunities (determined by analysis and forecasts of the organization's external circumstances), along with weaknesses and strengths (of the organization's internal state of affairs, in the present and future time frames), can be transformed into goal sets at appropriate organizational levels.

At the corporate level, goals are formulated to define the optimal collection of types of businesses in which the organization is engaged. The firm's data set can be the primary source of information about what types of businesses would be most conducive to future success. The internal portion of the data set highlights problems with existing operations; the external part points out merger possibilities as well as types of operations to avoid. Forecasts can identify potential problems with the present collection of businesses.

Existing business-level goals can be evaluated against the contents of the data set as well. Since business-level goals address business unit performance and competition, such factors as performance shortcomings, competitive position, latent capabilities, potential obstacles, and new opportunities can be discovered through the environmental and internal analyses and their respective parts of the resultant data set.

The data set is also intended to provide major inputs into decisions about the appropriateness of functional-level goals. At this level the portions of the data set that reflect internal strengths and weaknesses play a critical role in goal setting. One might find, for example, during financial analysis that the firm's selling and administrative expenses are excessively high as a percentage of sales. Further analysis might show that sales growth has slowed and that turnover of salespeople is high.

Goals could be set for the marketing department that reflect more desirable performance along these dimensions. Marketing action plans would then be modified to achieve the new goals.

Goal Formulation Theories

Many explanations have been offered in the management literature for how organizational goals are formulated. Mintzberg notes that, during this century, organizational goal formulation theories have undergone a complete reversal from the "rational man" view (one goal setter setting a single organizational goal) through the coalition bargaining view (many goals, many goal setters) to the political arena view (no organizational goals, power games among individuals).

Some examples of the influential goal formulation theories that have appeared over the past several decades follow, in chronological order:

Barnard: Organizational goals are formed by a "trickle-up" process in which subordinates' expectations are adopted by a consensus-based acceptance process.

Papandreou: A top manager forms the organization's goals as a multivariate function of the preferences of influential actors.

Thompson and McEwen: Organizational goals constitute a dynamic equilibrium that is constantly changing to reflect changes in the relationships between the organization and its environment.

Cyert and March: Multiple goals emerge from the bargaining among various coalitions that form out of the parrying for control and personal power by key actors.

Simon: Goals are constraints on profit maximization imposed by decision makers' bounded rationality.

Granger: Hierarchy of goals results from a process of screening, filtering, and narrowing broad expectations to more focused, specific subgoals in a reasonably logical fashion.

Ansoff: New organization goals are tried out iteratively

as means for closing gaps between present goals and hoped-for results.

Allison:

- Organization process model - reasonably stable goals emerge as incompatible constraints that represent the quasi-resolution of conflict among internal and external interest groups;
- Bureaucratic politics model - key players "play" politics to produce goals they agree with as individuals.

Georgiou: Personal goals of individuals come and go as organizational goals according to the short-term victories of key managers as they engage in political combat. There are no organizational goals as such.

Hall: Goals are set according to three processes, the appropriateness of which depends upon two contingencies, concentration of power and amount of goal-preference conflict: problem solving - concentrated power, no preference conflict; and bargaining - balanced power, preferences in conflict.

MacMillan: Organizational coalition members demand coalition commitment to personal goals; the coalition responds by developing commitment to generalized versions of individual members' goals.

These generalized goals (not the specific goals of individuals) become the organization's goals. Beyond these explanations, the models of decision-making processes presented also apply to goal setting.

It is safe to conclude that different people set goals in different ways. But there are at least two sets of influences that must be acknowledged and incorporated in anyone's goal setting activities. They are the power structure within the firm and the values of managers and other employees as they relate to acceptance of the new goal set.

POWER AND GOALS

A model of goal setting presented by Mintzberg in 1979 has endured in its ability to structure the complicated process of identifying political pressures that must be dealt with by managers. Although many of the hypotheses proposed in this model remain untested, it has a great deal of face validity.

According to this model, organizational goals result from the plays of power between two groups of organization influencers: the external coalition and the internal coalition. The external coalition is the set of groups and individuals who, from outside the organization, compete for influence over it.

These external influencers consist of owners (if they are not actively involved in management), suppliers, unions, and various subsets of the public at large which reflect current social issues.

They exert influence over the decisions and activities of those who are running the organization by means of social norms, specific (legal and formal) constraints, pressure campaigns, direct operational controls, and membership on the board of directors.

Three kinds of external coalitions (EC) are proposed by Mintzberg:

- The dominated EC, in which most power is held by an individual or a group whose members are acting in concert;
- The divided EC, where most of the power is shared by some key individuals or groups and the organization is faced with a concomitant set of conflicting demands;
- The passive EC, in which power is dispersed across a large number of individuals or groups and reverts to the internal coalition.

The internal coalition (IC) gets organizational business done, and through its efforts goals emerge.

The internal coalition consists of five influencer individuals or groups:

- The peak coordinator (the top manager);
- Middle or line managers who are delegated formal responsibility for actions and decisions of designated portions of the operating core or that organizational part of a business where its work is accomplished;

- Operators who make up the operating core are nonmanagers who get the work done;
- Analysts who are free of responsibility for conducting"line" activities and instead, advise, design, and run coordinative systems that bring about planning and control;]
- Support staff who advise on certain specialized activities and actually operate various ancillary processes. Analysts would include such jobs as planner, efficiency experts, expediters, accountants and computer programmers while support staff would consist of cafeteria workers, mailroom people, payroll specialists, legal counsel staff, and so on.

Power is distributed across these groups according to four systems of influence or more specifically, systems of control: The system of authority which is made up of the top manager's personal control system, by which the peak coordinator exercises authority and the bureaucratic (formal) control system (rules, procedures, performance control and evolution systems, training programs, etc.);

The political control system, which acts to displace the intentions of the peak coordinator, or the entire system of authority more generally, by exercising illegitimate power often arising out of conflict; the ideologic control system, which defines the personality or character of the organization as an entity apart from its group of participants and is based on the traditions, beliefs, and myths about the organization.

Lastly, thesystem of expertise serves to distribute power on the basis of skill or talent rather than according to authority, ideology, or even, in some cases, political activities. It seems that the perception of skill and talent tends to increase one's invulnerability to other control systems to a large degree.

Within these five sets of powers of the internal coalition, formal goals are formed. The peak coordinator, by exercising his/her personal and bureaucratic control systems, attempts to impose formal goals and a collection of subgoals on other participants and units of the organization.

But the political system works to displace those formal goals as other internal influencers seek to have their preferences adopted as formal goals.

Through a process of bargaining, formal goals are modified. Ideological goals, often the manifestations of mission, become adopted by individuals, and ultimately by the organization.

Depending upon the relative power of these systems, five types of internal coalition can develop. Actually, more than five could develop but, as Mintzberg notes, the five that follow are the most natural:

- The Personalized IC is dominated by the system of authority in which the top manager dominates. This is the case when the top manager exercises strong control over the IC, makes the strategic decisions, and closely manages and controls implementation. Although the system of ideology can peacefully coexist with a personalized IC as long as ideology is subservient to it, the other systems of power cannot.
- In the bureaucratic IC power is also concentrated in the system of authority but this time in the bureaucratic control system. Instead of the personal power of the CEO being the dominating force, the organization's standard work activities and procedures serve the insiders who have formal power. But since bureaucratic control systems are usually designed to serve the needs of top management, maybe even to protect them, this IC tends to concentrate power at the top of the organization.
- The organization's system of ideology dominates goal setting when an ideologic IC prevails. Although the top manager holds power if he/she mirrors the ideological principles of the organization, anyone who represents the ideology tends to share in the power created by personification of company beliefs.
- In the fourth type of internal coalition, the professional IC, the system of expertise dominates

so that power flows to those who are regarded as possessing the skills and knowledge that lead to success of the organization.

- The politicized IC is our final type of coalition. In it, power rests with the person who has the most energy and skill for playing power games, not with the legitimate systems of influence. There tends to be no focus of power. Instead, the dominant influence tends to rest with the most recent victor in one or another of a series of little power skirmishes that go on in a structure devoid of the other, more substantial power systems. Politicized ICs are characterized by conflict and fluidity with power going, at least temporarily, to the person who is willing to spend the most time playing power games.

Organizational goals are formed according to the nature of six organizational power configurations that emerge from the interactions among the various types of internal and external coalitions.

These power configurations are described by Mintzberg as six natural combinations of his internal and external coalitions. There are nine other combinations that he claims are less likely to form (less natural). All fifteen power configurations can be studied in the book from which this section is drawn by those seeking more complete development of ideas.

For our purposes, the most important elements of the model are the six natural power configurations because they occur most often. They are the instrument, closed system, autocracy, missionary, meritocracy, and political arena configurations, as explained in the following section:

- The instrument power configuration is characterized by the organization being controlled by one dominant external influencer or group of them. The internal coalition tends to emerge as bureaucratic attempting to optimize whatever goals were selected for it by the external influencer."Such a configuration tends to emerge when an organization experiences external power that is focussed and organized, typically around a critical dependency or key legal prerogative, wielded by an external influencer (or a group of them acting in concert) with clear and operational goals."

- The closed system also has a bureaucratic internal coalition like the instrument configuration. The difference is that the closed system faces no concentrated external power source. Instead, its environment consists of atomistic inflencers such that none emerges as dominant. In other words, the closed system's external environment is passive. This combination of bureaucratic IC and passive EC leads to domination by the most effective bureaucrats, usually senior managers and their analysts who understand the workings of the bureaucracy better than other insiders. Because of the absence of external influence, the closed system's IC tends to serve its own interests and may even control its environment. "The closed system tends to appear in more established organizations, typically large ones in simple, stable environments with unskilled operators and dispersed external influencers."
- The autocracy experiences a passive EC also, but its IC is dominated by the personal control system of the CEO. This close control precludes political games where insiders can either follow the leader or leave. the EC's passivity can be borne out of a long history of lack of response by the organization to external demands or influence or even to a sense of hopelessness. Thus a firm undergoing a long period of decline into which is hired a new "white knight" CEO may switch to an autocracy. In this case the new CEO may be able to formulate and implement strategies previously considered out of the question by the organization's key players.
- The missionary power configuration has a passive EC and an ideologic IC. Because the IC is dominated

by ideology, the external influencers' power is nullified. Insiders are welded together around the strong ideology so that control is unnecessary. Ideologic goals tend to be internalized by participants. There are few political games because involvement in them marks the perpetrator as "anti-ideology." Activities are directed toward preserving, extending, and perfecting the organization's mission and, therefore, the prevailing ideology.

- Power is centered on the expertise that defines the meritocracy and its professional IC. When there are more than one important expertise or skill that are involved in the conduct of work in the meritocracy, then the possibility exists for political games among skill groups. There may be squabbling about resources, location, top management attention, promotion candidates, and other actions that may serve to distinguish one skill group from another. But the focus on performance expertise tends to resolve most conflict in the true meritocracy, and that includes resolution of conflicting demands placed on the organization from the EC. The major contributor to the formation of meritocracies is the need for the organization's insiders to perform complex work that require skill and talent or some sort within the internal coalition.
- Conflict within a divided EC and a politicized IC lead to formation of the political arena, our last power configuration. Conflicting demands pressuring the organization from outside and the political conflict and its ensuing chaos inside lead to high turnover, low levels of loyalty, and, as Mintzberg said, loud voices. Political scheming tends to replace conduct of the organization's business. Until another configuration replaces this one, little goal setting activity takes place. Usually the personal discomfort engendered by a politicized IC motivates insiders to correct the situation. Degenerating performance may

prompt involvement of owners or a group of insiders to take a major corrective action. Often the political arena develops as a natural step in the transition between two of the other configurations. It may also form in response to a challenge to the organization's existing order of power, a change in leadership, or a competitive threat that is not constructively handled right away.

Once goals are set within any of these configurations, they can change as a result of changes in the intensity of coalition demands, aspirations of managers, and the mission of the organization.

Mintzberg's model serves three purposes. First, it represents an integrated set of hypotheses that offer plausible explanations of how goals may actually form in organizations. As such it is a useful analytical device for gaining understanding of how goals emerge in cases and in real businesses

Second, it can serve as a structure within which goal changes can be suggested for case studies. By identifying the relative balance of IC and EC power relationships, the most effective ways to "inject" suggestions into an organization can be at least tentatively determined.

Third, the model delineates an explanation of how power comes into play as a major determinant of organizational goal formulation (and action plan formulation as well). Students should learn to decide on the type of internal and external coalitions present in a case or later, in a business, to get an idea about what kinds of goals and action plans might be better received than others.

VALUES OF KEY MANAGERS

In addition to the power relationships between the internal and external coalitions of a firm, the value orientations of the people within the organization will also affect the degree of acceptance with which a new strategy will be received. But values are difficult to measure, identify, and define. This section offers a model of values that allows analysts to describe most types of value orientations they might encounter in cases and real businesses.

Shirley et al. define personal values as "one's 'conception of the desirable.'" People's values are determined by their experience, education, and family backgrounds and can be thought of as "a guidance system which the manager uses when faced with a decision."

Herein lies the importance of values to the strategy formulation process. Strategies have to be implemented. That requires acceptance of the new goals and action plans by a majority of managers and employees. Trying to implement strategies that run counter in one way or another to the values of those people who are required to carry them out, especially key people, will lead to failure.

Until the 1950s it was felt that strategic behaviour was value-free.

However:

Common observation and sociological research both show that behaviour is not value-free, that both individuals and organizations exhibit preferences for certain types of strategic behaviour.

They express such preferences by persisting in a particular behaviour, even if it means a sacrifice in the results.

Thus generalizations about which strategies are "correct" are difficult to make without considering the value orientations of managers.

The following six value orientations have been identified by Guth and Tagieri as major determinants of peoples' decisions:

- *Theoretical*: Emphasis on truth, knowledge, and rational thinking.
- *Economic*: Orientation toward practicality, usefulness, and the creation of wealth.
- *Political*: Emphasis on power and recognition.
- *Social:* Orientation toward positive relationships, affection, and the absence of conflict.
- *Aesthetic*: Strong desire for artistic factors such as harmony, composition, form, and symmetry.

- *Religious*: An orientation toward unit in the universe.

Although Guth and Tagieri found that managers tend to emphasize economic, theoretical, and political values more than the others, each of the six values can lead to the following types of goal preferences:

- *Theoretical value orientation*: Long-term research and development goals, emphasis on precision, and possibly an acceptance of detail and complexity even to the point of distraction.
- *Economic value orientation*: Growth and profitability goals, successful financial performance measures.
- *Political value orientation*: Emphasis on goals relating to size, such as total assets, sales volume, or number of employees, number of subsidiaries, and so on.
- *Social value orientation*: Goals stressing social responsibility, indirect rather than direct competition, or positive organizational atmosphere rather than possibly threatening congeniality. A disdain for rocking the boat that may even lead to stagnation of products, markets, or human resources.
- *Aesthetic value orientation*: Goals emphasizing product design, quality, and appeal even to the detriment of profitability.
- *Religious value orientation*: Goals stressing ethical matters, spiritual concepts, and moral obligations.

How top managers go about turning values into company-wide values, or as Ansoff describes it, into the strategic culture of the groups, is at the core of strategic management.

Deal and Kennedy explain that the real challenge for management is to imbue thousands and thousands of employees with a strongly ingrained sense of the company's values.

They explain six ways in which corporate visionaries, whom they call "heroes" (rare people who personify the aspirations of employees), can "reinforce the basic values of the (strategic) culture:"

- Make success attainable by employees by

demonstrating and rewarding the superior performance of outstanding employees who embody the critical company values.

- Provide role models by finding ways to transmit to employees understanding of how heroes attained their status.
- Represent the company's values to the outside world.
- Find a way to preserve the values that make the company special, to keep them current and in employees' minds.
- Set a standard of performance for employees that is appropriate to the organization's values.
- Search out and employ a means for motivating employees to perform in a way consistent with, and supportive of, organization values.

Implicit in three of these suggestions are ways for top managers to bridge the gap that may exist between values and goals or action plans.

In the first (make success attainable), positive reinforcement is suggested as the way to demonstrate to employees which goal achievements are consistent with values.

In other words value preferences must first be understood by top managers and then there must be follow-up work to identify and reward value achievement or manifestations.

The value orientations managers expect their employees to adopt should be displayed by the managers themselves. The personal goals of top managers then can be reinterpreted for lower-level managers.

Last, the sixth suggestion (seek motivational techniques consistent with company values) implies that careful thought about the value implications of raises, promotions, job restructuring, recognition, and other motivational approaches is necessary. These techniques should be selected on the basis not only of expected goal achievement, but also of expected value attainment.

These simple value structures make consideration of the important role of values in strategy formulation straightforward.

As part of an effective set of solutions to a case analysis, a section which addresses value attainment makes the suggested solution more believable.

A LTERNATIVE AND COMPLEMENTARY STRATEGIC POSTURES

Although a firm's set of strategies may in fact be unique, the essential nature of its set of goals and action plans tends to be one or some combination.

They are labeled strategic "postures" because each one represents a synthesis of, or tendency in, the elements and characteristics of strategy. Two firms could have the same strategic posture but they would be differentiated by their specific quantitative and qualitative goals, corporate- and business-level strategies, and functional strategies.

The offensive types are appropriate for growth-related goals; the defensive for goals that require constricting operations because of inefficiencies.

OFFENSIVE POSTURES

Offensive postures are employed by management to reach goals related to increases in sales or market share, and in some cases, profitability.

The five types are concentration, horizontal merger, integration, diversification, and joint venture. It should be pointed out that bringing about an increase in market share alone may not always satisfy performance expectations. There is some evidence suggesting that achieving high returns from high market share depends at least partly on some other considerations.

Woo studied businesses which had successfully established strong market share positions so as to identify the factors which differentiate the high return performers from the low return performers. She defined business as "a division, product line, or other profit centre within its parent company, selling a distinct set of products or services to an identifiable group or groups of customers, in competition with a well-defined set of competitors."

The factors suspected of contributing to performance are market stability, competitive strategy, demand characteristics, and degree of relatedness among SBUs within multi-unit firms. The question analyzed was whether factors other than market share alone explain performance differences between the two groups of high market share firms.

The analysis shows that whether gaining high market share will translate into high profitability is a function of three sets of factors.

First, higher returns accrue to high share businesses within stable markets than to high share businesses in less stable markets.

Within the market stability dimension, profitable share leaders had more competitors and older products with lower value added than more profitable share leaders. They also conducted business in regional markets in which their competitors were well-connected to suppliers and customers.

Offensive and Defensive Strategic Postures

Offensive

- Concentration Growth
  - Market Penetration
  - Market Development
  - Product Development
  - Horizontal Merger
  - Niching
  - Low-cost Leadership("Functional Rationalization")
  - Cost Focus
  - Differentiation
  - Focused Differentiation
- Integrative Growth
  - Backward
  - Forward
- Diversification Growth
  - Concentric
  - Conglomerate
- Joint Ventures

Defensive

- Retrenchment/Turnaround
  - Shallow
  - Deep
- Divestiture
  - Sell-off
  - Spin-off
  - Split-off
- Liquidation
  - Voluntary Closure
  - Assignment
  - Bankruptcy
- Harvesting

differed in terms of several strategic factors. Low returns were characteristic of firms with the greatest differential between the percentages of superior and inferior products—the operational definition of quality. Low return leaders also tended to have higher prices and higher direct costs than their competitors. For high return leaders the size of their price premiums over competitors was lower than for their low return counterparts and their costs were lower than competitors.'

Generally, the study shows that superior market share does not alone explain effective and high return performance. The additional factors of market stability, competitive strategy, and demand characteristics play important roles in determining the profitability of high share organizations. Thus, an attempt to generate high share alone might be unsuccessful only because these other factors were not considered.

Concentration Postures

Concentration postures are primarily marketing moves attempted to improve sales or profitability by getting more out of resources currently available within the firm.

There are some profound advantages to building a strategy around a firm's present products and markets. Drucker observes:

The belief has been held widely that the business that "diversifies" into many areas is likely to do better than the business that concentrates on one area.

The belief is sheer myth and is contradicted by all evidence... Complex businesses, despite their size and large resources, have again and again shown themselves exceedingly vulnerable to competition by a small but highly concentrated single-market or single-technology business.

First, a concentration posture allows the firm to develop heightened expertise in its products and markets by specialization. Many firms have dominated their industries by following concentration strategies. Among these are Holiday Inn, MacDonald's, and Xerox.

Second, by focusing on one segment of the market, or on one product or a limited product line, the company's visibility is enhanced. Chances are better for market leadership, especially when competitors have to spread their capabilities across multiple lines or segments.

Next, concentration increases operational flexibility by eliminating, or at least minimizing, interaction effects. Since multiple products in a line, or segments in a marketing mix, must compete for the firm's resources, nonconcentrated companies must balance resource allocation changes.

Before more funds can be allocated to the marketing effort of one product, managers first may have to determine from which other products or functions funds will be diverted. Such decisions take time and thus tend to reduce the efficiency of decisions in non-concentrated firms relative to concentrated ones. As long as demand holds for the product or line, or in the market segments of a firm pursuing concentration, the potential for growth may be greater than for the other choices.

Similar advice is offered by Lauenstein and Skinner who advocate focusing attention and resources—technology, knowledge, finances, assets, human skills, and management—on gaining competitive advantage rather than spreading and diverting those resources and eventually either weakening strategic position or preventing its development. Industry dominance is gained by first concentrating on limited fields of technology, product, or market; then reinforcing strengths like financial condition, experience, and share in these concentrated areas; until competitive superiority is achieved in the areas in which resource focus has been built.

Once competitive advantage is established, management can apply its superior resources to growth goals with far more dexterity than would have been possible without resource strengths.

In operational terms, pursuing resource concentration strategies means avoiding the tendency to "bounce around" from one quick fix—new product, subsidiary, or market—to another, and instead, building fundamental strengths in areas that may ensure the long-term success of the firm.

Students often sense the urge to try something new while analyzing case studies in which the organization has several functional weaknesses and few strengths with which to work.

A common reaction is to recommend diversification rather than figuring out what internal capabilities will be necessary for sustained dominance and setting out to develop those capabilities.

Market Penetration: This posture is followed to increase sales within the firm's present markets with its present products. It is essentially an advertising action that would normally follow a market analysis undertaken to gain insight into user and nonuser characteristics, as well as their perceptions of the product and its attributes. Obviously such an analysis would have to reveal sufficient sales potential to justify the effort.

Functional actions that might be designed to implement market penetration include the following:

- Increase present customers' usage rates by product modification such as"new improved,""longer life", or more effective versions.
- Find new uses for the product, which will increase sales. The discovery that baking soda would reduce odors in sink drains represented a new use that resulted in consumers turning over their stocks of the product more quickly.

- Increase the number of customers within a segment by intensified advertising/promotion programs. This choice normally calls for improving ads, increasing media coverage, or increasing advertising frequency, each of which would necessitate an increase in marketing budget, or at least a change in its application.

Market Development: Firms with strategies aimed at market development seek to expand the geographical regions or the number of market segments they serve with their product.

Examples include:

- Microcomputer manufacturers entrance into the commercial microcomputer market shortly after introducing their machines as home computers.
- Development by colleges and universities of continuing education programs in order to take their services to nontraditional students.
- Attempts by Volkswagen and Volvo during the early-1980s to appeal to the upper-income market by emphasizing that thrifty people are respected for their good judgment and that thriftiness is embodied in buying some models in their lines.
- Mercedes Benz, Lexus (Toyota) and Infiniti (Nissan) introducing models with lower price tags than their earlier high-priced luxury cars in order to make sales to people not willing or able to buy the high-priced models but wishing to own these pricey brands.

Action plans for marketing that can implement strategies involving sales increases through market development include:

- Identifying new segments of the existing market area to which an appeal will be made, and then appropriately modifying advertising budgets and related strategies to develop a new series of advertisements.
- Establishing the necessary supply and distribution systems, along with promotion and advertising strategies, to take the product to a different geographical area.

- Developing new versions of the product to appeal to a new segment.

Product Development. Product development is a way to increase sales in present segments by augmenting the present product line. A furniture manufacturing firm that adds a line of bedroom furniture to increase sales in its present market segments would be involved in product development.

Product development strategies can be operationalized by:

- Developing new features for present products as often seen with various detergents, toothpastes, and cosmetics.
- Designing additional models and sizes of the product as exemplified by the proliferation of different models of 35mm cameras by the same manufacturers.
- Creating improved versions of products as has occurred with some heating systems, window and door installation units for the home, and child-restraint systems for automobiles.

Of course, action plans would be developed for other functional areas besides marketing for each of the concentration strategies.

Horizontal merger. Horizontal merger is merging with or acquiring another company in the same industry. It is classified as a concentration posture because it involves increasing the firm's level of activity in its present products, markets, or both. The combination of American Motors and Renault was a horizontal merger. During the 1980s many horizontal mergers were allowed by the Securities and Exchange Commission. Some of the most notable were in the banking and airline industries.

Niching

Newman advocated developing "propitious niches" that optimize a company's position relative to its competitors and its resources. The resources possessed by a firm around which it might develop a niche could be its unique functional capabilities (strengths), technological knowledge and ability, and so on. When Porter described his now widely known generic competitive strategies of cost leadership, cost focus, differentiation, and focused differentiation, he did not refer to them as niche strategies. But if management of a firm sought to establish cost leadership, for example, it would actually be developing a niche based upon its ability to manage the costs of its operations better than its competitors. Similarly, a differentiation strategy would exploit a firm's marketing, production, R&D, or other area's knowledge and abilities and might thus be considered a niche-developing move.

Porter defines lower cost and differentiation as bases of competitive advantage that, if successfully developed, can lead to strategies of cost leadership or cost focus and differentiation or focused differentiation, respectively, as shown below,

Competitive Advantage	Broad Target Market	Narrow Target Market
Lower Cost	Cost Leadership Action Plan	Cost Focus Action Plan
Differentiation	Differentiation Action Plan	Focused Differentiation Action Plan

Adapted from Michael E. Porter, The Competitive Advantage of Nations.

Stated differently, firms that have the competitive advantage of lower cost operations can formulate and implement action plans of cost leadership or cost focus. Businesses that have the competitive advantage of differentiated products can pursue action plans of differentiation or focused differentiation.

Choosing between the two lower cost choices, cost leadership and cost focus, is a matter of choosing goals that define either broad or narrow competitive scope. Competitive scope identifies the size of the "piece" of a firm's market to which the low cost or differentiation strategy will be applied.

This decision involves identifying things like number of product models that will be made, number of different distribution channels that will be used, number of market segments (collections of demographic variables or geographic areas) that will be entered, and so on. With broad competitive scope (large mass market) the lower cost firm would strive for a cost leadership position by aggressively rationalizing its operations to maintain lower costs and concomitantly higher profit margins than its competitors.

Firms with lower cost advantages that are aiming at a narrow market definition, that is, a small niche, should embark upon a cost focus action plan. They might concentrate on a particular geographic area, well-defined group of customers, or a narrow set of demographics or needs while essentially abrogating the rest of the market to other competitors.

Both lower cost strategies requires making a product or service available more efficiently than one's competitors at the same quality level and doing it by functional rationalization.

Rather than controlling costs only in production, both necessitate rationalizing all functional departments so as to minimize the costs of their operation relative to competitors so that profit margins can be higher than those of competitors.

Successful rationalization of functional departments' operations would allow the company to achieve functional goals related to thinning the product line or reducing prices so that business level market share or profit goals could be reached.

The conceptual simplicity of functional rationalization masks its difficulty, attendant detail and possible behavioral problems. It is a tough thing to do in a company or business unit that has been riding a growth curve which has suddenly leveled off. This is because the organizational mind set is often slanted toward the almost jubilant extravagance that accompanies rapid growth.

There is a fine distinction between functional rationalization and shallow retrenchment, a defensive action plan discussed in a moment.

They differ largely in terms of the environmental circumstances within which they are formulated. Shallow retrenchment is a reduction in size or activity levels in response to financial or economic problems. Rationalization, on the other hand, is a positive, offensive action designed to keep the organization lean and efficient in the face of market, product, or industry maturity.

It may be thought of as a necessary element of an intention to reduce prices while maintaining profit margins as a way to compete in a mature or saturated market. As such it is not a reaction to adversity but rather, proaction for growth.

Examples of functional actions which might be included in a functional rationalization to develop a lower cost strategy are the following:

- Reduce operating expenses in functional departments as well as corporate level operations in order to achieve superior relative cost position.
- Thin product offerings to the best performers (determined by whatever measures are strategically relevant).
- Reposition marketing efforts to the potentially most successful markets or segments.
- Attempt to reduce cost-of-goods-sold as a percentage of sales by streamlining inventory or "buying better."

Differentiation is bringing about market supremacy by achieving higher quality, better customer service, or more appealing product features than one's competitors, or superiority or uniqueness in other characteristics.

It is achieved when product or service uniqueness is recognized throughout the industry and by buyers of the product. About $400 million in shrimp is exported to the U.S. and Europe from the South American country of Ecuador every year.

Ecuadorian shrimp growers are convinced that their product is the highest quality shrimp available in the U.S. They see no need to attempt to differentiate their shrimp in the U.S. on the basis of quality because, they say, it is the best available! But the buyers of shrimp apparently don't "understand" since.

Thai black tiger shrimp and Chinese eastern whites have, over the brief span of four years, reduced Ecuador's market share by nearly 50 per cent.

The industry may sense differentiation, but without customer-perceived differentiation, it doesn't carry through to the "bottom line."

As the diagram above demonstrates, companies with the competitive advantage of a differentiated product or service can formulate and implement action plans to differentiate within a broad market or to focus differentiation in a narrow market.

As with lower cost strategies, the difference between these two alternatives is one of market breadth and thus the scope of competition taken on by the company. Differentiation is striving for industry-wide uniqueness whereas focused differentiation aims at a concentrated market definition.

The premier example of broad-based differentiation is Mercedes-Benz' quality-based franchise in the worldwide automobile market. Focused differentiation has been achieved by New Balance by offering athletic shoes in widths so that people with wide feet seek New Balance shoes almost out of necessity.

Lower cost and differentiation strategies can be pursued in either a narrowly defined niche or a broadly defined one. This definition of Integration Strategies

Whereas concentration strategies are aimed primarily at sales increases, integration strategies seek mainly, but not exclusively, to acquire a service or product by merging with or acquiring the prior provider. Therefore, the process of integration should be implemented within a framework of goals that spells out the limits of such evaluative criteria as return on sales and investment, pivotal expense items, time, and cash flow.

Backward Integration. Backward integration entails gaining increased control over the firm's supply (or input) activities. It can be implemented through merger with or acquisition of the firm that produces the company's inputs or by "growing one's own" supply systems. However, it is often easier to finance an acquisition than internal expansion.

Forward Integration. Forward integration consists of obtaining control over the external portions of the firm's marketing systems. In most cases this means either acquiring a distribution system or establishing one internally.

Reasons for Diversity and Integration

Even though the advantages of concentration may be significant, certain forces cause integration and diversification to be favorable strategies for some businesses. Drucker categorizes them as internal and external pressures for diversity. Internal Pressures. First, there is often psychological pressure for expansion. Business owners as well as managers simply get tired of doing the same thing. The possibility of expanding by diversification or integration, of facing the challenges of a new set of business circumstances, is often too attractive to forego.

Second, businesses can reach a nonoptimal size which integration can rectify. As an example, Drucker explains that in the 1920s and 1930s, Sears, Roebuck emerged as a giant retailer needing supply commitments its suppliers were unwilling to provide without a permanent relationship. Sears integrated backward to the point where more than half of its products are produced by manufacturers in which it has an ownership stake.

To commit the desired volume of output to Sears, suppliers needed a permanent reciprocal commitment from Sears to, among other things, obtain adequate control. Without backward integration, Sears was the wrong size.

Third, integration can increase profitability by turning a cost centre into a revenue (and profit) producer. Firms that integrate can then operate the new business as a profit centre while also serving the needs of the old business. However, inefficiencies in managing the new firm along with the old can create unexpected and burdensome familiarization costs.

Integration by merger rather than internal development tends to reduce these costs. Without careful planning, however, the cost of inefficiencies associated with operating an unfamiliar business can be greater than the costs of purchasing the inputs. Many boat dealers in the Northeast attempted to build vessels in limited quantities during the winter for sale during the boating season, only to find that inefficiencies and unfamiliarity with this new activity made it unprofitable.

Finally, a related integration pressure is the desire to increase control of supply streams to correct inconsistencies in quality or delivery schedules, or unreliability of distributors, when they become intolerable. Sears is a good example of a firm whose huge retail demand, coupled with the need to regularize quality levels, necessitated backward integration.

External Pressures. Often more influential in diversification decisions are forces exerted on the firm from outside. There is first the pressure of reaching the growth limits of the firm's economic environment. Drucker gives as examples such countries as Belgium, India, Peru, Venezuela, and Japan, in which certain firms reached the local economy's growth limits. They then diversified into other industries in order to grow.

The same problem is faced by small domestic firms tied tightly into local markets. A local marina business, for example, that expands slip and mooring rental facilities to the point where all who want to pay the price to keep their boats there are doing so faces diversification as the only reasonable expansion choice. The owner might choose to open a restaurant, a ships store, or a bar, among others. In the marina case, practical local growth can also be limited by physical space limitations.

The second external pressure for diversification has been the expansion of domestic markets to international scale. Since World War II, country after country has developed similar demand patterns. Since demand determines supply, firms expand to meet developing demand patterns on foreign soil. Thus international corporations, based in countries around the world, have pursued demand across national boundaries.

Third, technological branching creates pressure for diversity. A new technology often spawns a whole family of technologies and a multitude of products and product lines for numerous markets. Management can design strategies to diversify along with technological branching, or even to develop the branch technologies through aggressive R&D.

The fourth external pressure for diversification is the nature of tax laws. Rather than pay taxes on distributed profits from the corporation they own, stockholders often prefer that managers reinvest earnings in the business. When there is limited need for such financing in a firm's existing line of business, managers are forced to seek merger partners to generate acceptable returns. Of course, tax laws were not designed to further industrial concentration in this way.

Finally, career expectations of managers, whose expertise is highly valued by their employers, create pressure for diversification. By acquiring subsidiaries a corporation can also acquire upper-level management positions for its upwardly mobile and talented junior people.

Profitability of Vertical Integration Strategies. Buzzell analyzed PIMS data to determine the profitability of vertical integration. He first explained the benefits and risks of vertical integration and then, on the basis of statistical analysis of 1,649 manufacturing firms, offered five guidelines for evaluating the benefits and risks of integration strategies.

The benefits of vertical integration are explained as follows:

- Reduction or elimination of transaction costs: This can occur when firms in different stages of a production process combine and reduce buying and selling costs among them.
- Assurance of continued supplies: Supply of critical input materials can be assured by ownership of suppliers.
- Cost reductions through improved coordination: Costs generated by the often complex logistics of coordinating production and inventory scheduling among suppliers can be reduced by integration.
- Easier innovation: Because integrated firms are involved in many production and marketing activities rather than only a few, innovation through improved coordinating of technical and marketing functions is easier.

- Creation of higher entry barriers: Because integrated firms obtain a greater "critical mass," they necessitate higher financial and managerial investments by would-be ccmpetitors.

The PIMS (Profit Impact of Marketing Strategies) project is an ongoing analysis by the Strategic Planning Institute (SPI) of over 1,700 product and service business units of the approximately 200 SPI corporate members.

Offsetting these pluses are the following costs and risks of integration:

- Capital requirements rise when a firm integrates either backward or forward as it supports the resource needs of the new activities. This increase in investment intensity leads to lower profitability by raising the breakeven point.
- Unbalanced scales of operation appear when different stages of production are combined. This happens when the input requirements of one stage (company) are less than the optimal production level of the producing stage. For example, a small boat dealer began its own line of sailing dinghies rather than buying them from a large national manufacturer. However, because of the small volume of this new operation, the dealer's per-unit costs for producing the boats were so high that he was unable to price them competitively.
- Limited flexibility accompanies commitment to the new stage of production. This is a problem when a change in technology or market conditions occurs and the company is unable to withdraw from the weak stage quickly.
- A firm that integrates is no longer specialized in just one stage. The added company requirements of the new production stage can be radically different from its traditional management competence. Learning the new stage's operating characteristics can be costly for the integrating firm's management.

Buzzell found that the profitability of vertical integration is situational; that is, sometimes it works and sometimes it does not.

Ne offers the following observations about integration:

- When an integration strategy can be implemented without greater investment intensity (investment-to-sales ratio), return on investment (ROI) is likely to rise.
- Backward integration of both consumer and industrial goods manufacturers improves ROI a small amount. Return on investment for consumer goods manufacturers is higher when they are more forward integrated than their competitors.
- Firms with large market share will tend to receive greater benefits from increases in vertical integration.
- The profitability of vertical integration strategies does not tend to vary with the stability of market conditions and technology.
- For firms that undergo rapid increases in materials costs, return on investment and extent of vertical integration tend to be indirectly related.
- Highly integrated businesses tend to produce more product innovations.

On the basis of these findings, the following guidelines were offered to help bring about more benefits than costs of vertical integration:

- Beware of increases in investment needs that tend to accompany vertical integration.
- Consider other ways of achieving vertical integration without outright ownership. An example is entering into long-term contracts with suppliers and joint ventures or strategic alliances.
- Do not integrate partway by taking an incremental approach to it. Instead define an integration goal and achieve it.
- Identify the scale requirements of the integration suppliers/customers and stay within those parameters.

- Do not integrate for purposes of reducing raw materials costs without careful analysis.

Diversification Strategies

Before the strategist embarks upon an external diversification strategy, several questions should be answered. First, have all reasonable avenues for intensive growth been ruled out as feasible ways to attain goals? They may constitute less risky methods for growth than diversification.

Next, is the firm diversifying out of strength in its present operations? Too often a management group looks to diversification as a way of covering less-than-satisfactory performance in its present activities.

Diversification has the best chance of success when the business chosen fits the strategy and when it is attempted by managements who have mastered their current strategies. Those who have been unable to successfully manage one business, or set of businesses, will probably find greater difficulty in managing an additional business.

Yet, as Drucker points out, "No matter how desirable concentration is, it may have to be harmonized with diversification. Otherwise it would become overspecification... Simplicity and complexity are both genuine needs. They pull the business in opposite directions."

There are two diversification approaches—concentric and conglomerate—from which the strategist can choose. The one selected should have the greatest chance of making use of the firm's strengths or external opportunities or dealing constructively with a correctable weakness or external threat. In other words diversification should make sense strategically, just as any other strategic choice.

Concentric Diversification: This is the development of a business with products that have marketing or technological synergies with the firm's present products. New classes of customers will be sought for these products. Minute Maid represented concentric diversification for Coca-Cola, whose marketing expertise, particularly its distribution capabilities, were brought to bear on Minute Maid's products.

Conglomerate Diversification

This is the combination of business units with products that:

- Represent no marketing, technological, or other synergies
- Appeal to new customer classes. It would be viewed as an investment of company funds in a firm with a correctable deficiency or in an environmental opportunity. A well known firm that practices conglomerate diversification as a matter of strategy is Textron. It has acquired such diverse products as helicopters, watchbands, chainsaws, golf carts, staplers, and machine tools.

Joint Venture

A joint venture or strategic alliance is a business unit or competitive effort established for a specific purpose and the ownership of which is shared by two or more businesses. It can be used as a way to own and control a business, product line, market, or activity that does not really fit the strategy of either parent.

Ideally joint ventures are formed by organizations with complementary or supplementary capabilities, which are unified in the joint venture. They get together because of a mutual need for the results of its operation.

The major reasons why managers involve their companies in joint ventures are to enter new markets and gain access to raw materials.

Killing explains that joint ventures are used to accomplish these objectives for four primary reasons. First, many governments insist that foreign competitors participate in joint ventures with local partners rather than set up a wholly owned subsidiary.

Second, managers may turn to joint venture when the financial risks of certain larger projects are too great for their company to bear alone. The Alaskan pipeline was a joint venture among hundreds of firms.

Third, when neither partner alone has sufficient skills or resources to make the business a success, joint venture may be an attractive avenue to success by making it possible to combine the needed attributes.

Finally, a joint venture may be the only way that the partners can reach acceptable economies of scale in research, marketing, or production. Killing notes that European auto makers may be forced into a series of joint ventures in the future because the volume of cars produced in Europe is too small to support ten different companies.

The three common types of joint ventures are unrelated partners, related partners, and dual-nationality partners.

Unrelated Partners: These are firms that are independent and usually are in different industries. They pool their respective contributions—resources, skills, technologies, and so on—in the joint venture and share contractually in the results of its operation.

In the 1920s General motors and Standard oil of New Jersey formed a joint venture of this type—Ethyl Corporation. Its ultimate purpose was to produce and distribute gasoline containing the additive tetraethyl lead, which was to prevent knocking in gasoline engines. The strategic importance of the joint venture is illustrated by GM's role in this partnership.

Its strategy involved mechanical activities. Yet the "knocking" problem with gasoline engines was limiting automobile sales. Rather than get into a different business—namely, chemical processing and distribution, a risky diversification for GM—it founded Ethyl Corporation as a joint venture with Standard Oil, which had the needed expertise. General Motors benefited from the sale of Ethyl's products, and also from increased sales of automobiles; Standard Oil participated directly in Ethyl's sales, but also in heightened gasoline demand.

Related Partners. Joint ventures by related partners are aggregations of similar activities or business units that could not survive alone. Aramco (Arabian American Oil Company) is a joint venture formed in the 1940s by Jersey Standard, California Standard, and Mobil.

Although perhaps an unpalatable goal to some by today's standards, its purpose was to monopolize the large Saudi

Arabian oil deposits that constituted a major marketing threat to each participant acting alone.

Dual Nationality. The last type of joint venture is the dual-nationality combination, whereby firms join forces to overcome political, social, or cultural obstacles. Many foreign governments allow U.S. firms to do business on their soil only as partners with the local firms in joint ventures.

Joint ventures can be further categorized in terms of the degree of management control or responsibility exercised by the partners.

Killing defines three possible levels of control that he calls dominant parent, shared management, and independent joint ventures, which can be used to identify the control relationships of unrelated, related, and dual nationality ventures.

Dominant parent joint ventures are those in which one partner is more active in managing the venture's operations than the other. Thus, a venture between two partners each of whose financial ownership amounted to 50 per cent would be a dominant joint venture if one actively managed.

Shared management ventures are those in which both partners take an active operational role. Typically the partners place some of their own managers in the venture to manage some challenging management problems that necessitate the following:

- Defined objectives for each parent and for the joint venture should be specified in an agreement similar to a partnership agreement.
- The agreement should also provide for a way to arbitrate deadlocks.
- Whenever possible the joint venture should operate autonomously of the parent firms.
- Conditions and methods of dissolution or spin-off should be outlined to the extent that it is possible to do so beforehand.

Variations of these offensive action plans have been proposed by several authors but most of them rely on the fundamental action plans in the concentration category. These variations differ largely in terms of the goals which they would be formulated to achieve.

Buzzell, Gale and Sultan define share increasing and maintenance strategies called building and holding, respectively.

Build strategies call for investment to raise market share; holding actions are directed at maintaining present market share. Both strategy types could be implemented with the concentration postures described above.

Similarly, sales maximizing is defined by Utterback and Abernathy as an attempt to increase sales and share primarily by marketing efforts.

Performance maximizinginvolves competing on the basis of superior product or service performance which can be brought about by emphasis on product development as well as market penetration where R&D might be stressed. Hofer and Schendel describe share increasing strategies as heavy investment in building market share, growth actions as investment in present activities to maintain share position in markets that are growing, and profit strategies as designed to increase net cash flow by investing in current products, markets or activities.

Some of the strategies proposed by Wiseman, et al can also be implemented with concentration actions. The explosion strategy, improving competitive position quickly, can employ a new product development action plan although acquisition would probably be a popular choice where time is a critical factor.

Longer term growth is the usual goal of their expansion strategy which can be accomplished by all the concentration approaches as well as by other offensive action plans described below. Finally, the continuous growth strategy aims at maintaining competitive position and, like the earlier mentioned hold and growth strategies, can use concentration action plans.

Porter's differentiation and focus strategies can employ market penetration and development and product development actions. Differentiation calls for establishing distinctiveness in product or service offerings and would likely be attempted by concentration action plans. Focus strategies are largely market penetration activities aimed at concentration on a particular segment or market. Differentiation based on quality and price are discussed by Porter as important primary goals.

The Lincoln Electric company has achieved differentiation on the basis of both quality and price. It has done this by a constant focus on maintaining its top quality position in the industrial welding equipment market while passing along R&D-induced cost savings to customers in the form of price reductions. As a result, it is recognized as a top quality producer of its products worldwide, and as the low-price leader. This combination makes it nearly impossible for its competitors to take away its market share.

The strategy of domain offense is explained by Miles mostly in terms of product development and market penetration and development action plans, as is Murray' sentrepreneurial strategy.

The latter example, however, also can be accomplished by the other action plans defined herein, depending on the condition of the organization at the time the strategy is formulated and implemented. Entrepreneurial strategy is "characterized by widespread and more-or-less simultaneous change in the pattern of decisions taken by an organization." Thus, it initially could be based on various defensive action plans in instances where the organization has experienced operating difficulties of one sort or another or it could be built upon a set of mainly offensive action plans for companies that shift emphasis to a higher rate of growth or profit generation.

Guth proposes seven strategies that would be formulated to achieve growth goals and which also emphasize offensive action plans. For both holding relative market position and increasing market share in growing markets, market development and penetration and product development are appropriate business level actions with key functional strategies (such as production and marketing) properly adjusted to handle the growth goals. In markets that are mature, holding relative position andincreasing share can be accomplished by functional rationalization or penetrating or developing markets either domestically (if there is room) or internationally.

Companies that have performed well in markets which are in the process of maturing can hold their strong relative position by applying their financial and other resources to new product or market development or market penetration action plans.

The same kinds of actions would likely be called for in firms that have already successfully entered foreign markets and whose managers attempt growth while maintaining strong relative positions within their foreign markets. Internal new product development aimed at diversifying product offerings in foreign markets may become appropriate as understanding of those markets increases.

Finally, Guth explains that to hold relative position with a diversified domestic product line, a likely action plan is market development aimed at market diversification.

DEFENSIVE POSTURES

Not all strategies have expansion orientations. Very often the strategist is forced to contract the firm's operations. Except for the rare attempt by a firm's owners to simplify their lives by shrinking their business's size, contraction is usually a defensive response to adversity. There are three basic types: Retrenchment, divestiture, and liquidation.

Retrenchment Strategies

These strategies are attempts to regain control of a faltering business or to prevent it from faltering in the first place by temporarily "reining in" its operations.Retrenchment can take three major forms: shallow retrenchment, deep retrenchment, and reorganization.

Shallow Retrenchment

This is a response to adversity characterized by small but

significant cutbacks in expenditures for expense items, asset investment, or both. It would normally follow a decision to lighten emphasis on sales growth for a certain time period.

To illustrate, this strategy would be appropriate for a growing firm facing a cash flow shortage. Policies accompanying shallow retrenchment in this case might include selling only to high-quality (fast paying) accounts, stretching payables, or simply cutting costs to reduce cash requirements. Shallow retrenchment would continue until a targeted level of net cash flow or some other goal was met. Then the former growth strategy, or a variation, would replace it. As such, shallow retrenchment is an emphasis-switching exercise to build internal strength.

The kinds of activities that would characterize shallow retrenchment generally include reducing hiring rates, laying workers off, delaying asset replacement, dropping narrow margin products or lines, reducing inventory levels, stretching payables or other moves aimed at decreasing operating expenses, increasing net cash flows, and reducing asset investment rates.

Deep Retrenchment

This involves severely curtailing operations as a defence against major economic adversity, financial reverses, competitive disadvantage, or a drastic threat to sales growth or profitability that cannot be met with an offensive move. For shallow retrenchment, management is willing temporarily to de-emphasize growth in order to "trim some fat" and there is usually an implicit expectation to reinstate the former growth strategy.

By contrast, deep retrenchment is characterized by the intention to change at least part of strategy, usually by surgery in the product, market, or business-definition areas. The company would plan to exit from deep retrenchment as a different company, with fewer or different product/lines, different (leaner) organization structure, fewer or different markets or segments, and so forth. Clearly the distinction between shallow and deep retrenchment is subjective and a matter of degree; the idea cf intended change in strategy provides a useful distinction.

To single outjust one example, Chrysler entered a period of deep retrenchment duyring the late-1970s while searching for a new strategy. It returned to the offensive in 1980 with redefined products.

By comparison, during the early-1980s William T. Cresson, Chair and CEO of the troubled Crown Zellerbach Corporation, responded to declining profitability by consolidating operations into fewer, more efficient plants; replacing several senior executives; reducing the size of the workforce; and exchanging debt for equity.

This example exemplifies shallow retrenchment (albeit an extreme case), even though the planned changes were major in their effects on the firm, because the expectation was to remain in the same business with the same product/market scope—that is, to retain the original corporate strategy. What should change is the level of efficiency at which it is implemented in the future.

Divestiture

Profitability shrinkages, sales declines, and other operational problems of a diversified firm may be curable by divestment when at the root of the problem is an ill-fitting subsidiary or business unit. Actually divestment is more a matter of abandoning a misfit than it is a strategic orientation, except in instances where it is part of a strategy designed to rehabilitate ailing acquisitions subsequently to be spun off.

Although diversified firms often have divestiture guidelines to handle the problem of separating ill-fitting businesses, divestiture can constitute a strategic posture for some firms.

For example, Singer labored under a divestiture strategy during the mid- and late 1970s for this reason. The unit had become so large that it had to compete head to head with the major computer firms.

By joining with Honeywell, the resulting company became big enough to support the large R&D programme, expensive marketing effort, and capital investment necessary to challenge the leaders.

The three fundamental types of divestiture are the sell-off, spin-off, and split off.

Sell-off: The distinction between a sell-off and a spin-off is blurred because both can be accomplished by the sale of a subsidiary. About the only consistent difference seems to be the intentions of the parent firm. If it sells a business unit that it had originally intended to keep, it is typically a sell-off. However, if the intention in acquiring or "growing" the subsidiary had been subsequently to sell it, then it is labeled a spin-off. Beyond this minor distinction, there are few general differences between the two cases.

In a sell-off the parent firm should attempt to find a buyer who constitutes a strategic fit for the salable business. Too often the idea is to "unload a loser" rather than to match the business to the buyer.

General Electric's sale of its computer business was a sell-off. Another example, but one designed to enhance the parent's immediate financial health (actually the most common reason for a sell-off), is GAF Corporation's sale of eight businesses during 1980-1981. Reducing GAF to its two best performers, roofing products and specialty chemicals, the sell-off strategy was an attempt to rectify a 1980 loss of $233.5 million on sales of $1.2 billion. By October 1981 GAF had expected to earn $20 million before taxes on lower sales of $700 million. The next step was to resume growth in its chemicals and roofing businesses.

Spin-off. In addition to the parent's original plan to sell the unit, a spin-off divestiture is usually one in which the business unit stands on its own after being separated from the parent.

A firm that used spin-off divestiture as a revenue-producing strategy is Heizer Corporation, a Chicago-based business-development company. Edgar F. Heizer, the public venture firm's chairman and president, developed the new strategy, dubbed "deconglomeration," to buy conglomerates in the $200 million to $400 million range, break up their business parts, and reintegrate the pieces into new companies to be spun off via public sales.

Split-off. By contrast a split-off is a divorce of two approximately equal-sized business units. An example of a split-off was the separation in 1980 of the toy and writing instruments divisions of Hasbro Industries, Inc.

The writing instruments division was incorporated as Empire Pencils, Inc., and stockholders in the original firm were given the choice of which division they would like to own after the separation. Once stock ownership was shuffled, the two businesses simply went their separate ways.

Liquidation

When a firm or unit of a firm is worth more dead than alive, it can be liquidated. Of course, when this happens, the firm ceases to exist; its assets are sold item by item and the proceeds distributed among creditors. Funds left over after creditors and liquidation costs are paid are distributed among stockholders.

Entire firms are rarely liquidated for reasons other than inability to correct financial distress and, obviously, failure to locate a buyer for divestiture.

Liquidation can be accomplished via one of three possible avenues: voluntary closure, assignment, and bankruptcy.

Voluntary Closure. This takes place when a firm simply pays off its creditors, closes its doors, and quietly goes out of business.

Voluntary closure implies that the firm or its owner has sufficient cash or liquid assets to pay off creditors. Typically voluntary closure is more prevalent among small businesses than large ones.

To determine the advisability of voluntary liquidation, the decision-maker can focus attention on the liquidating value of owner's equity—the market value of assets (called "liquidating value") less the amount of debt outstanding. Presumably if the firm's going concern value is greater than its liquidating value of equity, the owners will not liquidate. Instead they will seek to sell it as a going concern.

Assignment: This involves the transfer of title to assets to a third party. The trustee or assignee then sells the assets and distributes the proceeds among creditors, according to the magnitude of their claims.

It is a way of liquidating the debt of an insolvent firm while preventing mounting costs associated with formal bankruptcy proceedings.

There are three types of assignments: common-law assignment, statutory assignment, and assignment plus settlement.

Common-law assignment is not carried out under the auspices of a court, but is usually conducted through the adjustment bureau of a local credit managers' association. Debtors are not discharged specifically by common-law assignment from claims that are not paid by assignment. However, discharge may be brought about by meeting certain legal requirements.

Statutory assignment is like common-law assignment except that it is conducted under state assignment regulations and is a more formal procedure. The court oversees appointment of a trustee, sale of assets, and distribution of proceeds. Although discharge is not automatic, it can occur with inclusion of the appropriate statements on settlement checks. Assignment plus settlement refers to an assignment procedure undertaken in cooperation with a committee of the firm's creditors.

The local credit managers' association's adjustment bureau works with the creditors' committee to obtain a release of the debtor from subsequent claims.

Thus after assignment procedures have run their course and proceeds have been distributed among creditors, the creditors' committee may grant that execution of the assignment is in full settlement of the claims on the debtor.

Bankruptcy: Liquidation under the Federal Bankruptcy Act is appropriate when the liquidating value of assets is exceeded by debt; that is, when the firm is insolvent and the market (appraised) value of assets is insufficient to pay outstanding debt.

The primary feature of liquidation under the Federal Bankruptcy Act (as opposed to assignment) is that all obligations are discharged automatically and the owners can start a new business unhampered by the burden of prior debt.

Although bankruptcy assures equitable distribution to creditors and discharges the debtor from all obligations, the procedure is long and cumbersome.

There are two levels of insolvency. Technical insolvency applies when the firm has a positive net worth (its total assets exceed its total liabilities) but it cannot meet its currently maturing obligations.

Bankrupt insolvency is when the fair market value of total assets is exceeded by total liabilities (negative real net worth).

HARVESTING

"Harvesting' is the strategy of deliberately exchanging (percentage) points of market share for higher short-term cash flow and/or profits." In other words harvesting is the practice of squeezing cash from products or SBUs for which growth has been ruled out as a possible strategy.

Several opinions have been offered concerning the situation in which harvesting is appropriate. According to the Boston Consulting Group (BCG), a business with a low expected growth rate that also enjoys high market share is called a cash cow. Harvesting is the appropriate strategy for such a business.

The following conditions for harvesting have been suggested by Kotler:

- The market is stable or declining.
- The product is not strategically important.
- Attempts to increase market share would likely prove futile.
- Total sales depend little on the unit.
- Opportunity costs are significant.
- Chances are high that even with reduced support of the product it can continue to produce positive net cash flows, at least for a while.

Schoeffler cautions that harvesting can lead to sudden

collapse of a business and offers the following conditions for successful use of this strategy:

- Market maturity.
- Average or above average product quality.
- Reasonable market share.
- Average or above average price.

Without market maturity, high quality, and strong market share a product would be unlikely to possess sufficient continued cash-generating strength once support is reduced. High price normally allows a high gross profit margin and thus net cash flow generating ability.

CAPTIVE COMPANY

A captive company is a subcontractor that derives the majority of its sales from one buyer (the captor). Although being tightly linked to a source of a large proportion of sales may seem to be a comfortable situation, captives run the risk of being dropped as suppliers and of having too few compensating revenue sources.

Because they are heavily dependent on the captor, they may have little control over such factors as price, product characteristics, quality level, and delivery times. Consequently captive companies must be adept at cost control and at maintaining good relations with the captor and meeting its needs. It also helps to have a low need for independence!

Why would management of a firm opt for a captive strategy? Glueck suggests that some firms retrench into captive positions defensively. This would happen if a firm were to scale down its operations by closing its smaller accounts.

But some firms are captive companies by choice. They often are started to fill a specific need of a large buyer. As long as the captor continues to buy, captives can operate profitably while expending little of the energy and resources required by typical competitiveness.

Among the most often cited examples of captive company strategies are the firms that supply Sears. These include Kellwood Company, which sells 74 per cent of its apparel output to Sears; DeSoto, Inc., for which 70 per cent of its paint and furniture revenues is from Sears; and the Baltimore-based Easco Corporation, 82 per cent of whose sales in 1980 were to Sears. Easco produces Sears' line of Craftsman mechanics' hand tools such as wrenches and sockets. Easco's problems in the early 1980s demonstrate some of the shortcomings of captive company status.

First, a captive is obviously at the mercy of the market capabilities of the captor. This was the case for Easco, which, when Sears' growth started to slip in the late 1970s, decided to market tools under its own name. Although it has increased its private sales by one third, it is still hampered by its long association with Sears.

Second, Easco, by relying on Sears to do its marketing, allowed the introduction of competitors into prime retail markets. Now that it wants to do its own marketing, it faces a long, uphill battle.

Third, when linked closely to Sears, Easco did not need a marketing department. It took the company several years to develop the marketing know-how to venture out on its own.

SUMMARY

This chapter explains how goals fit into strategic management in the first part and enumerates the major action plans (strategy postures) available to managers in the second. First the terminology of goal formulation and its role in strategy formulation were explained. An organization's goal set consists of qualitative and quantitative goals. Quantitative goals, in turn, should consist of both interim and final components. In strategy formulation, goals or expected results, are formulated along with action plans that are the means for achieving goals.

Next the role of goals in the development and expression of mission and strategy at the enterprise, corporate, business, and functional levels was explained. Mission contains goals that express the basic purpose of the organization. For the four levels of strategy, goals are set that represent societal interactions, expected business portfolio characteristics, expected business unit results, and desired functional department outcomes.

Goal formulation processes were reviewed and the importance of present strategies, the firm's data set, and power relationships and value systems as inputs to goal formulation, was discussed. The first section closed with a discussion of ways to inculcate an organization's goal set with intended cultural characteristics.

The second part of the chapter categorizes the major orientations that strategy can have. They are divided into offensive and defensive strategic postures. Offensive postures have a positive valence, so to speak; they are growth-directed. Increased levels of sales, profitability, market share, size, control, or any number of other goals can be the hoped-for result of an offensive strategic posture.

The defensive postures are implemented to produce constriction of operations. As such they are strategic directions designed to recoup strength or to correct a deficiency in the way the firm is operating.

Chapter 4

Evaluating and Selecting Strategies

INTRODUCTION

The location of the activities of strategy evaluation and selection in the process of strategic management. After several likely strategy choices have been formulated, they can be evaluated by following the approaches described in the first part of this chapter. Six schemes are presented for identifying the most likely strategies from among a set of possible choices.

Confronted with several likely strategies, managers must next select the one(s) they believe optimal. The definition of what is optimal varies from decision maker to decision maker and even for particular decision makers (as they vary the decision approach or model they follow to make the selection). In the second part of this chapter, several strategy selection approaches are explained. Our purpose in doing so is to make students more aware of the decision processes they follow while analyzing cases.

The chapter closes with a description of the criteria the selected strategies should meet. This set of factors would apply regardless of the strategy selection approach followed.

SYSTEMS FOR STRATEGY COMPARISON

Although there are doubtlessly may rule-of-thumb approaches used by managers to compare strategy choices, probably the most often discussed techniques over recent years are growth-share matrix, General Electric's stoplight grid, life cycle theory and the related product/market evolution portfolio matrix, gap analysis, and directional policy matrix. Some of these models, especially those that attempt to portray the complex strategy comparison or selection decisions as a simple matrix model, have received increasing criticism.

Most notably, a 1984 Business Week article entitled "The New Breed of Corporate Planner" referred to their use as "formula planning." This brand implied that they are superficial shortcuts to management decision making. Pioneered in the 1960s by the Boston Consulting Group (BCG), they gained a wide following when stability of market structures and growth trends prevailed. Now, however, they seem to be oversimplifications for several reasons.

First, they caused an overemphasis on market share growth. Strategic planning degenerated into portfolio management problems instead of trying to figure out how to run successful businesses.

High-growth businesses are not necessarily high-profit businesses and many managements found themselves overburdened with imbalanced portfolios of SBUs. Second, a competitor who knows you are using a certain formula can anticipate your strategic moves accurately.

Dependence on formulas may even dull management's thinking about its competitive position and moves. Finally, use of matrices and formulas can cause managers to circumvent much of the environmental, internal, and industry analysis necessary for formulating and effectively implementing strategy. It is too easy to draw incorrect conclusions from incomplete or faulty data with some of these models.

The relationships addressed in the models that follow are important parts, but only parts, of understanding strategy formulation. However, they by no means should be used to replace or shortcut gaining a thorough understanding of where a firm is today or where it should be in the future.

The models are also excellent expository structures. That is, they are handy for explaining a point about portfolio issues or about strategy elements simply because they are oversimplifications. Their strength is in reducing complex variables to easy-to-understand dimensions and portraying them in readily interpretable terms.

Growth-Share Matrix (GSM)

The Boston Consulting Group developed the growth-share matrix to analyse the problem of resource deployment among the business units or products of multibusiness firms. The business units or products are analyzed by placing each one in the matrix according to their:

- Expected growth rate (vertical axis), measured by anticipated growth rate in sales,
- Relative market share (horizontal axis), measured as the unit's share divided by that of its largest competitor.

Thus businesses or products in quadrant I with low expected growth rates and low relative market standing are labeled "dogs" or "cash traps." They should be managed to minimize cash flow by retrenchment, divestiture, or even liquidation.

These units or products are likely to be characterized by high costs, low quality, less effective marketing procedures, and so on, which would collectively contribute to weak competitive position and low potential for profits.

High projected growth rates and low market standing, are interpretive problems. The reason is that although they are operating in markets with expected growth potential, they currently are experiencing competitive disadvantage. Management can invest cash to correct the market weakness so as to take advantage of expected market growth or, if not convinced of their ability to improve market share, it can retrench, divest, or liquidate to minimize the cash drain.

THE BCG GSM

Products or business units in quadrant III, the "stars," have both high market standing and high industry growth potential. They should receive heavy cash investment in order to maintain their market share. Successful resource deployment beyond cash requirements could lead to a superior market share when industry growth potential falls off. Such a product or business would then become a cash generator or "cash cow," as depicted by location in quadrant IV. Cash cows have a strong market position in industries that have matured.

These products or businesses can thus be "milked" by investing just enough cash to maintain market standing and applying excess cash inflows to the firm's other activities that are growth industries or products.

In addition to the above implications of the GSM for cash management, the matrix also suggests how competitors might be expected to behave in each quadrant.

To illustrate, a star performer (market leader with high market share in a rapidly growing industry) usually can expect a serious threat only from cash-rich competitors. Only they can afford to embark upon an expensive programme to challenge the probable market leader's cost supremacy and market differentiation.

In comparison with the position of the star performers, cash cows can expect little serious competition because of their relatively low expected industry growth rates. Competitors would likely be reluctant to mount a major offensive in the absence of significant industry potential. Thus a cash cow can enjoy a relatively secure market position, but only as long as sufficient investment in maintaining market share continues.

Quadrant II firms, "question marks," are highly vulnerable by virtue of their low share in high potential growth rate industries. They can expect diverse competitive challenges. Indeed, as small fish in a big sea, question marks can look forward to heavy cash needs to establish themselves as major competitive forces (stars).

Business units that fall in quadrant I are probably only marginally profitable and can anticipate little improvement in present markets.

They have two major competitive options:

- Get out of the market by the means suggested
- Develop a major innovation to redefine the market and their participation in it.

Although the growth-share matrix analysis can help in making strategic decisions about managing a portfolio of businesses or products, it has some shortcomings.First, not all businesses or products fit neatly into one of the four quadrants. Many businesses occupy middle positions between high and low market share and industry growth rate.

Second, other factors besides market share and industry growth rate affect strategy selection. These factors include "stage of product/market evolution, strategic fit among the different businesses, the presence of competitive advantages and distinctive competencies, emerging threats and opportunities, vulnerability to recession, market structure, capital requirements, and size of market. The BCG matrix does not give explicit consideration to these factors."

Third, a business's profitability, cash flow, and

industry attractiveness may not always be closely related to market share and growth rate. Some firms with low market share outperform their larger counterparts, and not all high-share businesses in low-growth industries generate surplus cash.

Finally, the GSM does not offer guidance for interunit comparisons. For example, in a firm with several cash cows, strict adherence to the matrix implies treating each one in the same way when some might be drained of cash ("harvested") and others managed for cash flow. Also, all stars are not necessarily "better" than cash cows.

General Electric's Stoplight Grid

General Electric's stoplight grid is a nine-element matrix used by GE to relate:

- Its SBUs' environmental opportunities and other factors determining industry attractiveness to
- Various measures of the SBUs' relative business strengths.

A business unit is located in the matrix by first determining whether its relative business strengths are high, medium, or low (vertical axis) through assessment of such factors as sales growth rate, market share, market image, and management capabilities. Its high, medium, or low ranking on the horizontal axis (industry attractiveness) is a function of the size and potential of its market; technological status, financial health, competitive structure, and social and political characteristics of its industry; and economic circumstances.

Rankings on both axes for each of GE's forty-three businesses are decided upon during planning review discussions and determine which of the nine cells in the grid it occupies. Business units with high or medium industry attractiveness in which GE has either medium or high strengths call for an "invest and grow" decision—a green-light strategy.

Medium or low industry promise coupled with medium or low strength of a GE business unit operating in that industry would indicate a red-light strategy—minimal additional investment by GE with expected continued earnings generation. The company may resort to retrenchment or limited technological support of red units.

Combinations of industry attractiveness and business strength scores that place a GE business in one of the yellow-light cells could be either a borderline case or composed of both red and green elements.

Hofer and schendel explain that the major shortcoming of GE's scheme is its ineffectiveness in portraying the circumstances of new businesses whose growth in new industries is just beginning.

Commenting on GE's use of the grid, Business Week notes, "After three or four critiques at various levels, the final grids—and decisions—are made by the corporate policy committee—the chairman, three vice-chairmen, five senior vice-presidents, and the vice-president for finance." Thus planning discussions, focused on the variables involved in the grid, may prevent costly mistakes and avoid reliance on gut reactions.

Life Cycle Analysis

Life cycle analysis relies on the belief that there are predictable relationships among the stages in product or business unit life cycles on one hand, and certain elements of strategy on the other.

The typical product life cycle curve is analogous to the life cycle of biological organisms . Note the relationship between unit profit margin and sales revenues at the different stages.

During preintroduction and introduction, the firm is investing heavily to build sales growth through product awareness and refinement, with emphasis on the latter. Thus profit margin is negative until growth begins to occur. If sales growth proceeds at a high enough rate, then unit profit margin will swing positive during the growth phase. Typically the firm's emphasis is shifted from product refinement to building market share, thus increasing the length and slope of the curve during this phase.

As more and more competitors enter the market, however, share is whittled away. Consequently the product's growth rate begins to level off and the product enters the maturity stage. During growth ever-increasing sales volume can drive unit profit margin higher and higher. As competitive pressures mount, though, profit margin is eaten away. Emphasis shifts to production efficiency as management attempts to maintain profit margin during the maturity phase.

Typical Sales and Profit Trends

In multiproduct firms attention is focused on the net effect on sales, profit margins, and cash generation of the performance of the firm's stable of products. Overall sales performance is a function of the balance of separate products' performance.

Multibusiness firms, that is, conglomerates or holding companies, can be viewed as a collection of multiproduct firms. Of course, the life cycle curves of the separate SBUs would not line up as neatly as they do in the diagram, but rather would be superimposed on each other in a complex network of curves. Corporate-level management is concerned with balancing the performance of a collection of SBUs. Overall conglomerate sales can be influenced by the addition or deletion of SBUs or by altering the performance of them.

Strategic Implications of Life Cycle Curves

Life cycle curves can be useful devices for explaining the relationships among sales and profit attributes of separate products, collections of products in a business, and collections of businesses in a conglomerate or holding company. Life cycle analysis has been suggested by some of its advocates as a basis for selecting appropriate strategy characteristics at all levels. It also may be viewed as a guide for business-level strategy implementation since it helps in selection of functional-level strategies, as discussed next.

Preintroduction and Introduction Strategic Implications

During the early stages of the life cycle, marketing strategy should focus on correcting product problems in design, features, and positioning so as to establish a competitive advantage and develop product awareness through advertising, promotion, and personal sales techniques. At the same time, personnel strategy could focus on planning and recruiting for new product human resource needs and dealing with union requirements. Also, one would expect the nature of research and development strategy to shift from a technical research orientation during preintroduction to more of a development orientation during actual introduction.

Financial strategy would be likely to address primarily sources of funds needed to fuel R&D and marketing efforts as well as the capital requirements of later production facilities. Capi'.al budgeting decisions would be outlined during these early stages so that capacity would be adequate to serve growth needs when sales volume began to accelerate.

Growth Stage Strategy Implications

During the growth stage, strategic emphases change relative to introduction. Marketing strategy is concerned with quickly carving out a niche for the product or firm and for its distribution capabilities, even when doing so might involve taking risks with overcapacity. Too often, firms have unadvisedly accepted quality shortfalls as a necessary cost of rapid growth. Widening profit margins during growth may even permit certain functional inefficiencies and risk taking. Communication strategy is directed toward establishing brand preference through heavy media use, sampling programs, and promotion programs, and strategy should emphasize:

- Resource acquisition to maintain strength
- Development of ways to continue growth when it begins to slow.

Personnel strategy may focus on developing loyalty, commitment, and expertise. Training and development programs and various communication systems are established to build management and employee teams that can deal successfully with the demands of impending tight competition among firms during the maturity phase.

General Electric tries to staff growth-stage product management positions with "growers" who have an entrepreneurial flair.

Maturity-Stage Strategy Implications

Efficiency and profit-generating ability become major concerns as products enter the maturity stage. Competition grows as more firms enter the market and the implication is that only the most productive firms with established niches and competent people will survive.

Marketing efforts concentrate on maintaining customer loyalty and in strengthening this with distributors personally selling to dealers, sales promotions, and publicity.

Production strategy concentrates on efficiency and, at the same time, sharpens the ability to meet delivery schedules and minimize defective products. Cost control systems are often put in place.

Personnel strategy may focus on various incentive systems to produce manufacturing efficiency. Advancements and transfers are used and some firms try to fit management positions to managers who have personalities more attuned to the belt-tightening needs of products and SBUs at the maturity stage.

Chase Manhattan Bank, for example, shifted a manager with recognized cost-cutting abilities so that he could streamline its European operations. At Corning Glass Company, when its television-tube business seemed to have reached maturity, a manager with cost-cutting skills was appointed as its manager.

Decline-Stage Strategy Implications

When a product reaches the point where its markets are saturated, an effort is often made to modify it so that its life cycle is either started anew or its maturity stage extended. When falling sales of a product cannot be reversed and it enters the decline stage, management's emphasis may switch to milking it dry of all profit.

Advertising and promotion expenditures are reduced to a minimum. People are transferred to new positions where their experience can be brought to bear on products in earlier growth stages (if management was skillful enough to have created such products).

Various strategies have been suggested for products that have entered the decline stage. Hofer and Schendel suggest four choices when sales are less than 5 per cent of those of the industry leaders:

- Concentration on a small market segment and reduction of the firm's asset base to the minimum levels needed for survival
- Acquisition of several similar firms so as to raise sales to 15 per cent of the leaders' sales;
- Selling out to a buyer with sufficient cash resources and the willingness to use them to effect a turnaround;
- Liquidation. Other variations of these are described by various authors at both the product and business levels.

Product/Market Evolution Portfolio Matrix

The product/market evolution matrix was formulated to allow the analyst to focus corporate- and business-level strategy decisions on the stage of product/market evolution and its relationship with market position.

Business units are represented by circles that vary in size according to their respective industry size; each circle contains a pie wedge that corresponds in size to its market share.

By locating a firm's SBUs on the matrix, the strategist can analyse the distribution of business units that make up its portfolio against the life cycle curve stage.

Life Cycle Analysis Limitations

Although life cycle analysis has been widely advocated, its critics suggest that it should be used with caution. Kotler explains that as a planning tool and a control tool, it is useful in outlining choices and monitoring progress, respectively. But its usefulness as a forecasting tool is limited.

The principal difficulties with life cycle theory are that:

- Its patterns vary too widely,
- Identifying the stage a product is actually in is difficult,
- It may be readily biased by marketing strategy decisions, and as such, the curve itself is a dependent, not an independent variable.

GAP ANALYSIS

In this approach attention is first focused on the gaps between the actual or anticipated values that certain variables take on and the values that are most desirable.

Once the gaps are identified, attention shifts to devising ways to close them. Gap analysis has been advocated for strategic choice decisions within the following four primary contexts: Environmental analysis, functional-level policy analysis, business-level strategy analysis, and corporate-level strategy analysis.

Environmental Gap Analysis

For purposes of environmental analysis, gap analysis is a way of focusing on differences between the firm's strategy set and resources and the threats and opportunities that make up its environment. More specifically it is used to identify gaps between where a firm would be if it continued with its present strategy and was subjected to expected environmental developments, and where the strategist would like the firm to be in terms of strategic goals. Thus this "planning gap" can be filled by implementing new action plans, or strategic goals can be altered.

Gap Analysis at the Function Level

A popular use for gap analysis is to compare actual and potential market variables for marketing strategy purposes. Webber proposes a form of gap analysis for analyzing the differences between industry market potential and the firm's own sales by product line.

This overall gap is made up of four segments as follows:

- Product-line gap: the portion due to each product in the full product line.
- Distribution gap: the portion caused by an inadequate distribution system.
- Usage gap: the part caused by less than full usage.
- Competitive gap: the segment caused by sales that are lost to direct competitors.

Each type of gap may be closed through its own set of strategic or tactical moves. They correspond to what we have defined as business-level goals and action plans or marketing strategy, depending upon the level of their organization.

Accurately determining the type and magnitude of each kind of gap is the difficult part of market gap analysis. However, this technique focuses attention on defining the various elements of a firm's sales shortfall.

Gap Analysis at the Business Level

There are profound similarities between gap analysis at the business level and gap analysis for environmental audit and functional-level analysis purposes. At the business level, however, the gaps of interest are those related to the performance of the business unit as a whole. The focus is on gaps between actual and planned-for results according to such criteria as various profit measures, cash flow generation, management expertise, company image, and relative product quality. Consequently gap analysis at the business level is very much like analysis of budget variances.

Gap Analysis at the Corporate Level

When applied to the corporate level, gap analysis focuses on the consolidated performance of the portfolio of business units. Differences between desired values of performance variables (gross, operating, or net profit on total assets or equity; growth rate of sales; geographical coverage; and so on) and actual values can trigger portfolio modification decisions (corporate-level strategic decisions) as explained.

DIRECTIONAL POLICY MATRIX (DPM)

The DPM is a method of business portfolio analysis formulated by Shell International Chemical Company. It has nine cells in which businesses are located depending upon their scores on each of the two axes: Expected market profitability and competitive positions.

The horizontal axis, labeled "business sector prospects" or "prospects for market sector profitability," is a measure similar to industry attractiveness used in the GE planning grid. A firm is rated on a scale from "unattractive," through "average," to "attractive" depending upon an evaluation of its industry's market growth, market quality, and environmental aspects.

Similarly, its location on a scale that runs from a "weak," through "average," to "strong" competitive position is determined by answering questions about its market share position, production capabilities, and R&D strengths.

The cell labels represent possible strategic choices or types of resource deployments most appropriate for the firm, given its score on each of the two axes. More specifically these cell labels have the following implications:

- *Disinvest*: Likely already losing money; net cash flow negative over time. Losses may be minimized by divestiture or even liquidation.

- *Phased Withdrawal*: Probably not generating sufficient cash to justify continuation; assets can be redeployed.
- *Cash Generator*: Equivalent to a "cash cow" in the GE planning grid. This cell would be occupied by a firm or product in later stages of the life cycle that does not warrant heavy investment, but can be "milked" of cash due to its strong competitive position.
- *Proceed with Care*: Similar to a "question mark;" firms falling in this sector may require some investment support but heavy investment would be extremely risky.
- *Growth* (*upper*) and (*lower*): Similar to a GE planning grid "green-light" strategy. A firm, product, or SBU in these sectors would call for investment support to allow growth with the market. It should generate sufficient cash on its own.
- *Double or Quit*: Units in this sector should become "high fliers" in the not too distant future. Consequently those in the upper rightmost corner of cell should be singled out for full support. Others should be abandoned.
- *Try Harder*: External financing may be justified to push a unit in this sector to a leadership position. However, such a move will require judicious application of funds.
- *Leader*: The strategy for this segment is to protect this position by external investment (funds beyond those generated by the unit itself - occasionally); earnings should be quite strong and a major focus may be maintaining sufficient capacity to capitalize on strong demand.

The DPM can thus be used to identify strategies for single businesses as well as for plotting combinations of units in multibusiness or multiproduct firms. Locating competitors on the DPM can provide useful insights into the nature of corporate-level strategic configurations. However, there is room for error in the positioning of a firm or product on the two axes, and thus DPM location should be interpreted with an open mind and not in isolation.

The New Business Familiarity Matrix

Roberts and Berry devised a technique for selecting optimum diversification action plans for firms wishing to enter new product-markets. Called the familiarity matrix it helps strategists decide which product-markets to enter and how. Its two axes, familiarity with market factors and technology or service, are both divided into three values: Base, new familiar, and new unfamiliar.

The market dimension refers to the amount of knowledge possessed by the diversifying company of various characteristics of the market and the competitors within it. The authors distinguish between the newness of, and the familiarity with, the market for a product-service. Newness of a market is the extent to which the company has previously targeted it. Markets with which the company has prior experience, conceivably by selling old or existing products in it, are called base markets. Markets with which no such prior exposure exists are called new.

Whether a new product is base or new to the diversifying company, it may or may not be familiar with it. Familiarity is the measure of the degree of understanding the company has of the characteristics and business patterns of the market, even though it may not have participated in it. Thus, a company's new product choice could represent new but also familiar, new and unfamiliar, or base market factors.

The other dimension of the matrix, technologies or services embodied in the product, may similarly be base or new. A new technology or service is one which has not been employed in the company's old or existing products whereas base technologies have been. Familiarity with the technology embodied in the diversification product/service represents the company's degree of knowledge in it. As with market factors, a diversification product/service can represent a new and familiar, new and unfamiliar, or base technology to the diversifying company.

Referring again new business proposals can be placed on the familiarity matrix by locating their position on both the market and technology axes. For both, the possibilities are base, new familiar, or new unfamiliar. Following this procedure a new business product/service would be positioned in one of the nine cells. The three subsets of cells (blank, dotted, and crosshatched) represent three levels of familiarity the company has with the markets and technology of the proposed new business entry with amount of familiarity indicated by the key.

Joint ventures: New unfamiliar markets and base technologies. Joint ventures can exploit the competencies of both partners and lead to synergies. They also serve to diversify risk for the partners.

In this cell, the company would have had no experience with the market factors in question but would have had vast experience with the technology involved since it would be the base technology of its present business. Thus a joint venture would be a feasible action plan for entering the Cell business as long as the other partner could provide the needed market expertise.

Venture capital or nurturing or educational acquisition: New unfamiliar or familiar market or technology. Businesses that fall in any of these three cells would involve both markets and technologies with which the company had either no previous involvement and no knowledge, or some understanding of knowledge with one or the other.

Venture capital and nurturing provided by the company to other usually smaller ventures would allow development of experience with a low level of commitment by the company. Venture capital funding alone by the company would be a less involved level of commitment than venture capital with nurturing, the provision of management assistance and support of various kinds along with infusion of funds.

The latter would tend to represent a higher level of interest on the part of the company in the new venture than providing venture capital alone.

Educational acquisitions are those in which the company acquires the new venture outright and thereby would obtain a faster rate of familiarization with the new venture than would normally be possible with venture capital or nurturing.

Internal market development, acquisitions, or even joint ventures: New familiar markets; base technology. That the new business involves the company's base technology in this cell along with familiarization with the markets involved, means that the company may benefit from the internal development of market expertise and of the entire venture. Alternatively, although there would be little technological advantage to relationships with others, the need for market expertise may necessitate acquisition of a venture which had developed a grasp of the market, or even a joint venture with a partner that had this expertise.

Internal ventures, acquisitions, or licensing: New familiar markets and technology. Businesses which are located in this cell represent markets and technologies with which the company has had no prior experience but with which it has some knowledge and understanding. Therefore with a high level of confidence in this understanding, the company might successfully choose to develop the business internally. With somewhat less confidence, managing an acquisition might be more appropriate. Licensing, as an alternative to outright ownership of a technology, would avoid the risks of developing it internally and could enable the company to acquire market knowledge from the licenser as well.

Internal base developments: Base market factors and technology. Business ventures involving the markets and technologies of a company's present base businesses would likely be successfully developed internally. Similarly, its experience with both sets of factors could enable it to successfully manage acquisitions involving the new business idea, a more expeditious way of entering the new activity.

Internal product development, acquisitions, or licensing: Base market factors, new familiar technology. When the proposed new venture employs a new technology with which the company has some knowledge, and markets within which it currently competes, internal development of the technology would probably be appropriate. Such a choice would be advisable if the company's confidence in its understanding of the technology was high. Internal development would allow it to exclusively take advantage of its experience and understanding of market factors.

Alternatively, technological expertise could quickly be obtained by acquisition and would be appropriate were time a critical factor. Licensing, too, would be a moderately expeditious action plan but would necessitate sharing of benefits through licensing fees and royalties.

"New style" joint ventures: Base market factors, new unfamiliar technology. The company could bring its base market knowledge and experience to bear on a new venture involving an unfamiliar technology by participating with a small venture that has the appropriate technical expertise. This type of relationship is called a "new style" joint venture and has become an increasingly popular action plan for large, market wise companies wishing to participate in new technologies.

PROCESS OF STRATEGY SELECTION: STRATEGIC DECISION MAKING

After comparing possible strategies, the manager must decide which will be the future strategies of the organization. Many different decision models have been proposed to explain how these decisions can be made. These decision-making contexts constitute different frames of reference a decision maker might take. It is important to note which frame of reference—context—surrounds a particular decision model and then to compare it only with other decision models within that context.

The manager may actually select more than one. In contingency planning systems, an action plan could be selected for the environmental scenario that is most likely to occur and/or the set of goals appropriate to that scenario. Another strategy would be selected for an optimistic scenario - a reasonable but very favorable set of environmental circumstances with a somewhat low probability of occurrence. Then a third strategy would be chosen for the pessimistic scenario, which also has a low probability of occurrence but carries unfavorable implications.

Cross-context comparisons may be faulty because of the different contexts. For example, arguing about the superiority of, say, Allison's organization process approach to decision analysis or Lindblom's incremementalism model is fruitless without first agreeing on the appropriateness of either the organization or the individual context. This is so because the context of decisions can change with each decision, and the applicability of a decision approach depends on the context.

Five contexts for decisions are described in this section—individual, group, organization, societal institution, and worldwide societal. Then several decision approaches within each context are discussed.

Context of the Individual

Many decision models focus on factors peculiar to the individual decision maker. The major ones are the rationality, bounded rationality, incrementalism, intuitive, and adaptive approaches.

Rational Decision Model. According to Steiner et al., "(A) decision is rational when it effectively and efficiently assures the achievement of aims for which the means are selected." A more general description is that rational decisions maximize net value achievement, where the sacrifice in one value necessitated by a decision is more than offset by an increase in the achievement of another value. Although many interpretations of rational decision making have been proposed that differ in their details, they tend to have the following common framework of basic steps:

- Establish a complete set of operational goals with weights.
- Prepare a complete inventory of values and resources with weights.
- Generate a complete set of strategy choices or solutions.

- Prepare a complete set of predicted benefits and costs of each strategy or solution choice.
- Compute the expected value of each choice.
- Select the choice that has the highest expected value.
  Organizational Decision Making Can Take Place

Note the use of the word "complete" in the first four steps. Completeness of these processes is important to ensure that one is behaving rationally. Stated differently, a decision maker could not lay claim to rationality were an incomplete set of strategy choices selected for evaluation.

If the decision maker could perform each of these steps completely, then a decision that maximizes net value achievement would result. For an economist, a rational, optimal decision might be the one that maximizes the value preferences of society as a whole.

Behavioral scientists might measure rational decisions in terms of personal need satisfaction. Indeed the definition of rational decision outcomes can change from manager to manager, or even from situation to situation. For business decisions some of the goals that have been used to define rational decisions are return on capital investment, realized positive profits, and profit growth, in addition to maximum profits.

How does rational, maximizing decision making work? Classical economic theory defines an economic (person) as follows: One who in the course of being "economic" is also "rational." This (person) is assumed to have knowledge of the relevant aspects of (the) environment which, if not absolutely complete, is at least impressively clear and voluminous. such persons are assumed to have a well-organized and stable system of preferences, and a skill in computation that enables (them) to calculate for the alternative courses of action that are available, which of these will permit... reach(ing) the highest attainable point on (their) preference scale.

Economic (persons) are assumed to make rational, maximizing decisions within closed systems in which minimum weight is given to the decision maker's environment and to the complexity of the decision process itself. Variables that cannot be computed within closed-system rationality requirements are "disregarded by assuming all other things are equal." Then marginal analysis is used to calculate the profit-maximizing solution.

Arguments in favour of striving to make rational, maximizing decisions include the following:

- Harrison notes that "despite the obvious divergence between theory and practice...(it) has some distinct advantages from the standpoint of understanding, prediction, and control."
- When the model is employed, failure to maximize the selected variable usually indicates economic inefficiency.
- Acceptance of the model by managers will undoubtedly cause them to select strategic options that will facilitate greater efficiency.
- When there is goal congruence between the decision maker and the organization, following the model should lead to maximum utility satisfaction as well as efficiency.

However appealing these arguments may seem, there are many detractors from the rational, maximizing model as a basis for business decisions generally, and for strategy choice selection in particular. First, managers are said to maximize their own interests rather than the goals of the firm at best, or to maintain the status quo at worst. Clearly if managers cannot be brought to aspire to corporate goals, their decisions will not approach those that would result from application of the rational, maximizing model to strategy selection.

Second, critics of rational, maximizing behaviour argue that because there is a wide divergence of interests, loyalties, and goals in organizations, "it is unlikely that the firm will achieve its objectives with anything resembling maximizing behaviour." Thus the tendency is for managers to stop analyzing strategic alternatives when a suitable, but not maximum, choice is found.

Third, objectively weighting organizational goals, even

if they can be agreed upon, usually requires more information than most managers have. The most that can be expected is for the implications of alternative strategies to be imperfectly known. The cost of attempting to generate perfect information is usually prohibitive so that maximizing itself becomes nonrational.

Finally, critics argue that the cognitive ability of managers is sufficiently limited so as to prevent rational, maximizing decisions. Managers simply cannot grasp all the information pertinent to complex decisions.

Bounded Rationality. Realization of the practical limitations of the rational model has led to the development of other explanations of how business decisions are made. Miller and Starr quip, "(P)eople simply don't have such an irrational passion for dispassionate rationality." One alternative, "satisficing," is proposed by March and Simon and rests upon certain assumptions about human behaviour described by Simon.

Satisficing is a modification of the strictly rational model that recognizes people's tendency toward settling for satisfactory rather than optimum means for achieving goals. March and Simon distinguish between optimal and satisfactory decision alternatives as follows:

- An alternative is optimal if
  - There exists a set of criteria that permits all alternatives to be compared,
  - The alternative in question is preferred, by these criteria, to all other alternatives.
- An alterative is satisfactory if
  - There exists a set of criteria that describes minimally satisfactory alternatives,
  - The alternative in question meets or exceeds all these criteria.

Harrison points out that the fundamental difference between these alternatives is that criteria of choice are applied to all the alternatives in the optimal case, but to minimally satisfactory alternatives in the satisfactory situation. Thus in the strategy selection problem, the satisficing manager would identify several reasonable choices and then select the best one. Conversely, rational maximizing managers would have to identify all strategy choices before selecting the best one. Simon's principle of bounded rationality can be viewed as an explanation of the conditions that lead to satisficing, rather than maximizing, decisions.

Accordingly the strategist's quest for information with which to analyse strategy choices rationally is constrained (bounded) by:

- His/her intellectual limitations in gathering all information,
- Limited amounts of time and money available for information gathering and analysis activities,
- "The virtual impossibility of obtaining anything close to perfcct information even if one had limitless time and money.

In keeping with the principles of bounded rationality, and recognizing the tendency toward satisficing behaviour, we can postulate the following bounded rationality decision model for strategy choice:

- Establish a reasonably comprehensive set of operational goals.
- Identify the important values and available resources.
- Generate a set of action plan choices that fall within the organization's capabilities and interests.
- Compute the critical costs and benefits of each choice.
- Select the choice with the greatest net benefit.

Incrementalism. Incrementalism is another approach devised to deal with the impracticalities of the rational maximizing model. Originally presented by Charles Lindblom as a model of public policy formulation, it has since been repeatedly described as a business strategy formulation process as well.

Disjointed incrementalism is explained by Lindblom as follows: The... (disjointed incremental model is) continually building out from the current situation, step-by-step by small degrees... (in the rational model one) start(s) from fundamentals anew each time, building on the past only as experience is embodied in a theory, and is always prepared to start completely from the ground up.

Disjointed incrementalism views strategy choice as a process of continuing past strategies with only incremental modifications. For example, zero-base budgeting, where the entire amount of a proposed budget is justified and analyzed, is roughly a rational process. Conversely incremental budgeting, in which only the proposed future increase in a budget is justified and analyzed but the present budget is tacitly agreed to, approximates the disjointed approach.

Disjointed incrementalism has generated much interest for about the same reason that Simon proposed the bounded rationality model: Recognition of the practical shortcomings of the rational model. Dye summarized the supporting arguments for disjointed incrementalism, as opposed to rationality, as follows:

- Decision makers do not have enough time, money or intelligence to behave strictly rationally.
- They tend to trust established strategies more than untried new ones.
- Heavy sunk costs in existing strategies make it difficult to accept radical strategy changes.
- Minor incremental changes in existing strategies are more politically expedient than the "all or nothing" commitment often necessary for new strategy.
- People naturally tend to "satisfice," not "maximize."

Of course, this kind of incrementalism carries the obvious risk of continuing a bad strategy all the way into bankruptcy. Manufacturing companies that, rather than discard and replace an unsuccessful product, choose instead to continue to change it in minor ways might be following the incremental approach. On the other hand, the incremental approach to management of a successful strategy might increase the level of success.

In summary, when existing strategy appears reasonable or strategy choices are close to the present strategy, then the incremental approach is probably appropriate. However, when the present strategy is not working or strategy proposals are radically different, then the rational and bounded rationality methods might be superior.

Logical incrementalism shares with disjointed incrementalism the sense of marginal analysis of strategy alternatives.

Quinn explains:

Strategy involves forces of such great number, strength, and combinatory power that one cannot predict events in a probabilistic sense. Hence it is logical that one proceed flexibly and experimentally from broad concepts toward specific commitments, making the latter concrete as late as possible in order to narrow the bonds of uncertainty and to benefit from the best available information.

Another interpretation of incrementalism is offered by Wu:

Disjointed incrementalism is essentially adaptive.

It adapts specifically to:

- Man's limited analytical capacities;
- The costliness of information;
- The interdependencies between the past and the present, and between the present and the future;
- The difficulty of coordination among subunits of organizations;
- The difficulty of analyzing and understanding the open system, such as that of a business organization.

In applying disjointed incrementalism to planning or decision making, planners start with considering only those alternatives that differ incrementally from the marginal changes for those alternatives being considered, and, finally, rank in order of preference the incremental consequences for making decisions.

In general decision making and problem solving based on the incremental adjustment concept may be described by the following steps:

- Define problems and (incremental) goals.
- Appraise the current situation and estimate incremental adjustments to be made to cope with problems.
- Quantify the consequences of incremental adjustments

and determine whether the conse-quences are satisfactory.

- If the consequences of incremental adjustments are not satisfactory to the decision maker, return to. Otherwise take action to implement incremental adjustments and return to.

Wu goes on to integrate this model with a budgeting system, and so provides an implementable model of the incremental decision process.

Intuitive Approach. Another individual-based decision model is the intuitive approach. Called the intuitive-anticipatory approach by Steiner, this decision concept has no explicit set of steps to follow.

Instead it recognizes that many managers make "gut-level" decisions about which strategy choice is the right one. Intuitive decisions generally apply within the short-term future and tend to entail little distant forecasting and planning. But this does not imply that managers make intuitive strategy selections in a void. Indeed such decisions typically come out of many years of management experience and a high level of confidence on the part of the decision maker.

Unfortunately good instincts cannot be readily acquired without experience. After stating that "the really effective and experienced people in both management and science typically operate in a largely intuitive manner and view with impatience attempts to make their methods explicit," Morris notes:

It does not appear reasonable... to suppose... that one could do very much more than modestly enhance the process of developing intuition... by providing decision models as possible targets for imitation when intuition is insufficiently developed.

It may well be that intuition or artistic skill is largely the product of imitation and practice, yet this process of development must have a beginning. Experience suggests that this beginning must include more than simply a familiarity with other people's methods.

This is why we so strongly advocate the use of case studies as a way, however modest and imperfect, of providing a strategy-selecting-and-implementing "beginning."

The Adaptive Approach. Ansoff proposes this approach as a way to apply probability estimates to the process of selecting strategy.

A form of "bounded rationality by elimination," it includes the following steps:

- Determine minimum threshold values for each goal. These are the minimum acceptable values of variables pertinent to goals. For example, for a firm with a return-on-investment goal, the minimum value of acceptable ROI would be its threshold value.
- Apply threshold minimums to strategy choices and reject those strategies that are not expected to reach the minimums.
- Rank strategy choices in terms of their ability to reach specified goal values.
- Assign probability of reaching each goal to remaining strategies assessed according to the extent to which they can be affected by expected environmental occurrences. The analyst would have already developed a data set. This step involves linking the data set to the strategy choices by use of either subjective (judgmental) or objective (if possible) probabilities.
- Compute the expected value of each strategy choice that remains in the analysis by finding the products of its feasibility estimate (for each goal) and its payoff.
- Select the strategy with the greatest expected value. When several strategies produce similar expected values, they can all be referred for subsequent analysis or selection according to other criteria.

This approach results in "adapting or changing one's strategy depending upon the way existing circumstances are perceived." As one proceeds through the adaptive process, certain rankings, payoffs, and probabilities can result in removing strategies from further consideration, modifying remaining strategies, or creating new strategies.

Group Context

Although business decisions ultimately are made by individuals, decision models within the group context focus on collections of people as the major influence in decisions. These approaches are the group and elite models.

Group Model. This model views strategy selection as a process of balancing the interests of groups. Thus the strategy selected from the various strategy choices represents a compromise among the proponents of those strategy choices.

Although group theory, as explained by Truman, applies to public policy, a CEO intent on balancing internal group influences in strategy selection also would utilize such an approach.

Balancing the interests of external groups in strategy selection can also be viewed as a group equilibrium problem. When the relative power of groups changes, strategy will change to establish a new equilibrium. Strategy "will move in the direction desired by the groups gaining in influence, and away from the desires of groups losing influence."

That power is frequently the basis of business decisions is well documented. Cyert and March identified the tendency for groups of people both within and outside organizations to band together into coalitions on the basis of their mutual interests.

The strategy selection process then becomes one of balancing the interests of coalitions. Mintzberg et al. report that managers often prefer the group/coalition process of decision making over rational analysis, even though it is slower and they do not like to admit using it.

Elite Theory. Dye states that in public policy making the assertion that policy reflects the demands of "the people" is often a myth.

Elites actually shape mass opinion on policy questions more than masses shape elite opinion. Thus public policy really turns out to be the preferences of elites. Public officials and administrators merely carry out the policies decided upon by the elite. Policies flow "downward" from elites to masses; they do not arise from mass demands.

Does the elite model of public policy apply to business strategy selection? Mintzberg explains that when the number of people or groups competing for power becomes large and power is widely dispersed, management often emerges as the dominant coalition. The odds are against one individual or group being able to control management, so seldom does such an attempt occur.

Thus relative to the perhaps hundreds of thousands of owners of a large, publicly owned corporation, management can constitute an effective elite. Management's decision and strategy selections can be largely implemented unilaterally. The elite group may come to view the mass of owners as passive, apathetic, ill-informed, and subject to manipulation. Preservation of the organization is seen by members of the elite as the way to perpetuate their own positions, autonomy, and wealth. This goal congruence between the elite and the mass of owners can be constructive.

Of course, the elite model can apply more neatly to public organizations than to private. A public university can be dominated by a state legislature, a board of trustees, a union or an administrative group, which allows faculty members to think that they are making strategic decisions when in fact they are not.

Organization Context

Within this context attention is focused on the organization itself. Easton explains the systems model as a descriptive model of public policy making. It has been used repeatedly as a conceptualization for business decisions of all sorts as well.

Two models applied by Allison also fit this context.

Systems Model: The systems model portrays decision making as primarily a function of a set of inputs, both organizational and external in origin, which, when processed by the organization, lead to a particular set of outputs. It addresses the organizational context of decisions and can be used to analyse them by comparing inputs and outputs across organizations. Outputs (selected strategy, for example) can be analyzed as a function of organizational inputs. Stated differently, strategy can be viewed as the dependent variable in analysis with organizational inputs treated as independent variables.

Thus, in a somewhat oversimplified example, a systems-oriented strategist might look at past environmental scenarios and company circumstances and identify ones similar to the present. Then, the strategy that worked best during past situations that are similar to the present would be selected for implementation.

As such, the systems model pays little attention to the internal machinations of the decision process itself, focusing instead on the relationships between inputs and outputs. Like the intuitive model, the systems approach relies on the strategist's experience and pattern recognition skills.

Some of the benefits of the systems model for strategy selection lie in the questions that it raises:

- What are the important elements of the environment that place demands on the organization?
- What characteristics of the organization allow it to transform demands into strategy?
- How do environmental inputs affect the content of strategy?
- How does selected strategy affect key actors in the environment through feedback?

The major benefit of this approach is that historical analyses of relationships between inputs of the organization or to the decision-making process and the characteristics of strategies associated with those inputs can be used to spot patterns with normative implications.

Organizational process model: Another organizational context model of decision making is Allison's organizational process model (Model II). It is actually a modification of Cyert and March's organizational choice model. Fundamentally strategy would be selected according to this model by:

- Interorganizational bargaining,
- Agreement on goals,
- Informal formulation of expectations,
- Selection of the first strategy choice that is seen as an acceptable means toward fulfilling expectations.

Allison's Model III is also an organizational context model in that it views decision making as the result of the political maneuvers of the organization's coalitions.Strategy would be selected according to the political interplay among the various internal and external coalitions of the organization.

Institutional Context

Within this context institutions are seen as the primary factors influencing strategy selection. In the public policy area: Political activities generally centre about particular governmental institutions - Congress, the Presidency, courts, states, municipalities, political parties, etc. The interests of individuals and groups, and their activities on behalf of these interests, are generally directed toward governmental institutions. Public policy is authoritatively determined, implemented, and enforced by governmental institutions.

Institutional Model. The institutional model seeks to explain the nature of institutional influence on public policy making. A policy in government is not implemented and enforced until it has been adopted by a governmental institution.

Most institutional studies in government have described the organization structure, duties, and functions of institutions. The point of studying public policy within the institutional model is to analyse the relationships between these institutional variables and the content of public policy.

Can the institutional model be applied to business strategy selection? Certainly Chandler's landmark analysis of the relationship between business structure and strategy can be labeled an institutional study. For example, the Hasbro (B) case describes how concerns and characteristics of the firm's board of directors were ultimately manifested in drastic changes in the company's overall strategy.

With reference to such institutional strategy analyses, patterns of past relationships can shed light on the problem of strategy selection choices.

Global Context

More and more attention is now being given to the question: "How can strategy be selected and implemented to optimize the firm's international competitive position?" Conceivably a strategy selection model will emerge in the near future that casts the selection decision within a global context. At present no such model exists.

However, work has been done that describes how to take global factors into consideration in the process of strategy formulation.

Porter explains that global influences enter strategy formulation through the structured analysis of competition in global industries. Global industries are those "in which the strategic positions of competitors in major geographical or national markets are fundamentally affected by their overall global positions." Stated differently, companies that have multinational subsidiaries can be nonglobal if their subsidiaries compete only within, instead of between, countries. Thus IBM is a global firm and Nestle is not.

What distinguishes effective global strategy is that it establishes competitive advantage in terms of four factors:

- Differences among countries in the cost of production factors.
- Demographic differences among foreign markets.
- Different roles of foreign governments in the competitive system.
- Cross-country"differences in goals, resources and ability to monitor foreign competitors."

The variables addressed in structural analyses of competition (suppliers, potential entrants, buyers, substitutes, and competitors) remain the same for global industry analysis and strategy formulation as for domestic industry analysis. However, the scope of each variable is greater for global than for domestic industries.

Consequently "structural analysis in global industries must encompass foreign competitors, a wider pool of potential entrants, a broader array of possible substitutes, and increased possibilities that firms' goals and personalities will differ as well as their perceptions of what is strategically important." These issues are addressed in the chapter on global strategic management.

Decision Model Summary

Decision models were discussed for several decision contexts: the individual (five decision models serve to structure or explain the thought processes of the decision maker); the groups of which the decision maker is a member (two models characterize decisions as a function of group interactions); the organization (the systems model takes the organization's decision process as a converter strategy decision inputs into decision outputs, and Allison's models rely on political processes); the institution (views strategy decisions as functions of business institutional variables); and the global (although no global strategy selection model has been widely acknowledged, criteria for the selection of global strategies were discussed).

The context of strategy selection models defines the conceptual level of variables addressed by the decision process; decision models identify the particular decision variables.

Decision Models in Perspective

Around these many different decision models swirls a controversy about how managers actually do make decisions and how they should make them.Understanding of the process of strategy selection ultimately rests upon development of a consensus on the larger issue of how decisions in general are made.

Discussions seem to centre first on whether decisions are made rationally or nonrationally. Those who choose the latter then ask, "How are nonrational decisions made?" Attempts to answer this question have generated many of the decision model choices currently available in the literature. What, then, can be said about the selection of decision models?

First of all, when the strategy selection situation is cast primarily in the context of groups, the organization, or institutional variables, then the group, system, or institutional decision approach, respectively, might be applied directly. Within the international context, strategy can be selected by the extent to which it addresses Porter's global strategy factors.

The hardest choices among decision models occur when the strategy selection decision lies securely within the individual context. Here there are no overriding group, organizational, institutional, or global influences on which to rely. Pertinent strategy selection criteria tend, in this case, to be more subtle and more personalized. Steiner advocates using the rational model whenever possible:

It seems apparent that there is no "one best way" for all companies, but there are better decision approaches given the constraints and characteristics of the situation. Even so, to the degree a formal, rational, structured approach can be used, the company will be likely to benefit.

CHARACTERISTICS OF THE SELECTED STRATEGY

Several structures have been proposed for testing the acceptability of a chosen strategy. They consist of lists of criteria that the goals and action plans should meet. They can be used as the elements on one axis of a matrix that has the strategy set choices arranged on the other.

Then each strategy can be scored on each criterion. The sum of criteria scores for each strategy can then be used to select the best one(s). In this way the criteria can be used in place of other measures of strategy acceptability in a modified rational model. The following strategy choice criteria have been synthesized from similar lists prepared by other authors.

- The selected strategy should be consistent with the
  - Organization's environment,
  - Internal capabilities and characteristics,
  - Available resources, and

  - Risk preferences
- The action plan choices should be aimed at clearly identified goals (objectives and targets) and should have a high chance of successfully reaching or guiding behaviour toward them.
- The selected strategy should have appropriate timing:
- The strategy choice should allow sufficient flexibility for adjustment to deal with competitors' responses and environmental changes.
- The organization's leadership should be committed to support of the chosen strategy.

Consistency Tests

Four consistency tests should be performed on the selected strategy.

Environmental Factors: The selected strategy should be consistent with the environmental factors identified during the environmental analysis. The selected strategy should address the major threats and opportunities, both present and future. After all, one of the major purposes of the strategy is to integrate the organization and the environment. By taking advantage of opportunities and either avoiding or overcoming threats, that integration can take place.

Internal Characteristics: The chosen strategy should be consistent with major internal characteristics of the organization, whose competencies and skills should be incorporated into the strategy so that they become emphasized; weaknesses should be addressed so that they can be corrected within an appropriate amount of time. Another internal characteristic is management capability.

Selected strategy must be implementable by either present management or new management people. Also, the ways in which the new strategy relates to past strategy should be clear. There is a strong relationship between past strategy and new strategy in most firms.The ways in which the new one is expected to improve on the old should be understood.

Resource Availability. New strategy should be consistent with physical facilities and financial resource availability in the present and future. Future resource needs should be within the organization's capability and understood in detail. Pro forma financial statements constructed to show the financial impact on the organization of the new strategy will help to demonstrate the ability of the firm to produce the necessary resources.

Risk/Return Preference: The final consistency test involves making sure that the selected strategy meshes well with the risk/return preference of management and owners. Risk-takers will be inclined toward strategies that involve relatively high levels of risk with commensurate high possible payoffs. They tend to stress organizational strengths and environmental opportunities, operate with confidence and aggressiveness, and tackle challenges head on; innovation is typically preferred over imitation. .

Alternatively risk-averters prefer more defensive, conservative strategies. They will try to stay within present capabilities without entering into projects requiring new strengths or skills, will balk at uncertainty, and will tend to be followers rather than leaders in their markets. When Friendly Ice Cream Corporation, a family-style restaurant chain with several hundred retail outlets in the Northeast, went public in 1969, the Wall Street Journal described Curtis and Preston Blake, the company's cofounders, as using both belts and suspenders to hold up their pants.

Their risk-averting orientation included such features as the discounting of every payable since the company's inception, refusal to use long-term debt, and reliance on extensive test marketing of minor product additions.

Clarity of Goals

The selected action plans should be linked with clearly understood objectives and targets, especially those related to profit performance. It will be difficult to monitor performance when action plans are not tied to goals that are widely adopted and understood.

In addition to relating clearly to goals, the selected action plans should have a high chance of reaching them by minimizing the effectiveness of competitors' counterattacks. There are two considerations here. First, strategy should avoid direct confrontation with rivals in areas where they are strongest. Rivals will often respond with less conviction when they do not perceive a direct attack on one of their strengths.

The large amount of investment necessary to mount a successful challenge to competitors' strengths may actually prohibit such a move.

If it is done with too little investment, it can carry a higher chance of failure than would typically be true if the competitor were weaker on this attribute.

Second, attacking a competitor's weaknesses, a less risky alternative, may carry insufficient return to justify the offensive.

For example, a primary weakness of major automobile manufacturers is their inability to produce truly "one-of-a-kind" cars. Many attempts have been made world-wide to capitalize on this "weakness," but only a handful have realized any success.

Timing

The timing of the selected strategy should be appropriate in two important ways. First, the length of time that will be necessary to implement the strategy should be appropriate given the company's present resources or the time it will take to get them. For a simple example, a firm's cash flow position can be deteriorating faster than its management's ability to retrench by collecting receivables, arranging a loan, or cutting expenses.

Second, the strategy must be timely in terms of environmental circumstances. When Chrysler decided during the early 1970s to try to strengthen its position in the large-car market, the oil embargo of 1974-1975 left it with a huge inventory of suddenly unpopular autos.

Flexibility

The selected strategy should allow sufficient maneuverability so that management can respond to competitors' reactions and minor environmental changes while still maintaining the integrity of the strategy.

One way to build in flexibility is to develop several contingency strategies, each of which applies to a somewhat different set of likely environmental assumptions. Then if the environmental assumptions begin to come true, the appropriate modifications can be made, having already been analyzed and pondered for their effects and requirements.

The same sort of contingency strategy set can be developed around likely competitor reactions.

Management Commitment

The selected strategy should have the commitment of all levels of management. In some organizations top management's advocacy of a strategy will soon lead to its support. In others, however, factions for and against a strategy will develop. With such division present, successful implementation of the strategy becomes difficult. "Successful strategies require commitment, not just acceptance.

How can the commitment of individuals be developed? Staw explains that commitment to a course of action is a function of the extent to which the action (strategy) is perceived as satisfying three needs: the need to justify past decisions (retrospective rationality), the need for consistency, and the need for positive subjective expected utility (prospective rationality).

To generate maximum commitment, the selected strategy in some way should confirm the correctness of decisions already made. Presumably managers at each level of the organization will react or proact to overall strategy with their own respective strategies. The more their responses can be seen as justifications of their past decisions, the greater will be the chances that they will sense commitment to, rather than merely acceptance of, the selected overall strategy, as well as their role in it.

Then, there are both cultural and organizational norms for consistency that apply to strategy selection as well as other decisions. According to Staw,

Motivation to justify decisions can be seen as a function of responsibility for negative consequences as well as both internal and external demands for competence... Responsibility for negative consequences leads to a motivation to justify previous decisions, if there is a need to demonstrate competence to oneself or others.

In other words some degree of consistency between the past strategy and the selected one is important in developing commitment because the similar new one demonstrates the correctness of the past one. This may at least partially explain why it tends to be difficult to get all the key actors in an organization to dedicate themselves to a radically new strategy. It may also explain why some boards of directors seem to replace CEOs when they feel that a strategy change is necessary.

Finally, the higher the prospective rationality of the selection, the more commitment is facilitated. Prospective rationality is the product of the perceived probability of future outcomes and the perceived value of those outcomes. It is roughly equivalent to the expected value of the strategy. A manager who feels that the selected strategy has a high expected value will be more committed to it than one who feels the expected value is low.

Thus for commitment to develop, all participants should be convinced that the organization has the resources, skills, time, and other attributes necessary to reach goals successfully with the new action plans, which together constitute a new strategy.

SUMMARY

Characteristics of the Boston Consulting Group's growth-share matrix, General Electric's planning grid, life cycle theory, the product/market evolution matrix, four variations of gap analysis, and the directional policy matrix were explained in the first section of this chapter.

Each of these techniques is a way of capturing the major determinants of strategy for the purpose of selecting the appropriate one. However, all of them leave room for the strategist to interject his/her own interpretation of the relationships among dependent and independent variables.

Strategy selection is a key management decision and its complexity is reflected in the many attempts that have been made to explain it. The second part of this chapter explains, first, the various contexts within which selected decision models have been derived - individual, group, organization, institutional, and global. Attempts to explain decision-making behaviour have tended to focus on one or another of these contexts.

Borrowing from the fields of economics and political science, as well as business administration theory, eleven decision models are explained within the contextual framework. In the individual context, five models are discussed: the rational, bounded rationality, incremental, intuitive, and adaptive approaches. Next the group and elite structures are described as characteristic of decisions made within the group context. Then the organization context's system model and organizational process approaches are explained. Finally, within the last two decision contexts, the institutional and global, the relevant strategic factors are presented.

Chapter 5

Formulating Functional Strategy: Implementing the Strategy Set

INTRODUCTION

In each functional area identified by the strategist as needing goals and action plans, the aspects of the domain of each and the degree of detail entered into are matters of choice. Management's concern in setting functional strategy should be to provide the firm's functional officers with sufficient guidelines to carry out the functional parts of implementing other levels of strategy. As one author explains,

Information about the selected (business-level) strategy can be transmitted by preparation of explicit goals and objectives... and immediate action for each of the major functional and technical areas within the firm. In turn... (this information) define(s) the individual tasks or jobs that are essential for strategic success, and the organizational structure and systems should then be designed to coordinate and integrate the performance of those tasks.

An autocratic CEO might wish to be highly specific in functional strategy. One with a participative or less directive style might select only a few key functional pressure points, so to speak, to guide the managers of each function.

Of primary concern in setting functional goals and action plans are the following decisions:

- Which functional areas must be addressed so as to most effectively implement enterprise-, corporate-, and business level strategies?

- Within each of those functional areas, what goals should be set?
- What action plans within each functional area would assure that the goals identified above would be reached?

Thus the major decisions confronting the strategist in setting functional-level strategy are roughly the same as those facing him/her in the process of strategy formulation at each of the other strategy levels, with one exception: A decision must be made first about which functional areas have to be dealt with. After identifying the appropriate functional areas, goal and action plan formulation follow the same process as the other strategy levels.

In this chapter the three stages of functional strategy formulation are discussed first. Then the major strategic variables are described for each of the functional areas of marketing, finance, personnel and union relations, production, research and development (R&D), and external relations. By the way, merger and acquisition strategy and global strategy may also be viewed as functional strategies since they have the role of implementing upper level strategies.

An organization might have functions other than those enumerated here but the principles of formulation remain the same. The strategist must identify the essential parts of each function and set goals and action plans to guide their implementation.

An example would be the real estate acquisition department of a large fast food chain. The function of acquiring locations for building new retail outlets would be a key element of growth strategy for such a firm.

Goals and action plans for selecting and purchasing locations would, if formulated and implemented effectively, represent the critical aspects of decision makers' thoughts and beliefs about how they will compete. Variables like size of location, demographics of the area, price, proximity to consumers' travel patterns and to competitors' units, and any number of other possible location parameters, would necessitate carefully formulated goals and action plans. If these decisions were made ineffectively, then the implementation of other functional strategy as well as business-level strategy, would likely prove to be suboptimal.

CHOOSING FUNCTIONAL AREAS

- To select the functional areas for which strategy has to be formulated, three steps should be followed:
- Enumerate enterprise-, corporate-, and business-level strategies and list the organizational units from which effort will be required for implementation of each.
- Compare the list with the present functional area structure of the organization.
- Note the organizational units for which goals and action plans will have to be changed to implement enterprise-, corporate-, and business-level goals and action plans.

For the first step, the functional requirements of higher-level strategies can simply be listed. The idea is to make sure that each strategy's functional needs are represented in the organizational structure. If a needed function is not currently part of the organization's stable of functions, then organizational structure would have to be modified, appropriate people trained or hired, and budgetary adjustments made.

A line of research has developed that focuses on linking certain operating characteristics with various functional emphases. Most cogent for purposes of deciding upon needed functional areas are a 1978 study by Miles and Snow, one undertaken by Snow and Hrebiniak in 1980, another by Hitt, Ireland, and Palia in 1982,and finally one by Gupta and Govindarajan. Their major purpose was to identify the relationships among various grand strategies and executives' opinions of the relative importance of several types of functional areas.

In the Hitt, Ireland, and Palia study, the first grand strategy, stability, refers to maintaining an approximately constant amount of improvement in annual functional performance without major changes in the mix of products or markets. In contrast to earlier studies, the authors found that "for firms implementing a stability strategy, no function was rated significantly higher than any other." They speculated that a possible reason for this result is that the stability strategy may precipitate a balance among functional areas. The absence of stability possibly would generate an imbalance in which one functional area would be emphasized more than others.

The study results showed that the general administration function was felt by the executive respondents to be the most important for internal growth. The researchers explained that this strategy requires strong, effective management, control, and leadership, and thus the emphasis on general administration was not surprising.

Next the grand strategy of external acquisitive growth—growth by acquisition, merger, or joint venture—requires emphasis on the functions of finance, marketing, and general administration. Finance is important to the analysis of the target firms' ability to achieve synergy through the combination. A strong administrative function tends to produce competent management of change, which is critical in order to join two firms successfully.

Finally, retrenchment strategies call for a strong marketing function. Marketing is important to monitor external relations, which are particularly sensitive for retrenching firms. Finance is important during retrenchment, presumably to analyse and monitor the financial condition of the firm.

Overall the study offered support for the contention that the relative importance of functional areas varies with strategy.

Both the Miles and Snow and Snow and Hrebiniak studies analyse the relative importance of functional areas across a different set of strategies from that used by Hitt, et al. The strategies they studied are the reactor, defender, prospector, and analyzer, which were first defined by Miles and Snow.

A reactor is a firm that tends to allow itself to be led into actions by environmental forces. Its products and market focuses change more often than its competitors' and they tend to assume less risk.

More aggressive firms—which frequently redefine their products and markets, value creative product and market moves, and respond quickly to environmental and competitive shifts—are called prospectors. Whereas prospectors may be thought of as darting in and out of various product/market combinations, often without attaining dominant positions, defenders tend to concentrate on narrow product/market definitions in which they seek a stable niche.

Last, analyzers combine the features of defenders and prospectors to some extent. They concentrate on a narrow product/market definition but quickly pursue new developments within their niche.

Both studies examine the ways in which these four strategy types differ in terms of distinctive competence (functional strategy) and organizational performance. Their findings suggest that the successful performance of firms following these strategies in the same industry depends upon their competence in appropriate functional strategy areas.

Miles and Snow suggested, first, that reactors showed no particular functional strengths but the other three types of strategies did. Defenders' strengths centered on general management, R&D, production, and finance; prospectors emphasized general management, product R&D, basic research, and market research; and analyzers stressed general management, production, applied research, and sales management.

The study by Snow and Hrebiniak showed that reactors have no regular pattern of competencies, but beyond that their results differed from those of Miles and Snow. In fact they noted that their study demonstrates the need to reconceptualize the distinctive competencies of defender, prospector, and analyzer strategies.

All three showed capabilities in general and financial management. Further, defenders were strong in the areas of applied engineering and production management; prospectors stressed product R&D and basic research; and analyzers showed too much variability in strengths across industries (beyond general and financial management) to allow generalizing about any of them.

Gupta and Govindarajan show that certain characteristics of the general managers of SBUs contribute to the effectiveness of some SBU strategies. In particular, the performance of SBUs with build strategies is facilitated by greater marketing/sales experience, greater risk propensity, and greater tolerance for ambiguity on the part of the business unit's general manager.

The opposite results obtained for harvest strategies; high values for the three general manager characteristics hindered SBU effectiveness.

Although these studies exhibit little consistency about the particular set of functional strengths associated with types of strategies, they do demonstrate that functional capabilities are developed by managers as important competitive tools. Managers seem to try to establish competitive strength by aligning certain functional capabilities with the strategy they have formulated. Thus they highlight the importance for strategists of understanding their firm's internal strengths and weaknesses while formulating strategy.

SETTING FUNCTIONAL GOALS

It can be seen that formulation of functional goals requires development of a data set by environmental analysis. The relevant environment of each functional area is analyzed and reduced to strengths, weaknesses, threats and opportunities. These positive and negative aspects are factored in with information about existing functional strategies, political processes, and

The Information Inputs, Processes, and Outputs of Strategic Management value systems at work in the organization. Present goals and action plans set for the enterprise, corporate, and business levels are also major information inputs to functional goal and action plan formulation, but probably the most important of the three is business-level goals and action plans.

In fact there is often a direct correspondence between business-level goals and the goals that are set within each functional area, and between business-and functional-level strategies.

For example, a business-level goal of increasing sales by 10 per cent will precipitate a set of, say, marketing, finance, personnel, and production goals, which, if met, will lead to reaching the business goal.

Similarly, if the business stracegy included concentration growth to reach the 10 per cent goal, then marketing strategy would have a different set of characteristics than would be the case had product development been selected as the business strategy.

The production, personnel, finance, and other strategies that might be appropriate would likely also differ according to the business strategy selected.

To set functional area goals, the following steps should be taken:

- For each functional area, compare present functional goals with new enterprise-, corporate-, and business-level goals.
- Decide what new goal areas (functional variables) are needed for each function.
- Set new goal levels (values for each functional area's variables).

FORMULATING FUNCTIONAL ACTION PLANS

To formulate action plans at the functional level, the difficult problem of deciding which functional areas to address already has been resolved in the goal-setting stage. So the strategist has only to decide which functional area goals (or set of related goals) for which it is necessary to formulate action plans.

A single goal might require action plans at several functional areas whereas others might require only one. The first step involves identifying what these functional area interdependencies are. It results in a list of the functional areas for which action plans have to be formulated for each functional goal.

To review these procedures briefly, inputs to formulation decisions consist of information about existing strategies for each functional area, environmental analysis and the data set it produces, knowledge of the extant political processes within the organization, and understanding of the values and preferences of its key actors and coalitions.

All of this information is analyzed in light of the new goals (or old ones, if they remain unchanged) that have been set for each function.

For the other levels of strategy—enterprise, corporate, and business—we have explained what the content of each should be.

For example, business strategy should address matters pertaining to the competitive niche and distinctive competencies of a single business or of an SBU for a multibusiness corporation.

But how can one generalize about the nature of topics that should be addressed in functional area strategy? Clearly the topical content of each functional area is considerably different from one function to another, and the nature of action plans required to meet goals for each function would also differ greatly across them.

Thus instead of stating generally what the substantive content of functional strategy should be, we must describe each functional strategy area's content individually. By the time most students take a course in strategic management, they have already taken various courses in each of the functional areas. Therefore, in the section that follows, we outline only the primary variables that would be given values by the strategist to guide the operation of each functional area in a way that is consistent with the other levels of strategy. The functional areas addressed are marketing, finance, R&D, personnel, production, and external relations.

MARKETING STRATEGY

Marketing goals and action plans should address matters of product/service, price, distribution, communication, and the process of new product development.

Product/Service

Product/service strategy would be set to:

- Define the key characteristics of the product or service.
- Locate it within the organization's product/service hierarchy,
- Select the quality level,
- Outline product/service support programs. This information would be specified when an old product/service is to be changed or a new one, or several, added.

These characteristics of a firm's product/service are determined by finding the best fit between the organization's various internal factors and its external factors as they relate to product/service.

Thus a university college might introduce an evening programme to broaden its asset utilization and extend its instructional capabilities (internal factors) in the face of increased numbers of nontraditional students with heightened demand for education (external factors), to help implement a product (service) development action plan to reach a goal of increased revenue.

Price

Strategy regarding product/service price would be set to accomplish one or some combination of four fundamental things:

- Change in profitability,
- Change in sales level or growth rate,
- Change in net cash flow,
- Maintenance of present sales, profit, or cash flow level.

Marketing goals and action plans deal with price by specifying the planned-for impact on company performance (as measured by the income statement) desired of a strategy. The task of actually setting price to yield that impact is normally the responsibility of the firm's marketing director where marketing is decentralized.

In cases where a profit impact is expected, marketing goals can set a target return on assets, net cash flow, return on sales, or some other evaluative criterion that would have been determined to justify the higher-level strategy. In small sole proprietorships or partnerships, the targeted return might be a dollar amount required to cover the spending needs of the owner/manager.

Some managers prefer to have prices set so as to generate a certain targeted dollar amount of sales, rate of change of sales, or market share. Although sales are more immediately measurable than profit, their use as a focus can lead to earnings or cash flow slippage that go undetected in the short term.

For example, a firm could allow progressively more liberal receivables policy and thus attract sales to meet a rigid sales growth or market share goal. Yet by increasing payables commitments, the firm could suddenly find itself placed on the cash basis by suppliers and unable to meet delivery requirements. Obviously sales and profitability would then be threatened.

Firms can also set a net cash flow target, which, when coupled with normal credit terms for an industry or geographical area, can dictate within narrow limits what price would be most appropriate. here a strong need for cash might require a relatively low price. This would be the case if buyers were unwilling to pay a higher price on short credit terms and the seller needed cash inflow to meet required outflows.

Finally, a strategist may feel that prices should be set so that competitive attention is not drawn to the firm or that risk is minimized. This equilibrium or "status quo"maintenance goal could be effective for a firm with stable returns on sales, for example, which is trying to avoid competitive retaliation.

Distribution (Place)

As with other marketing variables, the details of distribution system structure and selection are the province of the marketing director in a decentralized firm. Yet the corporate strategist's input to distribution system design is critical in that it sets the limits for subsequent distribution decisions.

The primary element of distribution goals and action plans is a definition of planned-for coverage or exposure of products addressed at higher levels of strategy.

Intended product exposure is a function of:

- The extent to which the firm is integrated forward or backward,
- Whether the output of intermediate steps in the production process will be marketed or retained only as components,
- Desired coverage, usually in geographical terms, of the items marketed.

To illustrate, a fully integrated home microcomputer manufacturer could limit distribution to sales of computers, the final products, to consumers. In so doing the firm would have foregone potential sales of separate intermediate products such as electronic components, individual hardware units, and software.

In this case distribution decisions would be a function of how wide a market area the strategist plans to cover with the finished product. If, alternatively, business strategy called for marketing the output of each step in the production process, then distribution strategy would address the coverage of variables for components, hardware, and software. Each one could have different coverage requirements, depending upon the density in the market area of potential buyers for each product class.

Promotion

The strategist's primary concern with promotion, or, more generally, communication, is to provide guidance to the firm's marketing specialists so that product communication assumes a form consistent with overall strategy.

There are four types of communication methods:

- *Personal sales presentations*: Direct communication between sellers and potential buyers.

- *Sales promotion*: Displays, exhibitions, demonstrations, and trade shows to complement other communication techniques.
- *Mass advertising*: Communication with large aggregates of potential buyers simultaneously.
- *Public relations*: Free nonpersonal communication.

In a decentralized firm, the job of selecting a particular combination of communication methods is usually the responsibility of marketing specialists.

To optimize congruence between communication methods and overall strategy, the strategist sets communication strategy in four areas to guide the specialist's decisions.

First, a set of quantitative communication goals specifies expectations of the programme ultimately designed. These goals are the planned-for results of the communication programme and are not necessarily the same as overall strategic goals.

Communication goals should be segment-specific such that the net effect of several communication efforts (say, one for each of several segments or markets served by the firm) is attainment of one overall growth rate in sales, market share, or profit. These goals should also clarify whether the purpose of communication is to educate, persuade, or remind.

Second, communication activities are aimed at either one or a combination of target market segments. A segment description is normally part of all marketing strategy subsets but has specific implications for communication specialists.

Third, while analyzing the firm's environmental circumstances, competitive position, and internal characteristics, strategic analysis (the process that would have led to the development of a new product or maintenance of an existing one) would have revealed a selection of possible selling points for the product or product mix.

A selling point is the collection of product or service attributes that constitute the primary message of the firm's communication programme; it is the information conveyed in the communication effort. Fourth, communication strategy should include the amount to be budgeted for the communication programme expressed in either dollars or percentage of sales or gross profit.

New Product Development

As products reach the decline stage of their life cycles, they must be replaced by new products in order for the firm to grow and prosper. Thus an integral part of a business strategy that stresses product development is a marketing strategy defining the way in which new product ideas will be generated. The product development process is summarized by Rabino and Moskowitz as four chronologically ordered stages as follows:

- *Formulation of product goals*: These may be thought of as the organization's requirements for new products; what must it "get out of" new product entries and therefore what are its purposes for generating new product ideas.
- Search, discovery, and evaluation of new product proposals. Procedures are developed and implemented to identify and screen new product ideas which may potentially heed product goals.
- *Product development and testing*: The number of new product ideas is reduced to the few tangible ones that have the highest chance of meeting goals and which fall within the company's strategic capability.
- *Market entry*: The commercialization phase is typically the province of the rest of the marketing function and requires expertise which resides there.

The rudiments of marketing strategy can be laid out by setting goals and action plans for each element above. For analysis of cases, students who formulate marketing strategy should follow the guidelines above for each element at a minimum.

FINANCE STRATEGY

The management of a firm's financial resources is intricately connected to the upper-level strategies of the firm.

That enterprise-, corporate-, and business-level goals normally include explicit financial performance criteria attests to the fundamental strategic nature of higher-order financial matters. So too financial resources thread through all the operational components of an enterprise in a manner that either enhances or constrains their contribution to overall performance. As such financial concerns are both directive and supportive in a strategic context.

Finance strategy is generally concerned with the acquisition and allocation of financial resources for the purpose of achieving goals at an acceptable level of risk. Thus the setting of goals and action plans for finance can be viewed as a problem relating the sources and uses of capital that is constrained, at least in part, by stockholders' wealth goals. In this section financial goals and action plans are treated from capital acquisition and allocation perspectives, though this distinction is only for expository purposes. Rarely are capital acquisition decisions made in isolation from those relating to how funds would be allocated, and vice versa. Indeed the familiar cost-of-capital notion has meaning in both regards.

On the matter of risk, we will find that it enters into both sources and uses problems. It is manifest primarily through the notions of financial leverage, operating leverage, liquidity, and working capital management. All are discussed in the present section.

Capital Allocation

Higher-level strategies normally involve certain current and fixed asset investments that represent short- and long-term applications or uses of funds. Specifications describing these investments are outlined in terms of capital budgeting techniques, cost-benefit analysis, and a cash budget, which serve:

- To determine the financial characteristics of strategic investments
- As evaluative criteria for monitoring the operation of the firm under the business-level strategy.

Of course, to determine the financial impact of strategic

investments, a comprehensive financial analysis (explained earlier) of the firm is necessary to define its preimplementation financial structure.

All subsequent changes can then be evaluated according to their expected effect on this financial profile. Business-level strategy will necessitate selection from among various expenditure choices.

Finance goals and action plans are needed to establish the expected outcomes and methods to be followed in such evaluations.

Related decisions involve the relative amounts of capital diverted to dividends versus reinvestment in the firm (the dividend payout ratio or its opposite, the earning retention ratio).

Investment Project Categories

Investment projects can be classified as follows:

- *Cost reduction*: Expenditures to increase the efficiency of labour or equipment would fall into this category. They commonly would be part of a retrenchment strategy or one targeting increased profitability.
- *Maintenance*: These expenditures are for replacement of worn-out or damaged equipment or facilities where no strategic change is intended.
- *Market development or penetration*: Expenditures for action plans requiring expansion into new markets or increased penetration of existing markets are included here. They would be for advertising campaigns, market research, geographical expansion, and so on.
- *Product development*: When expenditures are for the production of new or modified products, they fall into this category.
- *Compliance*: Expenditures are often required by government regulations, labour contracts, or insurance terms.
- *Miscellaneous*: Projects that do not fall into the other five categories are classified as miscellaneous.

Examples include office facilities and some employee benefit programs.

Authorization hierarchies: To evaluate investment alternatives, most managements establish expenditure authorization hierarchies by type of investment project, functional department, and/or division. Thus market development investments might have to be reviewed by the sales manager, the vice-president of marketing, a vice-presidential expenditure committee, the CEO, and ultimately the board of directors.

A dollar limit is usually established for each level. An expenditure above that limit has to be forwarded to the next highest level for authorization until it is either approved or denied. The magnitude of these limits and where they are applied depends upon the type of business, style of management, track records of individuals involved, and other factors, and should reflect the sensitivity of the firm's financial position involved, and other factors, and should reflect the sensitivity of the firm's financial position to losses. Authorization limits and the way they are administered become prime (though inconclusive) indicators of the type and degree of decentralization in an organization.

Project Selection Criteria

In all instances the capital allocation process becomes a budgetary matter therefore, we have the term "capital budgeting." But it is as much a process of selection as it is of submission.

Compliance and most miscellaneous projects, which usually involve no cash inflows, are evaluated by level of necessity and dollar amount. The other types of projects involve both cash inflows and outflows and can be evaluated by various measures of net return as well as size of outflow (or investment).

Most common among the various methods are the payback period, average rate of return, net present value, internal rate of return, and profitability index models. The model to be used to evaluate projects is specified by finance strategy along with the project selection criterion (or cutoff point) for approval.

Capital budgeting models allow the strategist to rank investment alternatives by profitability (or other bases). Establishing a cutoff point for selection from among the ranked alternatives is another strategic decision.

Two popular ways to determine the cutoff point are:

- To use the firm's cost of capital
- To compute other hurdle rates of return. Of course, some expenditures are simply necessary regardless of their return and would be selected accordingly. Compliance investments, for example, often fall into this category.

Cost of Capital. If investments are made in projects with returns below the rate paid to obtain capital, the earnings available to common shareholders will be reduced accordingly. The cost of capital for a firm is thus the rate of return on projects that is necessary to prevent changes in the earnings available to common shareholders and can be used as an evaluative criterion for selection from among strategic investment choices.

This definition does not imply that the concern is only with the cost of equity financing (which includes new common share issues as well as retained earnings). Debt and preferred stock are also sources of investment funds, both of which normally have different component costs from common equity sources taken alone. But the focus of cost of capital as an investment criterion is on the returns generated for common shareholders.

Establishing the firm's cost of capital is important to ensure that investments are not made with expected returns that are less than the amount the firm pays for capital. Thus the cost of capital can be used as a "hurdle" rate of return. This estimate is also used as the discount rate in computing net present value, internal rate of return, and the profitability index for projects.

Operating Leverage and Risk. All strategic investment decisions are going to involve some degree of risk. Risk entails not only the profitable versus unprofitable dichotomy, but also the variability in earnings or losses emanating from an investment project. One dimension of the risk-management question is captured in the concept of operating leverage.

Operating leverage is the degree of magnification of earnings or losses (expressed as cash flows or profits) set off by different levels of output. The magnification results from the variable cost versus fixed cost mix in an investment period. Generally the higher the level of fixed commitment in relation to variable costs, the greater is the leverage (and magnification). This, of course, is the central notion in the familiar break-even analysis, where concern is given not only to the break-even point, but also the levels of earnings or losses around it.

Operating leverage becomes a strategic issue because it affects such things as variability of anticipated sales, competitive strategy, and the degree to which the firm can absorb or tolerate variations in earnings.

The fact that differences exist across companies in their relative amounts of operating leverage may be largely a function of the industry in which each of them competes. The fashion apparel industry, for example, tends to display a good deal more demand volatility than does the tobacco industry.

The first, therefore, tends to be more labour (variable cost) intensive than the latter in its production processes (though there are other explanations for this difference as well). It is much more difficult to reduce fixed than variable commitments than in the short term to address temporary demand shortfalls.

Second, a firm's fixed versus variable cost mix is often a function of the competitive advantage it is trying to achieve. A firm choosing a technological leadership role would likely have comparably large fixed commitments to research and development.

This would raise its relative break-even point and magnify the levels of losses or earnings at other output levels. Or a firm trying to maintain a price leadership position might require automated (capital-intensive) production systems.

Here lower total costs at higher output levels allow the competitive price advantage and magnify earnings above break-even volume. Below break-even volume, the reverse is true. Finally, the tolerance for, or ability to absorb, earnings fluctuations affects the operating leverage profile. A marginal firm, intolerant of losses, would probably make as few fixed commitments as possible. Though this might impair its upside earnings capability, the firm's primary concern would be with downside risk.

Managers are also concerned with the degree of operating leverage when confronted with vertical integration decisions, since they usually represent the conversion of variable costs to fixed costs. One reason for integrating vertically is to capture the margins realized by suppliers or downstream distributors.

But in the process, additional fixed costs are normally incurred that alter the degree of operating leverage the integrator experiences. Any resulting variations in earnings or loss potential must be consistent with overall financial performance goals.

If not, the new acquisition might operate at a loss (below break-even). Losses could be avoided by margin/cost trade-offs between integrated units (absorption), or additional fixed-cost commitments may be simply insignificant in the grand scheme of things. In any case the operating leverage profile of a firm and that of individual investments pose risk, as well as profitability, questions.

Capital Acquisition

The second aspect of financial goals and action plans is determining the sources of capital to be invested in assets needed to carry out a higher-level (usually business-level) strategy. Long-term sources will affect primarily the firm's debt/equity structure; short-term sources its liquidity position. But, as we shall see, they are interrelated.

Financial choices will be made to optimize the firm's overall financial profile while also maximizing the likelihood that a new set of higher-level strategies will be implemented as planned. Making these choices is a decision process fraught with trade-offs. Using equity to raise funds may improve debt/equity position, but will dilute ownership. Use of short-term debt will preserve ownership but will threaten liquidity. Using internally generated funds will prevent interest expense increases, but may threaten dividend payout ability. Thus the strategist's primary concern is with setting limits or guidelines for key financial criteria within which a higher-level strategy's financial requirements must fit.

Considerations in the Capital Mix. Financing for strategic investments falls generally into two classes; short term and long term. For both the strategist must select the optimal type of financing—optimal in terms of cash/return trade-offs, relative costs, and control as indicated by the firm's mission and master strategy. For example, if stockholders through the board of directors were to oppose further dilution of holdings, the strategist probably would not consider equity financing, even if it was considered optimal for another reason.

Next the impact of the selected mix of financing sources is assessed on:

- The firm's liquidity position
- The firm's debt/equity structure.

In the process of selecting sources of funds and capital, managers have the opportunity to affect the firm's financial profile. They can take advantage of financial strengths such as strong liquidity or a relatively low debt-to-equity position. Conversely they can, within reasonable limits, strengthen financial weaknesses.

Weak liquidity can be at least partially ameliorated by generating cash through tightening credit collection policies, improving inventory control, or controlling operating expenses. These are largely working capital management matters.

Dividend Policy. In deciding between long- and short-term financing, the strategist must evaluate the firm's dividend policy. The proportions of earnings allocated to dividends and retained earnings can materially affect the firm's ability to meet debt repayment schedules with cash.

Over-commitment to debt could necessitate reducing, or not increasing, dividend payments, and thus lessening cash flows to stockholders.

Dividend policy generally will be one of three major types: stable dollar amount per share, constant payout ratio, or low regular dividend plus extras. Which of these is appropriate for an individual firm is a function of a financial interpretation of shareholder goals, including expectations of returns and risk.

It is therefore a matter of highest-level concern, and normally is treated by the board of directors. Decisions regarding dividend policy also eventually affect the liquidity and debt structure of the firm, as well as stockholder relations.

Consequently, students should carefully enunciate the potential impact of proposed changes in dividend policy of companies they are analyzing in cases by explaining how they will alter the firm's liquidity position, debt structure, and stockholder relations.

Financial Leverage and Risk. In addition to dividend policy, the strategist will be particularly concerned with financial leverage. Not to be confused with operating leverage, financial leverage involves the use of debt in the firm's financial structure.

Though it may be operationally defined and measured in a variety of ways, it essentially entails the use of debt to extend the earning power of funds committed by the firm's shareholders. When used properly financial leverage magnifies returns on committed funds.

Because of the nature of financial leverage, it carries within it not only the general types of risk associated with operating leverage, but also two others that have rather specific implications.

First, there is the risk of default—the inability to meet debt obligations as they come due. By definition, as financial leverage increases, cash flow requirements necessary to service additional debt increase as well. The risk of inadequate cash flow is, therefore, a primary concern in strategic decisions regarding financial structure. This, of course, suggests that liquidity and leverage are intricately intertwined in decisions of that kind.

Second, the informed strategist not only must consider the risk of default and the involuntary actions that failure may lead to, but also the priority of claims that attend a given financial structure. In the case of liquidation, voluntary or involuntary, shareholders normally hold a claims position subordinate to that of debt holders. Thus increased leverage can have a deteriorating effect on the assets available for distribution to shareholders upon liquidation. Therefore, this component of risk enters financial structure decisions as well.

Cost of Capital. The cost of capital is of major importance in investment decisions (as a discount rate or hurdle rate of return), but it also has strategic importance in capital mix decisions. Since a firm's cost of capital represents the combined influence of all of its individual components, it can serve as a useful criterion for evaluating the capital structure itself.

That is, the lower the overall cost of capital, generally the more "optimal" is the capital structure for a given risk profile. In planning the capital mix, the finance strategist is concerned with minimizing the combined cost of funds so that the funding of future growth can be accomplished most economically. Thus if the addition of long-term debt to the capital structure ends up reducing the combined cost of capital (through a marked increase in the price of common stock, for example), then the increased-leverage decision can be partly justified on that basis. Similarly increases in common shares issued may have a disproportionately negative influence on the cost of debt. In these cases the cost-of-capital concept offers a useful framework for establishing capital mix objectives. Further, it forces the analyst to consider the interactive effects of different forms of financing, rather than simply examine the individual component costs of the various forms of debt and equity available.

Long-Term Financing Instruments

The major classes of long-term financing are common

stock, preferred stock, various forms of debt, and convertible securities . Selection from among these choices is a function of the firm's dividend policy, leverage position, cost of capital, and earnings per share; target values for each of these, in turn, are a function of higher-level goals and strategy. The strategist can set financial goals for each of these risk/return variables so as to guide the selection of long-term financing instruments.

Leasing

Increasingly popular as a method of financing, leasing is loosely a form of leverage. Because of the debt characteristics of leasing, which normally extend beyond one year, it is included in our discussion of long-term sources of funds. One author refers to leases as "soft debt."

The Internal Revenue Service normally allows an income tax deduction for the full amount of a lease (annualized, of course, by the payment schedule). This amount is often greater than that resulting from an asset purchase where depreciation and related interest expenses are deductible. Leases may also prove a more expeditious method of obtaining assets than by an outright purchase, and may allow for greater flexibility in asset management and financial planning

The viability of leasing instead of purchasing an asset is largely a function of cash outflows and the cost of funds. Although there are several ways to analyse the lease-or-buy decision, the internal rate of return approach is straightforward and reasonably comprehensive. The internal rate of return of leasing is compared with the after-tax cost of debt to determine which has the lower cost.

WORKING CAPITAL MANAGEMENT

Working capital management is an integral part of a firm's day-to-day affairs and is guided to some extent directly by strategic choices. Since it entails the management of current assets and current liabilities, it involves both the allocation and acquisition of funds and/or their material counterparts. The focus of working capital is generally short term, although it interacts with longer-term decision-making in the context of strategy implementation, and insofar as short-term financing is used in lieu of long-term financing.

Cash—the Common Thread

The common thread in the management of working capital is cash or, more generally, cash flow, which leads to changes in cash balances.

In some cases short-term cash flow is a function of long-term commitments (a capital purchase, for example) that may require a series of short-term obligations (e.g., current portion of long-term debt) or a large, nonserial cash outlay. In either circumstance working capital is affected through its cash component.

The minimum cash balance carried by a firm is that which is necessary to conduct business in a manner consistent with the firm's strategies. This includes the ability to react to emergencies, to maintain compensating balances, and to take advantage of profit-generating opportunities, as well as to meet regular requirements for raw material or inventory purchases, operating expenses, debt service, and other day-to-day expenditures.

The management of cash balances and their near-equivalents (e.g., marketable securities) can become a critical component of strategy implementation. Certainly this would be the case for marginal firms embarking on survival or turn-around strategies involving divestiture, retrenchment, or financial reorganization.

Chrysler Corporation's experiences at the turn of the decade are representative here, since the company was not concerned just with its liquidity (in the accounting sense), but specifically with maintaining adequate cash as obligations came due within the accounting period. Alternatively the accumulation of cash and near-equivalents may be necessary to implement a growth strategy.

In gearing up for its latest generation of computers, IBM amassed an unusually large fortune in cash and marketable securities. This required close top management scrutiny to ensure that these funds were generating adequate returns until they could be effectively invested internally.

Other Working Capital Concerns

All this is not meant to imply that working capital management translates solely into the management of cash. The mix and magnitude of current liabilities and the noncash components of current assets also have direct implications for higher-level strategy and its implementation. Though normally aimed at achieving a desired liquidity position (with a keen focus on cash flow), working capital decisions must be carefully cast in the strategic framework that guides them.

PERSONNEL AND UNION RELATIONS STRATEGY

Personnel goals and action plans are set to guide the personnel department in major staffing decisions pertinent to business-level strategy. It has four primary elements. First, the nature of jobs that are required to carry out the business-level strategy and the characteristics of people needed to fill them are determined by job analysis. Second, a staffing plan is developed to forecast total employment needs of the strategy by job title over the relevant planning horizon. Third, the magnitude of the strategy's payroll budget is estimated over the planning horizon. Finally, union relations strategy is set to heighten the prospects of union acceptance of matters pertaining to the union.

Job Analysis

Sometimes a strategy has very specific implications for jobs. For example, Hewlett-Packard's high-quality, high-price strategy necessitates astute R&D, which, in turn, requires a wide range of R&D jobs. When an electric utility decides to develop a non-fossil fuel source of electricity, new technical jobs are created that previously were not in the firm's hierarchy of jobs.

To communicate expectations about job content, a job analysis is performed to gather pertinent information. The job-related data are then reported in a set of job descriptions;

people-related information is arranged in a set of job specifications.

The primary role of job descriptions and specifications to guide the process of hiring and placing people. When no new jobs are involved in a new strategy, job analysis can be conducted on existing jobs. Ideally job analysis data would already be available in the latter case; the strategist could simply refer to existing job descriptions and specifications and note the number of job titles required. Of course, the problem the strategist faces when a strategy necessitates creation of new jobs is having to decide what the content of jobs and employment requirements will be before hiring applicants.

Several sources of occupational information can be helpful in finding out about the nature of new jobs. The Dictionary of Occupational Titles contains condensed job descriptions for over 30,000 job titles. It can serve as a starting point for deciding on the content of newly created jobs.

Other sources of job content information are the Alphabetical Index of Industries and Occupations and The International Standard Classification of Occupations.Although they provide only the most basic information about the activities involved in thousands of job titles, they are useful initial sources of ideas about the nature of jobs and the type of work to which job titles refer.

Staffing Plan

The staffing plan presents the required numbers of employees by job title that will be needed over the strategy's planning horizon. This is a key consideration for the firm's personnel specialists. It tells them how many and when people will have to be brought into the firm to operationalize strategy.

Human resource planning procedures are followed to develop the staffing plan. Total employee requirements are determined by job title for the initial stages of strategy implementation. Then these totals are modified to reflect the numbers of current employees who can be transferred into the new jobs as well as expected normal outflows caused by retirements, deaths, out-transfers, and separations. The result is net incremental human resource demand by job title generated by the strategic change.

Payroll Budget

The cost of labour is a major strategy variable. It can be a primary consideration in determining the feasibility of a new strategy. The staffing budget is simply the sum of estimated total labour costs involved in the new strategy. It should be broken down by department. As such it represents the dollar limits that functional managers cannot exceed in hiring people to implement the new strategy. Personnel strategy (or a separate strategy category) can address union/ management relations whether or not the firm is organized by a union. By reducing the critical areas of labour/ management relations to strategy, the relationship between unions and management can be productive and comfortable in unionized firms. For nonunionized firms the relationship between labour and management can be prevented from degenerating into a strictly adversarial one.

Union Relations Strategy

After a new strategy set has been formulated, one of the last functional areas that must be addressed with functional strategy is union relations. This area should be the last to be designed because there can be union relations implications for each of the other functional strategies. The purpose of union relations strategy is to set goals and action plans that will lead to acceptance of the new strategy set by unions representing employees of the organization.

There are four phases in setting union relations strategy:

- Determine the relationships among elements of the new strategy set and the union contract.
- Enumerate the features of the new strategy set that are likely to be subject to formal and informal negotiations.
- Prepare a proposal for negotiations for each strategy set feature in item 2.

- Enter negotiations.

Let us look at each one more closely.

Relationships Between Strategy and Contract. There are many possible ways in which a new strategy set can affect a union/management contract. For example, a retrenchment strategy might involve layoffs, of which the circumstances either could be spelled out in the contract or would have to be negotiated before implementation. Similarly a product development strategy could necessitate a work-force expansion. The processes of increasing the number of jobs and employees could be subject to contract provisions or negotiations.

The National Labour Relations Board (NLRB) defines the range of topics subject to collective bargaining in the private sector, as matters of wages, hours, and working conditions. In the public sector, the items subject to bargaining are usually covered by statute. They differ from state to state.

When agreement cannot be reached as to whether an item is subject to negotiation, the NLRB can be called upon to make the determination. It defines three types of bargaining issues for determination: mandatory, permissive, and illegal. Illegal bargaining subjects are those that are prohibited. Closed-shop agreements are in this category. Permissive items include management rights issues over which management has exclusive decision authority. Examples are product choices, pricing decisions, and types of advertisements. Permissive topics do not have to be negotiated, but can be if management so desires.

Mandatory bargaining subjects include matters pertaining to wages, hours, and working conditions, and these issues must be resolved by negotiations. Whenever a new strategy requires changing any of these three factors, it may be necessary to negotiate the company's position with affected unions.

For case-writing purposes, the elements of strategy, at all levels, that might be subject to negotiations are likely to be mandatory items (wages, hours, and working conditions) and permissive subjects (product prices, product additions and deletions, advertising methods, etc.). Students should identify these items and prepare the necessary arguments for presentation to the union leadership. That is, elements of cost should be estimated, effects on payroll and wage rates determined, expected increases or decreases in overtime calculated, and so on. The idea is to develop the arguments that would have to be made to union bargainers so that strategy could be implemented without union interference.

Formal or Informal Negotiations. Some items might be better left to formal negotiations whereas others could be resolved by informal bargaining. Formal negotiations are those that lead to a new contract between labour and management. Informal negotiations refer to the day-to-day discussions by the two parties about how the contract applies to particular situations. Many of the issues that surface when new strategy is developed can be resolved by informal negotiations during meetings between union and management representatives.

Items that would have to be handled through formal negotiations probably would hold up implementation of the strategy until the next collective bargaining sessions. Therefore, in practice it would be most helpful if negotiable items could be resolved informally. For case analysis negotiable issues should be earmarked for either formal or informal negotiations.

Preparation of Negotiation Proposals. Preparing proposals for either formal or informal collective bargaining purposes is largely a matter of conducting the necessary research to support one's position and then presenting findings, in as convincing a form as possible, during the negotiations themselves.

For strategy-setting purposes, this means that proposals must be "airtight" when presented. The best strategy ever conceived can be nullified by the inability of management to gain the support of unions or failure to consider before negotiations what the implications of the strategy are for union leadership and members. A good example is the extent to which support of the auto workers was necessary for Lee

Iacocca to begin to turn Chrysler Corporation around during the early 1980s.

Entering negotiations: The final phase of implementing union relations strategy is the process of entering into negotiations. This phase is usually subject to convention within the organization involved. That is, in any firm negotiations proceed according to procedures understood by both parties or spelled out by law or agreement.

RESEARCH AND DEVELOPMENT STRATEGY

Industrial research can have one of two fundamental orientations. Scientific research refers to what one author has called "free-roving and analytical inquiry into the domain of unpredictable phenomena." This type of research activity is concerned with generating new concepts that may or may not have product applications.

The second orientation is "commercial development—the ultimate business outcome of successful industrial research, with its practical aura of economic and company values and restraints." Development activity can take several forms, but is essentially product, as opposed to concept, oriented. Thus it is a more pragmatic and market-centered form of R&D effort than scientific research. Although statistics are scarce, development work may account for over 90 per cent of all industrial product innovation costs.

Research and development strategy has four primary elements: R&D goals, extent of integration of the R&D function, amount of market coupling desired, and size of the budget.

R&D Goals

Goals are needed to specify the purpose of R&D is used as part of product or market development or market-penetration business-level strategies, the firm's desired competitive position can largely determine the amount and type of R&D needed. More specifically R&D can have one of four basic purposes that normally would be stated at the business level.

First, industry leader positioning can require both scientific research and commercial development capabilities but research emphasis is important for consistent generation of new concepts with development potential.

The industry leader has to maintain its product preeminence by outstripping its competitors' new concept initiation rates. Thus the leader tends to have a high R&D expenditure-to-sales ratio and state-of-the-art research facilities.

In addition its development capabilities must be effective and rapid. Effectiveness is largely a matter of production expertise, quality consistency, and marketing know-how. In brief, an industry leader, as one would expect, has to be good at everything and have the confidence to invest heavily in risky scientific research.

Another R&D position is that of follower. A follower is described as a firm that essentially duplicates the product innovations of the industry leader. Such firms usually strive to underprice the leader by avoiding the overhead burden of a basic research function that maintains high quality. In return the follower sacrifices time, wide profit margins, and prestige by always having to wait for the leader to make a move. The more quickly a follower can respond to the leader's new introductions, the more it can capitalize on the early adopter market. Thus the follower's primary R&D capability has to be in competitive intelligence, market sensing, and development.

The third R&D position is that of adapter. The adapter scans its competitors' offerings, not just those of the leader, and then modifies selected ones to meet the needs of its market segments. It actually is not duplicating competitors' products in a strict sense, but rather is adapting them to the specific requirements imposed by its customers. The adapter is not necessarily producing a lower-quality rendition. When Michelin was dominating the radial tire industry, several U.S. tire manufacturers introduced the all-weather steel-belted radial tire. They adapted the steel radial to the particular needs of their customers.

Adapters need strong developmental research capabilities and a keen understanding of market needs and sensitivities. Although the all-weather radial example demonstrates the essential characteristics of an adapter's product relative to an industry leader's, it fails in one important respect. Adapters modify products by means of strategic choice, not simply as part of a product development tactic. That is, they are adapters by choice, not incidentally. Consequently an adapter searches for products (among many competitors) to modify for its customers.

The final position with R&D implications is that of copier. Copying in this sense usually involves price competition with a leader, follower, or even adapter, which is made possible by production efficiencies, often resulting in reductions in quality. For example, certain brands of wood stoves developed widespread reputations for heating efficiency, safety, and dependability.

These features normally command high retail prices. Copies of some of the more popular high-priced, high-quality units appeared at prices far below those of the originals. They also tended to have shorter warranty terms and were rougher in appearance.

Their smaller profit margins and lower prices required higher sales volume, and thus more widespread distribution. Also, copiers need accurate market information and process engineering capabilities sufficient to quickly produce a high volume of less costly copies.

Intensity of R&D

Realistically there are seven choices of levels of R&D involvement. Larger firms will tend to have more of the different levels of R&D activity and smaller ones fewer.

The choices are as follows:

Level 1: Basic research is seeking new conceptual developments at the frontier of a discipline with little concern for product applications. Very few new concepts from basic research ever reach the market as successful products.

Thus it is a risky and expensive type of research effort rarely pursued in-house by businesses. Much basic research is conducted by universities under federal or private grants.

Level 2: Applied research usually refers to problem-initiated research. These activities are focused on solving a problem whose nature has possible implications for the firm's product lines or items.

Level 3: Advance development focuses on determining preliminary performance specifications for a new conceptual design that may have been produced by applied research. Output of this activity would be a detailed set of guidelines on how the new product should operate with tolerances and the necessary component configuration.

Level 4: Design engineering converts performance specifications into design specifications, which are used to make a prototype. With appropriate refinements these specifications are the plans used for manufacturing.

Level 5: Feasibility testing is analysis of financial or physical reasonableness of a product, process, or project.

Level 6. Equipment engineering results in the design and development of machinery and equipment peculiar to the manufacturing needs of a product or component.

Level 7. Process engineering is the design of production operations necessary to manufacture an item or to convert design specifications.

When creative R&D is required for a strategy, the tendency will be to implement an R&D programme that consists of advance development or applied research. Conversely a strategy calling for merely copying another product would not require these high-level research functions.

The firm could operate successfully with process, or possibly design, engineering functions alone.

In terms of their relationships to the finished product, basic research is the most distant, and process engineering is the closest. Selection of the level of integration of R&D identifies the type of R&D effort appropriate for a business-level strategy.

Market and Production Coupling

Market and production coupling is the practice of controlling the output of an R&D operation by the input of marketing and production information.

For example, an applied research group could be "managed" by systematically informing researchers of pertinent marketing data such as customers' preferences and competitors' product attributes, or production quality maintenance problems and cost structures.

This should result in their work having market relevance and reflecting production realities. The information normally would be transmitted at regular meetings between appropriate managers and key R&D staff people.

Particularly at the basic research end of the system of R&D intensities, there is danger that researchers will pursue their own interests with limited market or production applicability.

This could result in too few new product ideas even though the researchers' professional development would be considerably enhanced. For example, development of esoteric propulsion systems by an automotive R&D group could be professionally satisfying to the researchers.

However, the systems would be of little immediate value to the firm if customers would not buy them, or if they could not be produced.

Firms investing large amounts in basic research programs can destroy their creative effectiveness, though, by too much market coupling. Thus the extent of coupling is a critical determination for the strategist in designing and managing an R&D programme at all levels, not just in basic research.

The choices facing the strategist concerning coupling are straightforward. For each level of R&D activity, R&D strategy should specify:

- The presence or absence of a market and/or production information input system
- The type of data that should be so transmitted. Responsibility for designing and implementing this information system would normally be held by a functional manager.

R&D Budget

Research and development goals and strategy should also specify the size of the R&D budget. An R&D budget, which can be viewed as a limit for R&D expenditures, is often expressed as a percentage of sales. However, this basis for R&D expenditures can lead to financial difficulties because it ignores consideration of whether there is sufficient profitability to cover R&D costs. Alternatively, the R&D budget could be a function of a profit measure.

An R&D budget can also be set according to industry practices. But the average R&D expenditure of competitors is a minimum below which management could find itself at a competitive disadvantage.

PRODUCTION STRATEGY

Perhaps in no other functional area is the task of reflecting business-level strategic choices in functional strategy as demanding as it is in the production area. During the press of current operational snags, it is easy for production managers to exchange strategic relevance in operational decisions for tactical convenience.

An industrial equipment manufacturer, for example, having developed a strategy stressing high quality and rapid delivery at premium prices, may suddenly cut inventory levels or the number of workers, or both to meet period-end cash flow needs. The restaurant chain store manager stressing product quality will precook food for the noon rush hour to hasten service when customers arrive.

These short-term departures from higher-level strategy not only have the effect of shocking the production system, but they also can produce results that are in conflict with that strategy— in these examples, the creation of a reputation for high-quality products.

To guide manufacturing managers in the operation of the production function in a way consistent with other strategy levels, production strategy should at the minimum address capacity, facilities, product quality, process, technology, and control.

Production Capacity

When business-level goals and strategy involve manufacturing, production capacity required to meet sales and inventory requirements should be specified. Thus to begin to set production goals and formulate strategy, thc strategist must first forecast sales.

Capacity is the amount of labour and equipment that will be required within specific time periods to meet expected demand. The strategist can express capacity in either total or incremental terms, whichever is consistent with the scope of strategy. As for units of analysis, capacity is usually specified as units of output per time period for labour, machines, and plant space required to meet expected demand. More specifically, production system capacity can be expressed as system efficiency (SE), the measure used to describe a firm's actual output as a function of production capacity:

$$SE = \text{System capacity}$$

in which system capacity and actual output are expressed as numbers of units per time period.

The system efficiency ratio is also called utilization rate. It may range from 85 to 95 per cent, or even higher, depending on industry, investment levels, and economic conditions. Of course, the precise maximum output capability of a firm varies somewhat with conditions. But management usually recognizes a certain capacity utilization rate as the level above which the firm cannot produce without adding facilities. This capacity limit is the one against which a new business-level strategy's production expectations are compared to determine whether or not new facilities are needed.

The seven basic ways in which a firm can be managed in order to respond to an increase in capacity requirements are shown.

These management approaches actually constitute the fundamental thrusts of production strategy choices available to the strategist. Only one—vary physical capacity—involves a permanent increase in facilities.

They are goals or directions, not precisely implementable actions. In reality production strategy will tend toward one, or some combination, of them and selection is a function of business-level strategy.

Each approach carries distinct costs, as indicated, which can interfere with achievement of goals in other functional areas and in higher levels. Thus the approaches must be carefully evaluated in terms of potential adverse effects in addition to their immediate advantages.

Production Processes

Production strategy should also specify the type of manufacturing processes to be used to produce the products called for by business-level strategy. There are three basic types of production—repetitive (continuous), intermittent (job order), and project systems—and two hybrids, job lot and limited-quantity large-scale systems.Explanations and examples of each are presented.

Quality

Also as part of production goals and strategy, the strategist can guide the production department in reaching the appropriate product quality level by specifying values for inspection costs and defective unit costs. It may not be necessary to specify quantities for both, since they are highly negatively correlated.

That is, when inspection costs are low, the proportion of defective units of output is high; when inspection costs are high, defects are low.

For new products and new production processes, it is difficult to know a priori what values to assign for desired inspection or defective unit costs.

Standards for quality, which arise from strategic analysis and parts of marketing strategy, usually cannot be interpreted directly in terms of inspection costs or defective units. For example, with no experience in producing a new product item, the strategist would have no basis for setting inspection cost levels or defective cost proportions even though a desired quality goal in a general sense is clearly understood.

Thus a period of experimentation by acceptance sampling would be necessary to establish reliably what cost control guidelines are appropriate to produce the desired and affordable level of defective units. "A general guideline is to inspect when the cost of inspection at a given stage is less than the probable loss from not inspecting."

In the absence of quality guidelines set by management, individual employees will set their own quality guidelines at the stage of production in which they are involved. This inconsistency can lead to chaos in production processes as product move between stages or activities, and ultimately can result in an unacceptably low level of product quality.

For new entries or existing products in extant markets, either through market research or information gathered from customers by salespeople, data can be developed on competitors' proportions of defective units. Then relative quality goals can be generally determined and inspection costs can be set by acceptance sampling techniques.

Of course, responsibility for seeing that a desired product quality level is maintained rests with everyone who is in a position to affect quality.

One of the key reasons for the success of Japanese manufacturers in acquiring reputations for quality products has been their ability to develop this sense of quality responsibility among all employees. To do so strategic quality or service goals (or intentions) must be manifested in all activities, from the very top to the bottom of the organization, through production quality strategy.

Facilities

When more capacity is required to carry out a business-level strategy, whether it involves new construction or the upgrading of old facilities, guidelines are needed to evaluate facility proposals. In service businesses owned or leased buildings have to be evaluated.

Evaluating proposals properly requires cost data. Industrial engineering may supply labour and productivity estimates; accounting may furnish labour rates, overhead rates, tax rates, and cost-of-capital rates.

The proposal should also be supported by a demand forecast so that expected revenues or savings can be compared with costs. At least two stages of analysis are usually undertaken. Preliminary analysis is used to screen out unacceptable proposals by break-even analysis, payback period, simple rate of return, or average annual cost methods.

Those projects that survive preliminary screening are then analyzed in more detail. This detailed analysis involves consideration of the time value of money and results in a rank ordering of proposals. It normally follows the other capital budgeting techniques identified in the financial strategy section (net present value, discounted rate of return, etc.).

There may also be a final analysis stage, which requires selection from among rank-ordered proposals. The firm's cost of capital, historical rate of return, or industry averages can be used as cutoff points for selection of the best proposal.

Replacement of existing facilities is guided by calculations based on costs. Although replacement decisions are usually operational in nature and ongoing, a new strategy can involve replacement of facilities as opposed to new acquisitions.

Facilities' replacements, a capital expenditure problem requiring large amounts of capital, are different from the more common component replacement decisions associated with maintenance management. Component replacement often involves expense items, charged to the current period, or relatively small capitalized expenditures. Facility replacement expenditures tend to have longer-term effects on the firm than do those for component replacement.

A more comprehensive model of the categories of decisions which make up production strategy is proposed by Wheelwright. It consists of the following eight elements: Capacity, facilities, technology, vertical integration, workforce, quality, production planning/materials control, and organization. Although we agree with this proposal, the parts of this list not addressed in our elements of production strategy can be addressed in the other functional strategy areas.

For example, the question of organization of the production effort would be confronted in organization strategy; desired level of technology in production would be a matter of reflecting technological preferences delineated in business level strategy; workforce issues would comprise personnel strategy, and so on.

EXTERNAL RELATIONS STRATEGY

Strategies for external relations are formulated to guide the organization's direct involvement in the external social and political systems. Of course, the environment of a firm is taken into consideration in the formulation of all levels of strategy. But for external relations goals and action plans, we are concerned with direct attempts to use political processes to influence elements of an organization's environment.

Dickie studied the effect which several characteristics of organizations seem to have on the ability of those companies to influence Congress, regulatory agencies, and state and local regulatory bodies. Two variables, size of organization and economic sector within which the organization operates, determine the amount of influence a firm is able to exert on proposed legislation. Large companies have more influence than smaller ones, according to his results, where size is measured by total assets. Thus, smaller organizations can expect to have to work harder to influence legislation than larger ones.

As for the influence of a firm's economic sector, utilities and service companies are more likely to have great influence before Congress than retail and mature industry firms. High technology and energy companies exhibit levels of influence before Congress between the other two combinations.

Influence before regulatory bodies is a function of the tenure of the organization's senior public affairs officer (time in position) and time with company, as well as size of the company.

Among utilities and retail firms, people with the most time in position have greater influence over regulatory agencies than those new to their positions. The opposite results obtain for service and energy firms, though, for which new public affairs officers are most likely to have the greatest influence.

A similar pattern emerged for public affairs officers' time with the company. Firms with public affairs officers who have been with the company less than eight years have the least influence on regulatory agencies. However, public affairs officers with over seventeen years of company service report the greatest degree of influence with respect to regulatory bodies.

Size of company is also a factor with regulatory agencies. The large organizations have the greatest influence over them as is the case with influence before Congress.

Size and sector of firm also are important factors in determining the amount of influence of companies on state and local regulatory bodies. Utilities and service firms have greater influence than those in other sectors and larger companies exceed smaller ones in terms of influence on state and local regulatory agencies.

Starling explains that companies enter into external political processes for four purposes.]

They can attempt to oppose or advocate:

- A state, local, or federal government action or policy;
- An interest group action;
- Another company's action;
- A union action.

He goes on to outline four political approaches organizations can take to influence these four sectors of its environment, and then suggests several possible strategies for each approach. In the rest of this section, we discuss these sets of political action approaches and associated strategies.

Information Activities Approach

Organizations can attempt to influence public opinion by disseminating information in various ways. They can use advocacy advertising to enhance their image. For example, frequent appearances on national television by Chrysler's president, Lee Iacocca, seem to have bolstered the public's confidence in Chrysler's products.

They can also obtain media coverage by preparing and releasing research reports, press releases, and position papers on key issues, and having executive grant interviews and make speeches. One executive who is frequently in the public eye is Ted Turner, who owns several businesses, including the Atlanta Braves baseball team and Turner Broadcasting Company. Turner became a national hero of sorts when he skippered the 12-meter yacht Courageous to four straight America's Cup victories over the Australians in 1977.

Electoral Activities Approach

Organizations can try to influence the results of elections by encouraging managers to become involved in voluntary political activity, by making campaign contributions, and by forming political action committees.

Managers can become politically active by working for a party or other political organization, running for local political office, or getting appointed to a public administrative group. By first determining the type of political activity by employees that would be strategically advantageous to the organization, top management can develop performance-evaluation criteria that reward employees that would be strategically advantageous to the organization, top management can develop performance-evaluation criteria that reward employees for such activity.

Political action committees (PACs) can be established to collect and funnel funds to political candidates and issues. They can be formed by individual organizations or on behalf of entire industries. Companies are forbidden from donating their own funds to candidates but they can pay the operating expenses of PACs and set strategy about recipients of funds collected by the PAC for employees and others.

A PAC can contribute up to $10,000 to a federal candidate; $5,000 before a nominating convention and then another $5,000 afterward. Authority over the distribution of PAC funds can give the associated company a considerable amount of influence with candidates.

Governmental Activities

Governmental policy-making processes can be influenced by coalition building, letter writing, and lobbying. Basically these three methods can be used to inform decision makers of an individual's, a firm's, or an industry's preferences in regard to specific governmental policy.

Firms can build coalitions to influence public policy making by identifying a constituency and then developing support within it for a particular viewpoint. Constituencies that can be developed into coalitions include stockholders, company charge card holders, employees, suppliers, and interest groups that are unrelated to the organization except for some similar interest.

Once a coalition is formed around an issue or a policy, the appropriate elected officials have to be informed of its wishes. This communication process is usually accomplished by letter-writing campaigns in which members of the coalition write to the elected official. Alternatively the coalition may use a lobbyist to convey its desires or concerns to the appropriate officials. Lobbyists are used to influence legislation at mainly the federal and state levels.

Litigation Activities

Finally, organizations can attempt to influence governments, interest groups, other companies, and unions by taking legal action. For example, the Mansville Corporation and two smaller firms unsuccessfully sought congressional relief from growing numbers of personal injury suits contending that asbestos, a product they had sold for years, was either killing or seriously injuring people. The critical issue is that the effects of asbestos poisoning may take as long as thirty years to materialize. Thus, in addition to outstanding suits, asbestos manufacturers can anticipate possibly a great number of claims many years in the future.

The companies responded by developing external relations strategy that involved filing bankruptcy petitions. If they were granted relief under, they hoped to be freed not only from current claims against them, but also from any claims arising from possible future asbestos sickness suits.

So far the strategy has failed: the court rejected one of the petitions. Nonetheless this rather unusual case demonstrates how a firm at least can attempt to use legal action to influence government and interest-group actions. The Mansville and related cases are examples of direct judicial activity. Alternatively organizations can use quasi-judicial activity, in the form of arbitration.

Arbitration is usually an attempt to avoid or foreshorten litigation over a disagreement between two parties. Basically arbitration entails an agreement between two parties to abide by the decision of a third party, the arbitrator.

The most common use of arbitration is to resolve labour/management disputes. However, it is not restricted to this situation. As the cost of litigation continues to rise, arbitration may become a more popular form of settlement in all types of disagreements.

Strategic Parameters

To set goals and action plans for external relations, the strategist must first understand the purpose of the external relations effort. This insight can be gained from the process just as with other strategy areas. External relations goals should be case in terms of the expected results of the effort.

Action plans for reaching those goals should specify the approaches to follow. In addition, expected results should specify the approaches to follow. In addition, expected results should be enumerated along with budgeted costs.

SUMMARY

This chapter explains the processes of formulation and major dimensions of content of functional strategy that is the implementable manifestation of higher levels of strategy. To formulate functional strategy, the analyst must first choose the functional areas within which to set goals and action plans. Then goals and action plans are set. The steps for these processes are explained in the first part of the chapter.

In the second part, the major elements of the content of six functional strategy areas are described. These dimensions can be viewed as the typical set of topics that would have to be addressed in order to formulate strategy for each functional area. A particular firm may not have all of the six functional areas covered in the chapter; it may have more than these six. The ones presented are intended to be used as a starting point for analysts to decide on the content of functional strategy for specific applications.

Chapter 6

Strategy Implementation and Control

INTRODUCTION

Regardless of how well it may have been conceived, a competitive strategy without effective organization of human resources is doomed to sub-optimize, if not fail completely. Since strategies can only be implemented by and through people, the manner in which human resources are coordinated through hierarchical and lateral assignments of responsibility and authority becomes a central management challenge.

As Cannon notes, "Neither strategy nor structure can be determined independently of the other... If structure cannot stand alone without strategy, it is equally true that strategy can rarely succeed without an appropriate structure."

We do so in the context of external and internal influences on structural choices, and by examining some of the options in unit formation and linkages. The control process is viewed as a way to monitor goal achievement and resource conservation.

CONTINGENCY CALCULUS INFLUENCES ON STRUCTURE

Ideally a strategy/structure calculus would dictate appropriate organizational forms for different strategic postures. But researchers and practitioners have yet to formulate that normative, determinant calculus effectively. Indeed the best that can be offered at this point is the familiar "contingency" approach to the problem. By contingency approach we mean that the choice of an appropriate organization structure is contingent upon an array of factors, the combination of which is likely to be unique to the firm at hand.

These factors can be categorized as:

- Strategic thrusts,
- Environmental circumstances,
- Complexities introduced by growth,
- Management culture and style.

Strategic Thrusts

As part of its strategic decision making, a firm identifies its distinctive competencies (strengths) and then attempts to capitalize on these in identified niches or segments of the marketplace. In so doing, cutting edges for organization structure may naturally fall out.

If the growth prospects for the company hinge on the success of these efforts, then this organizational differentiation may be exhibited at the highest levels of the structure, as opposed to being subsumed elsewhere.

Similarly the firm relying on new product development as a major component of its strategy may find it advantageous to have authority and responsibility for research and development reflected explicitly at higher organizational levels. On the flip side, a firm going through retrenchment may organizationally de-emphasize those components of the enterprise being retrenched—by collapsing a declining product division into a more prosperous one, for example.

To a large extent, the concept of the strategic business unit (SBU) represents the organizational manifestation of strategic thrust.

By grouping "businesses" according to commonality of mission, related product/market segments, similarity of competition, size, and facilities/technology, adopters of the SBU concept explicitly recognize strategic thrust as an organizational cutting edge (size notwithstanding). Of course, in the case of SBUs, not only are differences between units magnified, but the existence of a coordinating mechanism (through the corporate executive office) becomes both crucial and organizationally distinct.

Environmental Circumstances

Glueck boldly suggests, "All organization forms work; the key is to match the organization form with the characteristic of the environment [emphasis his]." He goes on to conclude:

In general, functional organizations work best in stable environments, with less need for cross-department coordination and communication and less need for innovation... Divisional organizations work best in changing environments which require faster adaptation, more coordination and communication, and innovation.

Lawrence and Lorsch address the role of environment in organization design by suggesting that the degree of formality of structure (part of what they refer to as differentiation) is positively related to the degree of environmental uncertainty. Further, the more differentiated, the greater is the need for collaboration and coordination ("Integration"). Thus organizations, or sub-units, that face wide, indeterminate fluctuations in product demand would tend to be more highly structured than those facing more stable environments. And this would tend toward a greater need for lateral interaction across organizational units.

Finally, both environmental threats and opportunities can lead to the establishment of "boundary spanning" units specifically designed to deal with the environmental circumstance at hand. Concern over pollution in the chemical industry has led many member firms to establish corporate-level offices to deal with the matter.

Complexities Introduced by Growth

In his classic work Strategy and Structure, Alfred Chandler examined the structural evolution of 70 large firms over several decades. He generally concluded that structure follows strategy as a firm expands. Structural changes are necessary so that internal resources can be administered efficiently and effectively in light of changing market conditions brought about by expansion.

Chandler's work set off a string of research dealing with structural correlates of growth, many of which supplemented his model with additional contingency variables. Without going into the refinements of each, they may be summarized through the notion that firms evolve somewhat definable organizational forms as they grow—entrepreneurial, functional, divisional, and, occasionally, matrix.

This stage is characterized by the small, rather informal, enterprise. It is dominated by the entrepreneur who directly controls all or nearly all employees. Strategic planning, if any, is done by the central figure, who also carries responsibility for all important operating decisions. This is a common structure in small enterprises. It tends toward flexibility and nonspecialization and its success is dependent on the capabilities.

This form represents the first step toward formality and specialization. As a firm expands in size and scope of operations, delegation of authority and responsibility to managers of specialized units is called for. Here the role of the central figure (chief executive officer) becomes more refined, reflecting the need for coordination of functional units and more focused concern on environmental and strategic matters.

As the firm's strategic thrusts build around product and/or market expansion and differentiation, both the internal climate and environmental conditions become more complex. Here the need for decentralization and semiautonomy is amplified, as the time and capability of the chief executive become overstretched. A corporate office is established (which may include vestiges of functional departmentalization, such as the corporate financial officer) to plan, coordinate, and allocate resources. The divisions, in turn, carry operational burdens and functional responsibilities.

As complexity increases, through diversification, the divisions themselves may pick up increased responsibility for their own strategic planning, and possibly be grouped as strategic business units.

The matrix structure is somewhat of an aberration in that it is designed to combine the virtues of the divisional and functional structures without overly disturbing whichever has been chosen.

Often used in the context of project management, clusters are built around products, markets, and/or technologies. The objective in the matrix organization is to capitalize on combinations of expertise that exist in the organization, but which are stifled by normal hierarchical structures. This is accomplished by horizontal groupings of individuals or units into teams that operationally deal with the strategic matter at hand.

The last point is an important one, since matrix groupings often reflect either a temporary, or as yet unresolved, specific strategic commitment.

For example, a multiproduct trading company might establish an export research group to study international markets. Or an aerospace firm might establish a unique product group (e.g., special alloy turbine blades) for a limited-duration government contract. In some instances the matrix structure is more permanent—to establish business-line profit centers from vertical functional tiers, as at Dow Corning, for example.

Of course, the matrix structure suffers from problems of dual authority, among others, but it can creatively serve the needs of strategic change that otherwise might be constrained by more traditional structures.

Management Culture and Style

Though it may be argued that strategy should dominate the design of organization structure, the internal workings and styles of management are going to shape it as well. Mintzberg suggests that "power" factors play an important role. These include the personal needs of organization members, organizational "fashions of the day" (e.g., participative versus nonparticipative styles), and the presence of outside control (e.g., degree of control by the board of directors). He argues that pressures for centralization and formality arise from needs for personal power at the strategic level as well as from higher degrees of external control. And the culture surrounding structures "in fashion" leads to pressures for their adoption.

What this suggests is that the choice of organization structure is not simply a matter of weighing impersonal strategic, environmental, and technical circumstances.

Instead organization design is going to be tempered by the human factor, including the capabilities of those organizing and being organized, and their collective needs, aspirations, and expectations.

Here generic typologies give way to human complexities. Indeed it is this complex web that calls for creativity and insights on the part of the strategist when choosing a structure for strategy implementation.

STRUCTURAL OPTIONS IN UNIT FORMATION

The combination of strategic thrusts, environment, growth, and management style influences the conceptual perspectives of top management toward organization design.

Hierarchical placement of organization units, lateral differentiation between units, the formality or informality of authority/responsibility relationships, and matters of centralization versus decentralization are among these.

Though the process is not necessarily sequential, these grand perspectives at some point must be translated into the establishment of specific organizational units.

Deciding upon a divisional structure, for example, must be further refined to define what the divisions will be. Further, interunit coordination and decision making may be enhanced through lateral linkages beyond those inherent in the unit hierarchy.

Bases for Unit Formation

Thus far we have alluded to different bases upon which hierarchical and lateral assignments are made in an organization. This grouping or Departmentation of the enterprise represents the specific interpretation of the contingency relationships outlined. Generally grouping has four primary effects on the firm:

- It establishes work accountability.
- It identifies units that will share resources.
- It creates (or demands) common performance measures.
- It prompts mutual accommodation.

Though many bases for departmentation or grouping exist, there are generally six that stand out.

Function or Process: This represents grouping based on commonality of skills, abilities, and the nature of work or activity. Often it refers to the basic business functions of marketing, finance, accounting, production, personnel, research and development, and so on.

Departmentation on this basis suggests that there are fundamental categories of business operations upon which organizational differentiation should centre.

Somewhat extended, it can also refer to phase of activity, particularly where the operations of an enterprise are sequential. Here different processes are seen as discrete components of the operational sequence.

On a small scale, a furniture company's manufacturing department might be further subdivided into cutting, turning, sanding, assembling, and finishing. At a more strategic level, a vertically integrated firm may make a primary organizational cut according to the different stages in the vertical chain.

An aluminum producer might have mining, transportation, smelting, fabrication, and marketing departments or semiautonomous divisions, for example.

In the latter case, "function or process" is not used in the same sense as "functional organization" presented previously. A semiautonomous division by definition would represent a divisional structure, though the grouping itself is based on a "phase" interpretation of function.

Product: For product grouping the departmental configuration represents output categories instead of either input skills or location.

General Motors, for instance, has Chevrolet, Buick, Pontiac, Oldsmobile, Cadillac, and other divisions that reflect major product classes.

Small marinas often have slip rentals, repair services, retail stores, and fuel retail departments. In both cases departmentation represents the major product or service categories of the firm.

In larger firms especially, product units often have their own functional groups (marketing, production, personnel, research, and others) such that the functional specialties are subordinate to the major emphasis of output.

Of course, the choice of product (or service) categories becomes an important component of effectively departmentalizing this way.

Products can be grouped according to such diverse criteria as technology (e.g., electronic versus mechanical versus electromechanical), brand (e.g., Noxzema versus Cover Girl), product function (e.g., welding versus grinding equipment), size (e.g., low-volume versus high-volume pumps), and so forth.

These distinctions often become manifest in "product-line" decisions, which, in turn, have organizational implications. Again we see a strategy/structure linkage.

Client or Customer. Here groupings revolve around market typologies that define customer classes (or individual customers) to whom the firm sells.

Distinctions between commercial and defence clients are very often made in consulting and aerospace circles. Organizations are structured accordingly. In the extreme the organization can be based on individual accounts, as in advertising agencies.

For obvious reasons one often finds evidence of client or customer groupings within marketing or sales organizations, but these distinctions can also extend to the upper levels of the hierarchy as strategy calls for them.

Location: The basis for structuring normally refers to the territory covered by an organizational unit and/or its actual siting. Different manufacturing plans producing the same products, funneling into the same distribution channels, may be organizationally distinct by virtue of their location.

Or geographical distinctions may be more market oriented, such as with domestic versus international divisions (e.g., hotel chains) or the establishment of sales territories (e.g., consumer products companies).

Personal Skills or Attributes. Occasionally one encounters a firm in which individuals are the primary organizational bases. For example, medical or dental partnerships and clinics are often organized by physicians.

Similarly consulting firms can be structured around senior partners. This type of organization may be found where the product or service of the firm is extraordinarily dependent upon the particular skills and capabilities, or even personalities, of certain people.

The development of various forms of prepaid group medical facilities (often called Health Maintenance Organizations or HMOs), in which patients are served by whatever physician happens to be available at the time of the patient's visit, represents attempts to get away from the inefficiencies of organization by person.

Time. Grouping on the basis of time actually has two dimensions. the first is a function of when tasks or overall operations are performed. Shift work in a manufacturing plant is organized this way.

On a somewhat different level, some colleges and universities have day and evening faculties, and in some instances separate administrative units for them. To the extent that evening educational programs represent a method of diversification and/or market development, the time dimension for organizing (day versus evening) results directly from that strategic commitment.

Second, time has structural implications from planning and responsibility perspectives. Vertical divisions of labour and responsibility often carry with them differences in planning and execution time horizons.

Thus general managers tend to have longer-term planning and perspectives than operational managers. And operational managers generally realise greater responsibility for short-term results than would those responsible for long-term affairs. Indeed a general management/operational management hierarchy is established precisely so this can occur. Although these six bases for structuring an organization and its sub-units appear somewhat distinct, their distinctions often become clouded.

For example, units defined on the basis of territory (location) may be established that way because markets (customers) have been so segmented. Similarly it may be difficult to distinguish clearly between the product basis and personal skills basis, particularly when the delivery of skills is the product.

Or product classes may be defined in a way that parallels customer classes (e.g., the familiar "consumer products" versus "industrial products" breakdown).

Nonetheless recognition of structural options is often facilitated by considering each of these alternatives in light of strategic and sub-unit objectives.

Another caveat is necessary. Except perhaps in the entrepreneurial structure, one rarely finds the instance where one, and only one, of these bases is used to structure an entire organization.

As the components of strategy are translated and retranslated downward, their organizational interpretations demand structures to match them.

The organizational tiering that results is likely to show evidence of any combination of the structural bases outlined.

Finally, lateral combinations are possible, and may be particularly useful at the upper levels of an organization. Strategic thrusts, environmental conditions, growth influences, and human characteristics may call for the mixing of structural bases at a given organizational level.

Thus a vice-president for research and development (functional) may sit at the same organizational level as a vice-president for a geographical division (location).

If properly conceived, this would suggest that neither basis alone was adequate to reflect the firm's strategic and internal circumstances at that level.

Additional Lateral Linkages

The implementation of strategy through structural design implies more than the somewhat mechanistic process of establishing organizational units.

Inherent in the process is the specification of unit objectives and responsibilities, boundaries of authority, and interunit interactions. To some extent the last of these derives simply from the hierarchical nature of organizations. Subunits are blended together in the context of the higher-order unit of which they are a part. Thus organization design is as much a matter of aggregation as it is of disaggregation.

But desirable interunit interactions often go beyond the strictures that might be imposed by the structural groupings we have discussed. Often additional coordination, decision making, and informational mechanisms are necessary.

These can extend from the informal communications between employees to the formality of the complex matrix organization presented earlier. In between lie company rules and procedures, and the establishment of liaison roles and committees.

Company rules and procedures cross-cut departments for the purpose of standardizing behaviour, and to that extent coordinate.

Liaison roles are established to bypass vertical communication channels; they are largely an information-flow device and are particularly useful in conflict resolution. Committees, of course, are institutional collections of people that can be either informational, coordinating, or decision making in their purpose.

CONTROL IN STRATEGIC MANAGEMENT

Control of the organization within a strategic management system is concerned with achieving goals by carrying out strategies effectively and efficiently.

Thus the strategic management control process addresses two broad issues:

- The adequacy of performance in fulfilling organizational goals (the effectiveness of the organization)
- The efficiency with which strategies are carried out.

The "correctness" of goals and strategies is evaluated during earlier stages of the strategic management process. Therefore, attention during control can be restricted to organizational performance.

That is, failure to achieve goals is viewed as a performance problem, not as a matter of faulty goals. We thus are concerned in control with determining the degree to which:

- Goals are achieved
- Resources are conserved.

EFFECTIVENESS AND EFFICIENCY

Effectiveness refers to how well an organization achieves its goals—produces expected results. Similarly Hofer and Schendel define effectiveness as the optimal relationship between a firm and its environment.

Thus effectiveness relates to the organization's goals. Efficiency, however, is the amount of output per unit of input and relates more to the nature of internal operations. It is not specifically related to goals.

An efficient organization is one that does whatever it does with the minimum consumption of resources. Ideally organizations carry out their activities both effectively and efficiently; that is, they do the right things in the right way.

However, the other three permutations are possible. Indeed a company could be neither effective nor efficient in the conduct of its business. Such a firm would experience competitive disadvantages as well as low productivity. In other words, it would be doing the wrong things wrong.

All this suggests that a number of structural options exist that can be overlaid or used in conjunction with traditional hierarchical relationships. As with other structural matters, however, the equation is underdefined—there is no single best way.

Somewhat better off are firms that do the wrong things right (that is, are efficient but not effective). However, while citing Drucker, Hofer and Schendel note that this is a less advantageous situation than doing the right things wrong (attaining effectiveness without efficiency). Organizations that do the right things wrong will outperform those that do the wrong things right.

It is clearly better to be both effective and efficient at the same time. But when effectiveness and efficiency are in conflict,' then positive external relations that lead to effectiveness should be stressed instead of internal efficiency. Although strategic management in its entirety emphasizes organizational effectiveness, the control process is concerned with both effectiveness and efficiency.

In this section we discuss:

- The type of control systems can be used,
- Phases of the control cycle,
- Typical employee responses to control methods,
- Some suggestions for making a control system work.

TYPES OF CONTROL SYSTEMS

Managers use either steering, yes/no, or postaction control systems, or some combination of the three, for monitoring the organization's progress.

Steering controls generally involve making predictions of expected results in the form of a set of standards and then comparing performance, as it occurs, with standards to detect deviations. The near simultaneity of performance and deviation detection enables timely corrective action.

The process of keeping a moving automobile on the road is an example of steering control. Similarly new employees' fellow workers will push, prod, scale, and instruct them until they begin to conform consistently to work group norms (standards).

Another example is high-frequency sampling of items produced on an assembly line for purposes of quality inspection. As soon as samples whose tolerances deviate from the standards are detected, corrections can be made in the way they are manufactured.

Yes/no controls are tests a piece of work must pass to go on to the next process. Examples include automobile inspection systems in some cases, "core" academic programs that must be completed before other courses can be taken, and the preflight tests of an aircraft.

Postaction controls consist of tests conducted on completed processes to determine whether or not results meet a standard. An inspector's evaluation of a long paper, end-line quality control inspection of manufactured products, and the use of review by peers to select articles for publication in journals and magazines are examples of postaction controls.

Of these three steering controls best meet the control needs of strategic management systems. They can be put in place to monitor the performance of an organization while its operations are under way.

Information about unmet goals, especially interim targets in the form of key variables, can be fed back to each stage in the strategic management process so that corrective action can be taken. The frequency of measurements is an important question when using steering controls. When measurements of performance are taken often, deviations from goals can be minimized.

However, the cost of such a system can be great when compared with the costs of infrequent measurement. But the costs of too infrequent measurement can also be excessive.

Therefore, control system management costs must be evaluated against the costs of such factors as high product failure rates, lost customers, and competitive disadvantage. In these terms even high short-term costs of control can be small when compared with its long-term benefits.

PHASES OF THE CONTROL CYCLE

The control process consists of the following four phases:

- Select key variables that will become the major evaluative criteria for determining whether goals have been achieved and strategies appropriately carried out.

- Set standards for key variables that represent levels of satisfactory performance.
- Measure performance against standards to detect deviations.
- Take action either to reinforce correct performance or to correct substandard performance.

Next we discuss each of these stages in more detail.

Key Variables for Control

Control systems are most often designed to measure profitability because it is a dominant goal in most companies. However, the particular measure of profitability of interest in a particular firm can vary across several interpretations of the various forms of gross profit, operating profit, and net profit.

But control systems may focus on other measurements (besides profitability), called key variables ["(a)lso called 'strategic factors, 'key success factors,' 'key result areas,' and 'pulse points'!] Usually only a few key variables are used for control purposes, "six being the number most commonly used."

Key variables have the following characteristics:

- They capture the essential elements of success (or failure) of the organization's strategies.
- They change dramatically with changes in organization performance.
- Changes in them are not easy to predict.
- They can be measured directly and objectively.

To arrive at a list of possible key variables for strategic control, the analyst first can ask the following three questions:

1. What management decisions will be critical to successfully carrying out strategies?
2. What factors are important as inputs to these decisions?
3. From what sources of revenue will the firm recover costs associated with these factors?

In answering, a set of variables will emerge that are possible key variables. Then this set can be pared down to a select few by screening them according to the above criteria (success elements, dramatic change, prediction difficulty, and measurability).

The resulting set of key variables that become control variables is peculiar to the firm. These variables reflect its major strategic thrusts and can be as different in various organizations as are people's fingerprints.

However, there are some common ones that are peculiar to certain functions. The list that follows is intended merely as an example of the kinds of key variables that may be ultimately selected for purposes of monitoring performance in ways consistent with strategy:

- Marketing variables: Sales, bookings, market share, gross margin, key account orders, lost orders, promotional indicators, new customers
- Production variables: Cost control (output per labour hour, overtime), percentage of capacity utilization, backlogs, quality, yield, raw materials cost, percentage of on-time delivery
- Finance variables: Inventory, accounts receivable, investment return

Within the strategic management process, major objectives and targets established for each level of strategy are also prime candidates for key control variables. For example, a management team striving to increase market share by one percentage point per year for three years can take these interim values as key variables.

If, at the close of the first year, implementation of the selected strategy has failed to produce the one percentage point increase in share, then corrective action can be taken. The team might establish six-month criteria, say, one half a percentage point, if appropriate, and gain even closer control of strategy implementation.

Too often management will set a long-term target and wait until it is not met before taking corrective action. Of course, it is then usually too late to change operations in a constructive way. Timely, feasible, understandable key variables are essential for effective control systems.

Setting Standards

After selecting key variables for monitoring organizational performance, standards have to be set for them. Standards are the levels of key variables that will be accepted as satisfactory.

Anthony and Deardon describe three types of standards: predetermined standards (budgets), historical standards, and external standards. Predetermined standards or budgets are the goals set during the goal formulation process of a strategic management programme.

A targeted five-year growth in return (operating profit) on sales from, say, 8 to 13 per cent, defines a direct key control variable.

Annual standards, or interim targets, would probably be set as part of business-level strategy. Whatever annual values were given to expected return on sales goals would be the standards against which subsequent annual performance would be compared for control purposes.

Similarly budgets, another form of predetermined standard, are often established as part of the functional strategy formulation process.

Functional managers, along with top-level managers, decide upon the size of budget necessary to carry out strategy when functional strategy goals (and action plans) are established.

Historical standards are set by using past performance as a comparative base. Thus current performance is compared with past performance. Historical standards are often used to evaluate performance. Management may wish to maintain a current ratio of 2 to 1, for example, or a certain inventory turnover ratio.

Use of historical standards is recommended only when it is determined that conditions have not changed so as to invalidate the trend and when prior performance is known to be acceptable.

External standards are those whose values are derived from sources outside the firm or SBU. Examples are other firms' performance characteristics the object firm's management wants to exceed, such as market share, return on assets, to earnings per share.

The shortcoming of this type of standard is the possible noncomparability of firms. Of these three types of standards, the one best suited for strategic management control purposes is predetermined standards.

Comparison of Actual Performance Against Standards This stage involves measuring actual key variable performance, comparing results against standards, and informing the appropriate people so that deviations can be detected and corrections made or reinforcement given.

Financial or management accounting systems are usually relied on for measuring actual performance. There are, however, many other measurement methods available, including product sampling, various predictions, observation by managers, meetings, and conferences.Whatever measurement methods are selected, they should be timely, accurate, and cost effective.

The need to inform people of measurements results necessitates a system of reporting. Anthony and Deardon identify two types of reports for control systems: information reports and control reports.

Information reports tell managers what is happening around them and may or may not be intended to precipitate action. Managers study them to determine if it is necessary to take corrective action. Control reports are those directed at actual versus planned performance comparisons and can take many forms.

Reinforcement or Corrective Action

Detection of negative deviations from standards usually leads to analysis of problems, decisions about how to correct them, and adjustments to operations.

Sometimes a control report will precipitate starting a new strategic management cycle. This new cycle may lead to the reformulation of goals or action plans, or both. Usually, however, strategies remain intact while operations are adjusted.

The control process should be continuous so that control information is constantly fed back to the goal and action plan formulation stage. Deviations, therefore, should prompt immediate analysis so that a timely decision can be made about whether to change goals or action plans or operational management.

It is important too that performance that exceeds standards be reinforced. Too often management focuses attention only on negative deviations from expectations.

EMPLOYEE RESPONSES TO CONTROL

Control systems themselves can trigger an array of human behaviors, some of which are positive in their impact on the organization and some of which are negative. Positive reactions such as voluntary compliance or even active acceptance can be expected when control criteria demonstrate relevance through operational significance and lead to results that can be:

- Affected by employees
- Directly measured.

Further, positive reactions to control can be precipitated by employee participation in the process of setting standards, especially when standards are perceived as achievable but not challenging.

Negative reactions to controls can take several forms. First, employees can resort to fudging records or even sabotage in order to distort performance measurements favorably. This result often stems from lack of participation in the process of developing standards as well as misunderstanding of the importance of control.

A large book printing company installed various types of production-counting devices on its printing and binding machines to determine which tasks represented production bottlenecks. At the end of each work day, the counters would be broken, reset before readings could be recorded, or disconnected altogether. Management was never able to install and use mechanical counters.

Another example of how control systems can be thwarted is a furniture factory in which the canvas bins containing the output of lathes were weighed to estimate the number of turnings produced.

Lathe operators stopped discarding defective pieces and instead threw them into the finished goods bin to maximize their respective counts.

Similarly a university administration that measures enrollment in classes according to course registrants rather than enrollment after the drop period usually will receive distorted class-size information.

Trading of favors among organizational units can take place when there is an imbalance between staff people responsible for measuring or reporting results and line people responsible for generating those results.

One might find a production manager vehemently supporting the promotion of a cost accounting manager and expecting more lenient treatment in return. This expectation clearly demonstrates the absence of understanding of the purposes of the control system.

A control system that emphasizes short-term results can jeopardize achievement of long-term goals. Failure to replace obsolete machinery may prevent short-term declines in return on assets but may also reduce long-term profitability.

Finally, absenteeism and turnover can be manifestations of tension and pressure caused by an overly strict control system.

SUGGESTIONS FOR CONTROL SYSTEM DEVELOPMENT

These negative results of control can be minimized by following Steiner's suggestions for developing control systems.

They are as follows:

- *Enlist top management support*: The involvement of top management can enable appropriate assignment of resources to the control effort as well as lend legitimacy to the system.

- *Have a clear organizational structure*: A well-defined and well-designed structure will help managers and employees understand their responsibility and authority and their various interrelationships within the control system.
- *Establish clear control responsibility*: Someone should be appointed as director of control operations so that accountability for its phases is clearly assigned.
- *Do not permit control to become an end in itself*: If the control system is allowed to dominate decisions, then creativity and initiative can be thwarted.
- Keep accounting "buzzwords" to a minimum. Use of esoteric accounting terminology may alienate those employees who do not understand it. Even a widely understood concept such as profit can evoke negative reactions from employees. A profit goal will often be interpreted by employees as an attempt to get more out of them with nothing given to them in return. For this reason positive reinforcement is important as a control method.
- *Keep it simple*: Before very long a control system can evolve into a "can of worms." When this is allowed to happen, frustrations, resentment, and then inaction can result.
- Communicate the purposes and limitations of control. Fewer negative results will develop the more employees understand and see an opportunity to benefit from the control system.
- *Encourage participation*: Especially in the standard-setting process, participation fosters understanding and commitment to the control effort.
- *Keep controls simple and few in number*: The easier control variables are to understand, the greater will be chances of acceptance and support by employees.

Also, control variables should be kept to as few as possible to prevent unnecessary complexity, confusion, and cost.

- *Make controls meaningful*: There must be widespread recognition of the importance and significance of control variables and their standards for the system to be accepted.
- Customise the control system. "Canned" systems should be avoided in favour of ones that reflect the idiosyncrasies of the organization.

SUMMARY

The processes of implementation and control of strategy are critical for successful strategic management. Through implementation responsibility for the various elements of an entire strategy set is assigned to people throughout the organization.

Thus the principles of organization design are integral elements in strategy implementation. The section on organization structure has two parts. First, the influences on structure caused by major strategic thrusts or emphases are discussed. These thrusts normally should be highlighted through organization structure. Also, various environmental factors can influence the nature of organization, as discussed next. In the second part of the section on organization, the types of structures available to strategists are explained and the lateral linkage options are presented.

Most tend to view organization structuring as largely a matter of working out vertical authority and responsibility relationships for a particular strategy.

However, lateral relationships also must be thought through and specified so that the appropriate cross-unit integration takes place.

The second section of the chapter addresses the process of controlling strategy implementation. Managers are primarily concerned with two factors in designing control systems.

Progress toward achieving goals specified in strategy at all levels is monitored to determine whether or not strategy is effective. Then control systems should be set up to monitor the extent to which resources are conserved. The section explains several types of control systems, the elements of the control cycle, and how employees can be expected to respond to different control configurations.

Last, some principles for the development of control systems are enumerated.

CORPORATE CULTURE AND BUSINESS ENVIRONMENT

We are currently experiencing enormous changes in corporate culture and business environment. Command and control strategy for managing business is giving way to autonomous business units with power to develop and implement their own policies.

The silo-based strategy is being replaced by collaboration and knowledge sharing not only within an enterprise but also with customers and suppliers. New products are no longer developed in isolation by one department but by a team of experts from different departments. Furthermore, there is now increasing pressure from top management to convert data into knowledge so that better decisions can be made.

The current technology has provided massive amount of data, but not enough efforts are being made to translate the data into intelligence. The changes in corporate culture and environment are causing changes in the way forecasts are prepared and communicated. The breaking down of functional silos has given rise to collaboration both within and outside the enterprise. There is now more openness among different functions than ever before. More and more decisions are now made collectively rather than individually.

The S&OP (Sales and Operations Process), which many companies now have in place, is an example of collaboration within an enterprise. In a regularly scheduled S&OP meeting, people from different functions often get together to build a consensus on forecasts; if there is a gap between supply and demand, decide on the action plan to match them; and determine capacity needs.

The programs such as VMI (Vendor Managed Inventory Program) and CPFR (Collaborative Planning, Forecasting and Replenishment) grew from the spirit of collaboration. Under both these programs, retailers not only provide access to point-of-sale data but also agree to share information about changes in their store layout, opening and closing of stores, promotional plans, and forecasts.

At present, Retail Link, Wal-Mart's electronic data interchange system, provides weekly forecasting data to more than 3500 of its 5000 vendors. If vendors know what is happening on the consumer end, as well as what retailers are planning to do, they can do a better job in preparing forecasts.

PERCEPTION ABOUT FORECASTING

Perception about forecasting is also changing. Although businesses have been using forecasts all along, they never called them as such. They prepare a budget, which is based on some estimates about the future. They prepare a production plan (how much to produce, and when and where), which is also based on some estimates about the future. In fact, every business decision is based on some expectations about the future. Businesses are now beginning to recognize forecasts and their need in decision-making.

Forecasts can be prepared intuitively (based on gut feeling) or systematically using a well-structured procedure. In the past, forecasts were mostly prepared intuitively. With this kind of process, forecasters are less likely to know where they went wrong. But if they were prepared systematically, using set procedures and processes, forecasters would have a better chance of recognizing the problem and then fixing it. More and more companies are now moving in the direction of preparing forecasts systematically.

FORECASTERS

Forecasting is not new, we have been doing it from time immemorial. What is new is a change in people involved in forecasting. In early days, forecasting was within the domain of prophets, seers, astrologers and fortunetellers, because they were the ones who were involved in forecasting. Prophets made prophecies about the world and the people - when there would be famine, prosperity, rain or war. Astrologers, seers and fortunetellers made predictions about business and personal lives of their patrons.

Then we see the emergence of professionals who were basically economists specializing in macro type forecasting. They basically forecasted the state of economy and its effect on the overall health of a company. In recent years, we have been seeing the development of a new breed of professionals who specialize in micro type forecasting, e.g., sales forecasting.

Since all functional plans such as of production, sales, finance and marketing are driven by sales forecasts; many companies felt that they would add substantial value to business by bringing in professionals who specialized in this type of forecasting. As such, many large corporations have created such positions, with titles ranging from Forecast Analyst to all the way to Vice President of Forecasting.

APPROACH TO FORECASTING

The approach to forecasting has also changed in a significant way. In the past, prophets and seers used their vision to make prophecies about the future, because it was believed that they had a perfect vision. Astrologers made predictions on the basis of movements of stars, moon and sun. Fortunetellers used and are still using all kinds of tricks of their trade. Some can tell the future by reading tealeaves and tarot cards, and others by the very feel of vibration coming from a patron. The professionals of today are becoming more and more scientific. Forecasts are now based on hard facts, crystallized by statistical tools and enhanced by informed judgment.

USES OF FORECASTS

The uses of forecasts have also dramatically changed.

Forecasting is now used not only for predicting social, political and economic changes but also for making business decisions. In recent years, business forecasting has changed in two significant ways: One, there is a shift in the emphasis from forecasting the general health of a business to forecasting specific aspects of a business.

In the past, the emphasis was primarily on forecasting the state of the economy and its overall effect on a business. Now the emphasis is on forecasting different aspects of a business such as demand, shipments, cash flow, and capacity and manpower requirements.

Two, there is a shift in the emphasis from strategic (long-term) to operational (short-term) forecasting. Both are important, but the operational forecasting plays an important role in running day to day operations, as such forecasts are used to drive production, logistic, procurement, sales, marketing and financial plans.

TECHNOLOGY

The innovations in technology have also changed the forecasting landscape by improving:

- Data processing,
- Data accessibility
- Data warehousing,
- Data mining,

which are vital to the forecasting function. The advancement in data processing has greatly improved the accuracy and speed at which data are entered, stored, exchanged, manipulated and analyzed.

Advances in data accessibility have given forecasters not only access to data previously unavailable, but also the speed and accuracy at which they can be retrieved. Now data can be accessed from any part of the globe in a matter of seconds and minutes. The innovation of EDI (Electronic Data Interchange), where one computer talks to another, has made it possible for the forecaster to obtain data from any corner of the world.

The Internet has also made it possible to retrieve data

from any part of the globe easily, quickly, accurately and inexpensively. As such, the forecasters now have access to a wealth of information/data. Scanning technology gives vendors access to consumption data, which tell them rather quickly how consumers are responding to their products in different markets, and also how their products are doing in relation to products of their competitors. The EDI and web-based technology also allow partners to communicate interactively about forecasts.

The improvement in data warehousing has enabled companies to store huge amounts of data that can be easily queried. Today, Wal-Mart's data warehouse system stores 7.5 terabytes (1 Terabyte = 1 Trillion bytes) of data including data of inventory, forecasts, demographics, markdowns, returns and market baskets. The system can handle as many as 35,000 queries in one week.

Data mining is like digging gold from dirt. There is a tremendous amount of information hidden in the data that can be helpful to forecasters. Data mining helps to dig out that information. It provides corporate intelligence and answers questions such as: How responsive are customers to our price and promotion? How does their purchasing behavior differ at different times of a year? What products do they tend to buy together? What lifecycle do sales follow as a product matures?

Advances in computer technology have made it possible to solve even the most complex mathematical problems in a matter of seconds - something we could not even dream of before. It also contributed to the development of forecasting software and systems that made it possible for forecasters to concentrate more on how to improve forecasts than on how to compute them.

Index